FOR SUCH A TIME AS THIS

And who knows whether you have not come to the kingdom for such a time as this?

Esther 4:14

For Such a Time as This

*Twenty-Six Women of Vision and Faith
Tell Their Stories*

Edited by

Lillian V. Grissen

WILLIAM B. EERDMANS PUBLISHING COMPANY
GRAND RAPIDS, MICHIGAN

Reprinted, May 1992

Library of Congress Cataloging-in-Publication Data

For such a time as this: twenty-six women of vision and faith
tell their stories / edited by Lillian Grissen.
p.   cm.
ISBN 0-8028-0611-2
1. Christian Reformed Church — United States — Biography.
2. Reformed Church — United States — Biography.   3. Women in the
Reformed Church — United States.   4. Women in church work —
Christian Reformed Church.   I. Grissen, Lillian V., 1926–   .
BX6841.F67   1991
285.7'092'2 — dc20
[B]   91-27422
CIP

Contents

v

Contents

Contents

Contents

——— X ———

Foreword

The Christian Reformed Church — like many other churches — is living between the times. The old is passing away, but the new has not yet come. What we thought was God's will for women is now being questioned. We have begun to affirm the new, but much of the new is still unknown.

What will happen to our marriages, to our children, to women themselves when they begin to dream dreams, follow visions, and prophesy; when they break the barriers and follow the call of God into these brave new worlds? Men ask: Will women become less feminine? Living with a prophet has never been easy, as many women can testify, but what will it be like for a man to be married to one?

Women too ask questions. Will I have to work outside the home — with long hours, few breaks, and little family time? Will I become defined by my work? Will my husband leave me if I can support myself?

We who live between the times need to hear what happens to women who follow the call of God to become prophets, visionaries, and dreamers. We need to hear what happens to their faith, to them as persons, to their families, to their relationships with men, and to their place in the community of the faithful. Pioneers write letters home to inform those who have yet to make the trip what life on the frontier is like. The stories in this book are such letters.

Faced with the new, we all need reassurance — especially perhaps those women, young and old, who are now dreaming dreams and hearing the Spirit's voice urging them to speak a word of prophecy. Such women need to hear about the extraordinary lives of ordinary women. Such stories may encourage them to join the ranks of the prophets, to know that they belong, and to become bold disciples.

Three women, trailblazers on their own, are not featured in this book because they gave genesis to this project: Joan Flikkema, keeper of the vision for the Christian Reformed Church; Dorothy Van Hamersveld, supporter of the dreams and visions of others, a woman who makes their journeys possible; and Lillian V. Grissen, the editor and author who followed her vision through Africa and Iowa to this place on the new frontier. She has edited this book for women in the Christian Reformed Church, perhaps for women in many churches, and it stands as a powerful sister to the book that Studs Terkel wrote about working men and women. Lillian's story, like those of Joan Flikkema and Dorothy Van Hamersveld, is yet to be told.

Melvin and Sylvia Hugen

Introduction

Some mothers choose to work outside the home. Others must; economics no longer allows them to remain at home. Mothers usually receive — both internally and externally — the message that their duty is to devote themselves to caring for their family and rearing their children well.

Some mothers who stay at home do at times feel bored, trapped, or unfulfilled. They envy their "working" sisters. On the other hand, mothers who do pursue careers sometimes accuse themselves of being selfish for not being with their children all day. These women are caught in a no-win dilemma, one that only they and their Lord can solve together.

This book is about women — women both single and married, women who have worked at home and women who have worked outside the home. It is not about women who seek fame. Or power. Or wealth. These women have not built cathedrals, written timeless novels, or ruled countries. Yet they have accomplished much. This is a book of stories about Christian Reformed women who have recognized, developed, and used their gifts in a century of transformation and transition.

They are wearing new shoes, stepping outward and forward into places, tasks, and opportunities unknown to our grandmothers. Grandma might have worn similar shoes had they been available in her day. These twentieth-century shoes are fashioned of gifts from the world's greatest Giver, the Holy Spirit. The styles vary greatly.

In the early years of this century, when our forefathers

pioneered Christian education in private, parentally controlled schools, they established a practice that would eventually transform women's thoughts and lives. Christian schools did not and do not separate the curriculum into masculine and feminine. The curriculum is designed to develop the minds and gifts of girls as well as boys, young women as well as young men.

In no century prior to this one have women been so widely and well educated. For many women, this is the century of birth. Like a child who develops in a mother's womb for nine months before birth, so women for centuries have slowly been preparing for this century of transformation. The preparation has been mostly invisible and quiet; only in the last few decades have their contributions been discovered. The pregnancy is finished, and the birth pangs are subsiding; more abundant life in God's kingdom belongs to their daughters.

It has become increasingly clear to Christians that education has made possible this new birth. But new life — transformation through education — brings exciting challenges. Education has enhanced women's abilities to love God with their *minds*. Education is not only privilege; it is also challenge. It is not only opportunity; it is also responsibility.

For many women — either by choice or by circumstance — there has been no altar; they have remained single. Many of them have accomplished much, sometimes more than would have been possible had they become wives and mothers. But the lives of *women* do not automatically stop at the altar. For many women, motherhood is the beginning of a lifetime of rewarding devotion to, even self-sacrifice for, their families. It often requires the giving up of other aspirations and dreams. Others, however, in addition to keeping a home and nurturing children, have gone beyond the family and have ably used their gifts in church and community.

Marriage and family are not and may not be the center of existence for either Christian women or Christian men. God is and must consciously be first, the core and center of our purpose and role on earth. How does a woman love God with her mind as well as with her heart, with her strength as well as with her soul?

Who are some of these women who have understood the responsibility of God acting in and through us? How do women use Spirit-given gifts? Who are the women who have been blessed not only with knowing what God has expected of them but also with the privilege of using their gifts in special ways?

These women have not ignored the beauty of their ability to give birth, to mother, and to nurture. They have cautiously rejoiced in their transformation and courageously followed the Spirit's nudging them to share their gifts with others so that others may rejoice too.

In this book the Committee for Women of the Christian Reformed Church (CW-CRC) shares the stories of some of these women. The purpose of this book is threefold: (1) to recognize the women whose stories are included; (2) to record for the archives of the Christian Reformed Church some of the stories of women who have developed the gifts God has given them, using them to serve family, church, school, and/or community; and (3) to provide role models for Christian young men and young women.

In their research for this book, Dorothy Van Hamersveld, the project director, and Joan Flikkema, CW-CRC executive director, searched for stories about Christian Reformed women who have used their gifts in exemplary ways. They found little information when they first pursued the typical avenues for finding it. But these women were not to be deterred. The excitement of sharing such stories led Joan and Dorothy to nurture the idea until it reached maturity in this book.

The committee for this project sent letters to more than eight hundred Christian Reformed churches in the United States and Canada. Each church was invited to nominate a woman, deceased or living, whom the committee could consider for inclusion. The committee also advertised in *The Banner*, the weekly publication of the church, and queried the church's many agencies, ministries, and committees. From the nominations received, the committee chose twenty-six women whose stories appear on these pages.

The thread that ties the stories together is not first of all the accomplishments of these women but rather their use of God-given gifts. Sometimes Christians speak of "special gifts," but are not all of God's gifts special? Reformed theology emphasizes that Christians fill a threefold office: prophet, priest, and king (or should we say prophetess, priestess, and queen?). In this book the writers have concentrated on women as prophets. In a conference paper entitled "Tasks of a Prophetic Church" (*Detroit II Conference Papers*, Orbis, 1982), Jacquelyn Grant has identified a prophet in part as a Christian who has the ability to discern the will of God for her life, who stands for justice and transformation, who is not afraid to confront evil, and who seeks to build a community of faith, partnership, justice, and unity.

More than half a century ago, Dr. Louis Berkhof, who was then a professor at the seminary of the Christian Reformed Church, made an illuminating comment on the prophetic office in the *Manual of Christian Doctrine*: "There are two sides to the prophetic office, the one receptive and the other productive. . . . The receptive side is the most important and controls the other. Without receiving the prophet cannot give, and [s]he cannot give more than [s]he receives. Yet the productive side is also essential." The women whose stories are included here have been receptive to God's voice and have used their gifts to serve, to be productive in his world.

If Jesus tarries, Christian women look ahead to yet another century on earth. Women's gifts are many, their privileges great, their responsibilities growing, and their challenges immeasurable. May the stories in this book encourage the reader to love God with all of his or her heart, soul, strength, and mind.

Lillian V. Grissen

I

I will pour out my Spirit on all people.
Your sons and daughters will prophesy. . . .

Acts 2:17

Initiators

Prophets and Dreamers

Priscilla. Phoebe. Junia. Lydia. Julia.

We do not know much about these women. We do know that they ministered in special ways to Paul and to the churches. Paul greets them as servants of Christ. God called them as surely as he called Paul himself to help build God's kingdom.

Johanna. Marguerite. Mary. Christine. Henrietta. Jacoba.

God called these women too. He called them to minister in special ways in the Christian Reformed Church in North America. They responded to the prophet Micah's command "to act justly and to love mercy and to walk humbly with [their] God."

They explained God's Word; they parented the orphans; they cared about and for the sick of mind; they ministered to the poor in spirit. God called them to create Christian institutions committed to truth, to justice, and to mercy.

Here are four stories of women God called for special tasks in advancing his kingdom on earth.

3

Johanna Timmer
First acting president of the Reformed Bible College
Grand Rapids, Michigan

Called to the foreign mission field, she could not go. Called to
teach the Word of God, she started a Bible college.

Johanna Timmer, daughter of the village barber, was born
in 1901 in Graafschap, Michigan. She earned her bachelor of
arts degree from Calvin College in Grand Rapids, Michigan.
Using the funds from a prestigious scholarship (she was the first
woman to win it), she obtained a master of arts degree from
the University of Michigan in Ann Arbor. After a year at Calvin
Theological Seminary, she transferred first to a Presbyterian

seminary and then to the University of Chicago Divinity School. In 1927, at age twenty-six, Jo became the first dean of women at Calvin College and an English instructor there.

Her appointment to Calvin created considerable conflict for her. For one thing, she had since childhood committed herself seriously to becoming a foreign missionary. She had focused much of her academic work on that dream. Planning for the day when she would teach Scripture in a foreign land, she had taken two years of Greek. Even after she became dean of women, she continued her seminary studies.

Besides struggling with her calling, Jo found that her role at Calvin confronted her with problems endemic to the position. Her files reveal what vexed her most. She was forced again and again to grapple with the matter of "worldly amusements," a burning issue in her day. What was she to do with young women who attended the theater, played cards, or danced? Jo's own ideas about the problem were remarkably flexible and thoughtful; her attitude was never legalistic. For example, when Marianne Radius learned that her application to teach at Grand Rapids Christian High had been turned down because she had, in her Presbyterian youth, attended movies, Jo went to the board to plead for her. The earlier decision was overturned, and Marianne was hired.

Rumors about goings-on at Calvin brought letters and questions from the constituency. One pastor, complaining about a rumor concerning Calvin coeds who attended a movie while in Chicago at a convention, closed his letter with the line "Where there is smoke, there's undoubtedly fire."

Such conflict drained Jo. In 1937 she requested a year's leave to regain her strength, and in the end she did not return to Calvin. At some point, perhaps because of her health, she must have concluded that foreign mission work was not what God had planned for her. But if she could not go to the mission field, she would teach God's Word in the United States. But not at Calvin College.

Her unexpected departure from Calvin shocked and surprised the board, her colleagues, and her students, past and present. Many wrote to her expressing their gratitude for her rigorous English classes, her provocative chapel talks, and her faithful guidance. She saved one letter from the late Rolf Veenstra, a Christian Reformed minister:

> Should your work have been discouraging — and I cannot but think that it was, at times — you can assure yourself that for every noisome critic there have been a dozen in the silent majority who approved of your policies and activities, but who thought it beneath them — as is always the sad story — to throw their smelly nightcaps into the air and crow with great to-do. As one of such majority, may I offer my mite of tribute in behalf of a task superbly done, and a task which only God can adequately reward, when with his "Well done!" he shall approve of work which was, we are all hoping in the next few years to learn, a stepping stone to a bigger one.

The new home — the "bigger one" — was the Reformed Bible Institute (now the Reformed Bible College) in Grand Rapids, Michigan. The RBI was born amid controversy, and from the beginning Jo Timmer was involved. The possibility of offering courses in evangelism at Calvin had been studied. In the late twenties, however, the Christian Reformed synod rejected the possibility. But form a separate institution to teach courses in evangelism and Bible from a Reformed perspective? Ridiculous! One person at that time described the product of such a school as a "tin can preacher."

Nevertheless, meetings to discuss the possibility continued, and these meetings included Jo Timmer. She explained her support in an article published in *The Banner* in April 1939, a month after a board of trustees had been organized for the school:

> A fact that is, I fear, often forgotten is that the less we know about the Word of God the less we know whether we are subjecting our view of God, man, and the world to the Word of God. Ignorance hinders the progress of truth seriously. . . . Knowledge is indeed spiritual power. It is not sincerity but the truth that makes us free. We need both. To the extent that Sunday school

teachers, leaders of societies, the wives of ministers and of missionaries, mission workers, and others are ignorant of the truth, no matter how rich their sincerity may be, to that extent they hinder the truth.

Jo's dedication was total. In 1940 she became the RBI's acting president, a position she held for the first four years the school was open, and its first dean. She also taught Reformed doctrine, and everyone — were they her students at Calvin or RBI — agrees that Miss Timmer was a brilliant teacher. Besides her other responsibilities, she administered the RBI's Christian Service Department. "She *was* the RBI," said Rev. John Schaal, a member of the board.

During her years at the RBI, Jo also was responsible for the creation of young women's societies throughout the denomination. Eventually these grew into a federation that held national conventions. Later the federation joined with the young men in the denomination to become the Young Calvinists of the Christian Reformed Church. She encouraged the dreams and aspirations of her students — especially two young women who had undertaken the task of providing shelter and love for unmarried mothers and their children, an activity that led to the founding of Bethany Home.

Jo left the RBI in 1943 — but not to retire. The Reverend Dick Walters had been appointed to become the first RBI president. For the next five years Jo worked as principal of Ripon Christian School in California. She then moved to Philadelphia, where she founded a Christian high school at the request of the Orthodox Presbyterian Church. When she finally did retire in 1963, she settled in Holland, Michigan. Still she busied herself — with as many as six different Bible study groups.

Johanna Timmer, called by God to foreign missions, never left the States. No matter. She created her own mission field wherever she went.

Johanna Timmer died from a heart attack in January 1978. She had finished her mission.

7

Marguerite Bonnema and Mary DeBoer VandenBosch
Founders of Bethany Home
Grand Rapids, Michigan

Two young girls, living in widely separated parts of the country, each dreamed of starting an orphanage.

Marguerite Bonnema, born February 8, 1913, was one of eight children, the daughter of an accountant. As a teenager in Cleveland, Ohio, she passed a Catholic orphanage every day as she walked to the junior high school. She often stood and watched, fascinated by the activities, the children's uniforms, the *idea*.

More than a thousand miles away, in Denver, Colorado,

lived Mary DeBoer, just a few years Marguerite's junior. (She was born on February 2, 1916.) As a young girl she amused her family with talk about starting a Christian home for children who had none.

After high school, Marguerite entered nurses' training to prepare herself — not for nursing but for the realization of her dream. She had read many stories about nurses working in mission fields or in orphanages in foreign countries. "Maybe," she thought, "I have to become a nurse in order to start a home." Graduating in 1935, the heart of the Great Depression, she spent the next five years as a private duty nurse. She wondered whether her dream would ever materialize.

Mary, one of seven children and daughter of a gardener, went to work after finishing the ninth grade. She continued to talk about her desire to start a Christian home, despite being considered a bit crazy to entertain such a notion. True, she had a problem: she did not know how to go about starting a home!

In January 1940, these two young women became roommates in Grand Rapids, Michigan, in a small room above a heating company on a street named Wealthy. Although penniless, they were willing to clean houses and babysit to make their way. Both of them were students in the first class at the Reformed Bible Institute (which, providentially, charged minimal tuition). Mary had taken a bus from Denver and had been greeted by Miss Johanna Timmer and Mr. P. B. Peterson, a local businessman who would later become important to both girls. Marguerite, having arrived earlier, welcomed the newcomer — and gave her the top bunk. Neither knew of the other's dreams.

One day, only a few weeks after the girls arrived in Grand Rapids, Marguerite asked, "What do you plan to do when you graduate, Mary?" Mary wondered, "Shall I tell her about wanting to start a Christian home for children? Maybe she'll think I'm a little crazy, just like some others do." Despite her misgivings, Mary spoke of her dream. Marguerite looked at her in astonishment. "Why, that's exactly what I want to do!"

How could they have known then that in time their dreams

would merge, and together they would make the idea of a Christian home a reality?

After graduating in December 1942, the two women moved into a small apartment on Sigsbee Street. Both young ladies became workers in local missions.

One day an American Indian family came to Marguerite for help at the Sixth and Broadway Mission. The father, dishonorably discharged from the army, was threatening to kill the family's infant girl because, he claimed, she was not his child. After much prayer, Mary and Marguerite agreed to care for the baby in their tiny apartment. To protect the baby, Mary and Marguerite withheld their address. They set up a meeting with the family in a lumberyard at the end of the local bus line. "When we arrived," says Marguerite, "the grandma was sitting against a tree with the baby in her arms. Mama stood a bit further away. A basket containing a few bits of clothing rested on one spot and the bottle on another. We gathered everything, spoke a few words, said good-bye, got on the bus, and went home." Their first child, tiny Regina Madeline, became "Jeannie" to her new mothers. A babysitter took care of Jeannie during the day while Mary and Marguerite worked.

More children followed: an infant whose mother could no longer care for her; a sixteen-year-old blind girl who had been in and out of foster care and now had no place to go; two little boys, Tommy and Johnny. Together all lived in the young women's small apartment. Not enough room. Not enough money (especially since Marguerite now stayed home with the children). But plenty of love! "You never saw two such tickled old maids in your life," says Marguerite. Their faith was firm: God had called them to this work, and he would provide.

Calls for help continued. Mary and Marguerite reassured each other with Philippians 4:19: "God will meet all your needs according to his glorious riches in Christ Jesus." A day came when word reached the young women that part of what was called the Ferris estate on the north side of Grand Rapids was for sale. Mr. Peterson, Andrew VanderVeer (who earlier had become interested in the young women's growing ministry), Marguerite, and Mary walked to the property. The building had been used as a *roadhouse*. But Mary and Marguerite didn't care; no matter what a roadhouse was, the house, set on nearly fourteen acres of land, was perfect for the children! "It had a great big room, 25' × 25', I'm sure," recalls Mary, "and two walls with large plate-glass windows. 'Oh,' we thought, 'what a wonderful playroom for the children!' There were two large bedrooms, several showers, and a nice bath. Downstairs was a large kitchen and a big dining room. We saw many possibilities."

Two weeks later Mr. Peterson offered them a loan to buy the property. "It was a miracle!" Mary says simply. Mr. Peterson paid for the necessary repairs. Nellie Kuipers, one of the volunteers who had worked with the women earlier, came with mops and pails and her junior high class. Together they cleaned the house.

On June 21, 1944, 901 Eastern Avenue became home for eight children. Each child had two mothers.

It *was* a miracle. Marguerite and Mary did not know that one day that house would be torn down and replaced with five buildings which would house Bethany Christian Services, an organization that still provides homes for children, nationally and internationally, besides offering (among other services) help to pregnant women and assistance with foster care, adoptions, and family counseling.

As was required, Marguerite and Mary applied for a license on March 9, 1945, to incorporate Bethany Home, as they had named it. They thought they had taken care of everything. Not so! The state required approval by the Council of Social Agencies. A dozen people — including a representative of the council, the fire marshal, and a judge — attended a meeting set up for the council to critique the work and the home. The questioning proceeded, and the meeting seemed to be going well. Then someone asked, "How will this home be supported financially?"

Mary and Marguerite had few answers that they thought would satisfy their reviewers. The Lord had provided them with satisfactory answers all along, but would these answers satisfy the state of Michigan? They admitted that they were totally dependent on donations: venison, canned goods, clothing, and cash (including tuition for the children's Christian education) came from friends and supporters.

The judge, the Honorable John B. Dalton — a stranger to both Mary and Marguerite — spoke up. He assured the inspectors that he was acquainted with the church represented here. "Don't worry about their support base," he said. "What the Christian Reformed Church starts, its people will support."

Bethany Home was given a license. "Again we thanked God for his wonderful provision. But, you know," says Mary, "I still wonder whether we ever thanked the judge."

When Bethany Home was incorporated, Andrew Vander-Veer was named president, Mary DeBoer the vice president, and Marguerite the treasurer. The home later obtained a license to provide adoption services. The Christian Reformed synod gave its blessing to the venture.

For five years Marguerite and Mary worked without salary. "It was the Lord's work. We just made ourselves available," Mary says.

Marguerite had realized her dream. No wonder she hated to leave in 1951, when she returned home to nurse her mother, who was recuperating from surgery. But Marguerite rapidly became involved in establishing a mission in Warren Heights near Cleveland. She also started Bible classes there and worked as an aide in the Christian school. Through this work she discovered that she loved teaching. The field was exciting, and it maintained her involvement with children. By taking classes at night and during the summer, Marguerite added a degree in education (from Western Michigan University) to her nursing degree. Before retiring in 1975, she taught for four years in Grant, Michigan, and for three years in the public schools in Grand Haven, Michigan. Marguerite now spends her retirement enjoying gardening, homemaking, and reading.

Mary stayed at Bethany Home until 1956, when she married John VandenBosch, a widower with three daughters — Yvonne,

Carol, and Joan. John and Mary became parents of a daughter, Helena Joy, and a son, John Peter, with Down's syndrome. Besides rearing their own children, John and Mary invited foster children to share their home. All told, thirty-one children experienced Mary and John's love and parenting.

John died on January 1, 1982. Mary and her son now live in Dorr, Michigan, where she has taught Sunday school and vacation Bible school and leads group Bible studies.

For Marguerite and Mary, God's promise to "supply all [their] needs according to his riches in Christ Jesus" was more than sufficient. Called by God when they were young to start a Christian home for children, they obeyed.

Hundreds of children, teenagers, and parents now rise and call them blessed.

Christine VanderLaan Beezhold (above) and
Henrietta VanderLaan Mollahan (opposite)
Founders of Elim Christian School
Chicago, Illinois

While Johanna Timmer was teaching at the Reformed Bible
Institute and Marguerite Bonnema and Mary DeBoer were
caring for as many as seventeen children at Bethany Home, two
sisters living in Chicago, Illinois, undertook another kind of
venture of faith and daring.

It was the spring of 1948. In the basement of the Second
Christian Reformed Church of Englewood, two sisters, Hen-

rietta and Christine, opened a small school on a trial basis for children with disabilities.

Henrietta was born on October 1, 1925; Christine on July 25, 1920. They, together with Pearl and Cornelius, were the children of Rudolph VanderLaan and Jeannette Bieze.

When Grandma Bieze had died in 1926, Grandpa Henry Bieze had come to live with the family. Henrietta — "Babe," as the family called her — was six months old at the time, and she soon became Grandpa's favorite. When she was older, Babe, inspired by countless visits to the sick with her grandpa, decided she wanted to become a nurse. Upon her pastor's advice — "You're too young and too naive for nursing school" — Babe spent a year at Calvin College. Her chemistry professor, Dr. John DeVries, suggested she apply to Chicago Presbyterian Hospital School of Nursing. "You want the best," he told her. Babe took his advice and was accepted. She graduated in 1947 and became a staff nurse at the hospital.

After graduating from high school in 1938, Christine worked in the loan department of a Chicago bank. She taught Sunday school, played the piano at the Helping Hand Mission on Chicago's Skid Row, and sang in the church choir. She attended night school for three years.

Until this point in their lives, the story of Christine and Babe is not unusual. They were children of Dutch immigrant parents who were hard-working and devoted. They were secure in the love of their parents and in their faith. The girls did what was expected of them.

God's call to them to do special work in his kingdom came through Rev. William Masselink, then pastor of Second Christian Reformed Church. He asked the two young women if they would start a school for mentally retarded children. What an idea! Why would the minister make such a request of them? Babe was a nurse, Christine a clerk in a loan department. What qualifications did they have? Well, none, apparently. But Rev. Masselink had a special reason for his strange request. His son, Paul, was a young boy with mental handicaps who was attending a public school. Paul was learning all sorts of undesirable habits there, Rev. Masselink said; he needed to be in a place where Christian values were taught. In fact, so did other children like Paul. And Rev. Masselink had confidence in Babe and Christine — more than they had in themselves.

The obstacles were many. Could two women teach such students — when neither one was trained as a teacher, especially not a teacher of mentally retarded children? Would people accept them as teachers? Would parents send their handicapped children to such a school? Would people support such an attempt? Would the consistory of Second Christian Reformed Church approve this use of their facilities?

Christine and Babe thought of a child in their church who had been trained to hide in the basement or a bedroom of the family home whenever the doorbell rang. Only her family saw her. At that time many people believed that handicapped children were sent from God as punishment. The children were hidden, ignored, and often neglected. Would that change?

After many discussions and meetings and much prayer, Babe and Christine decided to leave their positions and accept the greatest challenge they had ever faced. Together — with God's help — they would start a Christian school for children with disabilities.

By April 1948 seven children were enrolled for a six-week term, a trial period for the sisters and their school. The sisters spent the summer of 1948 at the University of Chicago learning as much as they could about children with disabilities. The University of Chicago evaluated the children and supplied the classroom materials needed to teach them. Christine and Babe comprised the complete staff of the new Christian school. Christine drove the "bus" — really her father's Cadillac — to pick up the children. Averaging fifty to seventy-five miles a day, she drove in all kinds of weather. She also collected the tuition from the parents, usually while she was transporting the children.

In the evening Christine and Babe prepared individualized lesson plans. They also explained their program at local churches and requested the churches' support.

And all day, of course, they taught seven children, most of whom had never before been inside a school. A few of them had never left their homes until now; they did not recognize an object as familiar as a child's swing. Babe nursed some of the children when they suffered grand-mal seizures. Because the children were frequently sick, Babe and Christine became both janitors and laundresses. At lunchtime they became cooks. On special outings to the zoo, the park, or the beach, they became recreational directors.

The days were long. Exhausting. But "the love shown on the faces of the children" made it worthwhile, the sisters say.

The parents of the children also "expressed great appreciation, many times with tears," notes Babe.

The six-week trial period was an unqualified success; at its end, many of the sisters' initial questions had been answered. Indeed, the need for their work was great. Parents were overwhelmed that their special children could go to school. Members of the Christian Reformed Church found funds to support the school.

Heartened by their early experience, Babe and Christine agreed to continue their labor of love. Seventeen children were accepted for the fall semester.

It was only two years until their small school, begun with seven children in a church basement, needed a building and specialized teachers. At this juncture Christine and Babe resigned. They had answered God's call and had "suffered the little children to come unto [God]."

From the work of these two sisters, Elim Christian School was born. Today Elim Christian School serves children with physical and mental handicaps, children from all over the United States, and provides facilities for children to live on campus.

After their groundbreaking work with the handicapped, the two sisters took separate paths. Babe went back to nursing. Eventually she married and had three sons. Today she lives with her second husband, Frank Mollahan, in New Port Richey, Florida. She is still nursing. Christine married shortly after leaving Elim and had four children. She and her husband, Chris Beezhold, live in Bradenton, Florida.

Today, as before, God continues to use both sisters in their churches for his work.

Jacoba Beuker Robbert
Envisioner of Pine Rest Christian Hospital
Cutlerville, Michigan

One morning Jacoba Robbert looked out the front window of
the parsonage in Kalamazoo, Michigan. A somewhat elderly
lady was walking back and forth. She was, she said after Jacoba
invited her in, looking for a "Dutch church." Her search had
brought her to the parsonage of First Kalamazoo Christian Reformed Church, the home of Rev. Jan Robbert and his wife,
Jacoba. The woman said she wanted to go to church. Jacoba

19

learned later that the woman had walked away from the state mental hospital in Kalamazoo, something she often did on Sunday.

Jacoba Robbert understood the woman's desire. As a minister's daughter who was now a minister's wife, Jacoba had spent her life in the parsonage. It was a special place, she thought. She had witnessed many of the pains and problems that people bring to their pastor.

Born in 1863 in Zwolle in the Netherlands, Jacoba was the daughter of Rev. Dr. Henricus Beuker. In 1885 she married Jan Robbert, a graduate of the Theological School at Kampen and a close friend of the Beuker family. According to Jacoba, "The year of 1885 was the crowning year of our earthly enjoyment." Their marriage was happy, and it was blessed with seven sons and three daughters. As a minister's wife, of course, Jacoba continued to live in the parsonage. In 1893 Jan accepted a call from First Roseland Christian Reformed Church in Chicago, and the family moved to the United States.

Subsequently, in 1901, the family moved to Kalamazoo. Here Jacoba became acquainted with the state hospital for the mentally ill and the retarded. Her compassion ran deep for the woman looking for a Dutch church and for others like her who were hospitalized in the state institution. Twice a week Jacoba went to the state hospital to minister to women there. Her concern inspired her to write an article in 1906 for *De Wachter,* then the weekly Dutch magazine of the Christian Reformed Church, about the need for *Christian* treatment for the emotionally and mentally ill. Her challenge was simple: "Can there be true healing of the soul without the Great Physician?"

Later Jacoba explained that she and other volunteers "saw and heard much at the Kalamazoo hospital which convinced us that Christian treatment was necessary for the patients. . . . The necessity became plainer to us from week to week. Body and soul are so closely related. The need of Christian love for those poor patients was so great."

Jacoba understood that the greatest gift which could be

given to people who suffered from mental and emotional illnesses was the assurance of God's forgiveness and his love. The Reverend John Keizer, pastor of Second Kalamazoo Christian Reformed Church, said that many Christian Reformed patients in state mental hospitals "suffered from anxieties about having sinned beyond the power of God's grace." He, like Jacoba, argued that such people needed ministers and counselors who understood Reformed theology.

A crusade was mounted for a Christian hospital to serve the mentally ill. In 1909 a group of seventy men and women met at LaGrave Avenue Christian Reformed Church in Grand Rapids, Michigan, and through that meeting the Christian Psychopathic Hospital Association was established. The Reverend John Keizer was elected the first president of the new board of directors. The association purchased the Cutler farm in Cutlerville, a small village south of Grand Rapids, to use as the hospital. By this time Jan and Jacoba Robbert had accepted a call to Niekerk, Michigan, a farming town that was some distance — by horse and buggy — from Grand Rapids.

Some people, of course, shrugged at the suggestion of a Christian hospital for the mentally ill. Still, wrote Jacoba, "the plan received the love and support from our people, and Cutlerville is a proof of this." When it first opened in 1910, the Christian Psychopathic Hospital employed four nurses, a cook, a solicitor, and a farmer. A year later Dr. J. G. Stuart became its first doctor and administrator.

Jacoba's vision of a Christian institution to help the mentally and emotionally ill was now realized. The hospital worked steadily toward becoming a highly respected institution. Today the multimillion-dollar complex now called Pine Rest Christian Hospital serves hundreds of people from every walk of life in both the United States and Canada, people suffering from a wide spectrum of emotional and mental problems.

Niekerk was not Jan's last pastorate. Jacoba moved to several parsonages as Jan accepted various calls. In 1918, ill and distraught because four sons had been called to fight in World

War I (and a fifth was waiting to be sent overseas), Jan accepted emeritation (honorable retirement). He died four years later. For the first time in her life, Jacoba could not live in a parsonage.

Jacoba spent her remaining years in Holland, Michigan. When she died in 1957, Dr. Jacob Hoogstra, her pastor for the last seventeen years of her life, called her a "mother in Israel."

Indeed, Jacoba was a prophet in her own country.

II

Her children arise
and call her blessed.

Proverbs 31:28

Eunice Meyer Vanderlaan

Voice in the Parsonage

"The prophet has an impatient temperament. Impatience can get you into a lot of trouble. You look like a troublemaker so easily. The very act of trying to bring about change may tear the social fabric that holds us together. Precisely here is the frightening part of it all."

25

Eunice Meyer Vanderlaan was born on March 25, 1940, to Martha Ulferts and Leo Meyer, a rural schoolteacher and a Minnesota farmer. As a child she attended a Christian school made up mainly of Dutch families. School wasn't always fun, during the years immediately following World War II, for a little girl who was the granddaughter of German immigrants. But this was only one of many challenges Eunice has faced, and she is equal to the task, heir to the sturdy notions of her forebears.

Early in life she learned that not everyone is considered equal. One's value, however, is not something granted by the government or by one's Dutch compatriots. A person's worth, her parents taught her, is God-given and irrevocable.

Leo Meyer's faith dictated that he be the very best farmer possible — and it also dictated that he have an impact on the society around him. He was an outspoken critic of any relaxation of Prohibition in his county. A man of strong opinions, he offered them freely to his children.

When Eunice was in high school, the Young Calvinist Federation of the Christian Reformed Church held oratorical contests. When Eunice and her brother Galen entered one year, Leo Meyer coached his children in the farm's long hoghouse. (It was the season between herds, so the hoghouse was empty.) Eunice's father made a speaking platform and rows of "pews" from straw bales. While Eunice gave her speech from the straw stage, her father and brother criticized and advised her from the straw seats. Then Eunice and Galen switched places. The coaching worked. For two years both Eunice and Galen won first place in their church, and both went on to participate at the league level.

After high school, Eunice went to Dordt College in Sioux Center, Iowa, for two years. She completed her education at Calvin College in Grand Rapids, Michigan, graduating with a bachelor of arts degree in secondary education. Again and again in the service of school and church Eunice has used her education and the elocutionary skills she developed in the hoghouse. The Christian Reformed synod of 1984 appointed her to a study committee on the withholding of income taxes as a form of conscientious objection. Synod 1985 placed her on a committee to study the nature and authority of the office of elders and deacons. Synod 1988 appointed her to the Inter-Church Relations Committee.

The art of communication and language itself are especially dear to Eunice. She has had several articles published in *The Banner, Christian Home and School,* and *Origins,* and she has written a workbook for the text *Basic English Revisited* (1983).

She looks and listens for the teaching in everything. The design on a package of fish crackers, for instance. "Look at this. There's a whole crowd of little fish crackers floating downstream," she points out. "No eyes. No mouths either. One little guy is going the other way. He's the only one with an eye. And look at the determined set to his mouth." An eye. A mouth. And a determination to swim upstream. Alone, if necessary. Like that one little fish, Eunice has chosen to swim against the tide of abortion. Publicly and privately, she has become an advocate for the voiceless unborn.

To be willing to swim alone is a prerequisite for prophetic witness. Still, to insist on swimming alone is not necessarily heroic; it can be neurotic. Recognizing this, Eunice joined the Right to Life organization. Geraldine Oftedahl, a speech and language pathologist who is the Roman Catholic chairperson of the Right to Life organization of New York state, worked with Eunice in Rochester. "Eunice probably facilitated as many as ten doors being opened to Right to Life in various churches. She's a woman for all seasons," says Geraldine.

When Eunice reads that to stop funding for Medicaid abortions would be to discriminate against poor women, her sympathy for the poor does not impede her reasoning. "On the contrary," her letter to the editor of the local press asserts, "a thoughtful and courageous advocacy for the poor will not deprive them of their young. It will assist them to care for them. . . . Affluent women do not have to destroy their offspring to attain quality of life. Poor women shouldn't have to either!"

A serious charge levied against people with pro-life convictions is that of unconcern about the futures of "unaborted" but unwanted children. But Eunice and her husband, Rev. Jim Vanderlaan, have opened their home to such children. The couple gave birth to three children: Miriam, 24; Naomi, 20; and John, 16. After that they began to adopt children. Neither one of them believes, however, that they should receive any special admiration for their decision to adopt. "I wish we had done it for some high-flown ideal," Eunice says. "But it was simply this insatiable hunger to be parents."

Eunice had complications with each of her pregnancies.

Eunice and her husband, Jim, have three children by birth and four children by adoption. Neither one of them believes, however, that they should receive any special admiration for their decision to adopt. "I wish we had done it for some high-flown ideal," Eunice says. "But it was simply this insatiable hunger to be parents."

This risk and the awareness that she and Jim had of the many children in need drew them toward adoption. "We love the baby stuff," Eunice says. "The smells, the bottles. We delight in a baby's cry and in the stepping of baby shoes across the floor." Today Eunice and her husband have four adopted African-American children: Timothy, 12; David, 10; Lydia, 8; and Nathan, 6. Each child's birth-mother had been confronted with the solution of abortion, and each had rejected it.

Wherever Jim and Eunice have gone to serve a congregation, they have made a difference. When they have moved on they have left behind them people ready to adopt, people sensitized to others with handicaps (Jim has been blind since birth), people waking to a life of commitment.

When Jewyl Bierma, a member of Webster (New York)

Christian Reformed Church at the time Jim was its pastor, gave birth to a daughter with spina bifida, her world changed. "I went through all the intense emotions and feelings of guilt," she said. "Whenever I was really up against the wall, Eunice would show me the positive points of the experience, but she's not a Polly-anna. I believe she faces reality better than most." Jewyl and her husband, Richard, have since adopted a daughter from Korea and an African-American son.

Pam Nyhof, of Parchment (Michigan) Christian Reformed Church, has one child by birth and one by adoption. Eunice's love for children and her creativity in expressing that love concretely have had a strong impact on Pam. The Vanderlaans' "Annual Family Awards Dinner," at which Eunice gives each child a Christmas ornament, seems especially significant to Pam because the awards are not for typical successes.

Eunice chooses each award to celebrate a child's personal achievement or victory over something difficult. One year Lydia and Nathan both suffered from nightmares, and often one of them would crawl into bed with their parents. Then they discovered they could comfort each other if they pushed their cribs right next to one another and slept close to each other. Their ornaments that year were two little cribs, each holding a little bear wearing a nightcap.

"On that day, we have a fancy dinner in the dining room," says Miriam. "Mom frequently invites our grandparents and special people. It's always a big event."

Virginia and Mark Lenz in Ithaca, New York, found that Eunice and Jim regarded people with handicaps in a refreshing way. "There was no undue sympathy," notes Virginia. "In fact, I've heard that once Jim got caught in a department store's revolving door. Instead of helping him, Eunice crossed the street, watched him, and laughed."

"That isn't what happened," protests Eunice, laughing. "A revolving door? That's too easy for Jim. No, it was the back exit of a large department store, a glass door in a glass wall." Jim and Eunice were dating at the time, and Jim had been teasing her by putting the tip of his cane in the back of her shoe. She decided to get back at him. Both of them were laughing so hard that Jim couldn't concentrate on finding the door, and Eunice left him groping for the exit. Eventually a stranger fought his way across traffic to help Jim out and then glared at Eunice.

Wherever Jim and Eunice have gone to serve a congregation, they have made a difference. When they have moved on, they have left behind them people ready to adopt, people sensitized to others with handicaps, people waking to a life of commitment.

That sometimes outrageous humor has influenced the way entire congregations have responded to Jim's blindness. Jewyl remembers that when the Vanderlaans first came to Webster Christian Reformed Church, the congregation was a bit uncomfortable. Their interaction with Jim, who is quite reserved, was awkward. After Jim had led a part of his first congregational meeting there, it was time for an elder to take over the rest of the meeting. As he was ready to sit down, Jim said, "Euny, I'd like you to come sit with me." Eunice, sitting somewhere in the midst of the congregation, said, "Well, Jim, I think you should come sit with me." There was a pause. Jim said, "But Euny, I don't really know where you are." With a silly grin on her face, Euny invited, "Well, Jim, come find me."

"The congregation burst into laughter," Jewyl remembers. "Eunice led the way to our seeing that Jim is a person like anyone else." This lightheartedness doesn't perturb Jim. "It's important for a person with handicaps to feel that the people he deals with most directly don't distort that feature," he says. "Right from the start Euny didn't do that. My blindness fascinated her, but she didn't treat it as a reason for pity. It's like any other characteristic that you acknowledge. You don't ridicule or accentuate it, but humor is a way of keeping it in perspective."

Jim and Eunice's relationship seems to have a unique flavor. There is little about it that is ingrown or self-indulgent. Eunice is often busy with her own projects, but when she and Jim work together, as they do during joint presentations at conferences, they are a genuine team. "That has been our interaction in everything we do," says Jim. "Euny is like a foil to me, as I am to her. She challenges me, and I challenge her — not in a destructive or competitive way but, as the Bible says, as 'iron sharpens iron.' We keep each other on our toes."

Eunice has given herself the freedom to choose which feminine trappings she will invest in. She is not ruled by vanity. The streaks of gray in her short, fluffy brown hair cause her no distress. "It's going to be tough in the twenty-first century to be a woman with pure motives and a pure life," Eunice says. "In department stores I'm struck by the space devoted to women and to all of the stuff that goes into making us presentable." For her, the word *femininity* evokes a variety of images: a married woman bending over a child; the wind catching the veil of a Catholic sister tending to an orphan; the articulate expression of a woman participating in a congressional hearing on behalf of people with handicaps.

Humor and uniqueness have also marked Jim and Eunice's

"Euny is like a foil to me, as I am to her," Jim says. "She challenges me, and I challenge her — not in a destructive or competitive way but, as the Bible says, 'as iron sharpens iron.' We keep each other on our toes."

---

roles as parents. It was when they already had five children — their three by birth and two adopted children — that Eunice experienced a nearly irresistible urge to adopt another child.

Jim was certain that she was already weighed down by the demands of a large family. Eunice was grief-stricken. She'd already bonded to a baby who was available for adoption, and whenever she saw a baby of the same gender, she could not control her tears. Later that week, when Eunice again saw such a baby, her empty arms ached. When she returned home, she went right to Jim's study to tell him how desolate she felt. "I was quite a sight because I'd been crying for several days," she says. Just then the doorbell rang, and Jim went to the door. Eunice heard Don Boner, one of the church elders. "May I speak to you for a moment, Jim?" All Eunice could think was "I can't let him see me like this or we'll have to tell him, too." So she dodged under Jim's desk.

Jim and Don came into the study. Eunice soon realized that the two men were discussing private church business that would take much more than a minute or two. As she crouched under her husband's desk, she knew that she couldn't eavesdrop on their confidential conversation. She knew that she'd have to say something like, "Jim . . . Don . . . excuse me, but I'm here under the desk," and she'd have to stand up. So she did.

At Jim's urging, Eunice confided her distress to Don. A little later she and Jim watched Don leave, dressed in his plain clothes, getting into his battered station wagon to go home to his very large family of birth, adopted, and profoundly disabled foster children. "Our problem must have seemed a bit silly to him," says Eunice.

She and Jim decided to adopt again, so Eunice's mothering urge was satisfied . . . temporarily. "Mom celebrated each child," explains Miriam. " 'You're only young once,' she would say. Whenever we went to a new parsonage, Mother always set one room aside as a *play* room — not a family room — and it was always close to the kitchen. It was only for toys and always for children. She always encouraged us to do things."

But Eunice's celebration of children and her tremendous desire to adopt again and again doesn't mean that motherhood has always been easy or a continual delight. "Probably the hardest thing I've done is to rear four little children after the age of thirty-nine," she says. "It's a lonely business. Few women as old as I am have little ones anymore. Late motherhood, though, is not a horror in my book. The most important job for us all, men and women, is to see that the next generation is cared for."

"Mother worked hard at encouraging all of us to develop our own identities," adds Miriam, "and I never felt that we competed for her attention. She is helping the younger children especially relate to their backgrounds. Timmy has Indian blood, so my parents are exploring his Cherokee heritage with him. They visited the Trail of Tears National Monument, which marks the end of that tragic forced march of Indians from the southeast United States to Oklahoma. They celebrate adoptive as well as regular birthdays with the younger children. She talks about their birth mothers."

Like all parents, Eunice yearns to shield her children from trouble. The Vanderlaan children too have experienced struggle. Miriam spent her high-school years confined twenty-three hours a day in a brace to correct her scoliosis (curvature of the spine). "It cut me to the quick," says Eunice, "but the Lord has used it for her good. Much of life is anguish. Parenting is showing children how to deal with it and how to express both pain and happiness."

The Vanderlaans' three dark-skinned sons have also sensitized Eunice to the fact that, in the eyes of white society, the black male is two things: threatening and invisible. And this fact she protests vehemently. She collects examples of advertising that excludes black males. She scans magazines and the TV screen, noticing the virtual absence of the black male and, when he is included, his relative size and placement in the scene. Then she speaks and writes. Local department stores, national corporations, catalog producers, and Christian publications hear from her frequently. She rebukes gently. The striking characteristic in each confrontation is her ability to empathize with the complexity of the other's life.

Sometimes, of course, she is criticized. Sometimes she feels insecure. "It's a lonely business," she says. "The cutting edge is never attractive, but the challenge is to evaluate yourself, to ask yourself, 'Am I unattractive for good reason? Is it my own fault that this is a lonely business, this obedience?'"

Her own internal "critics" also attack her. Eunice sometimes sees herself as indolent because she doesn't accomplish all her goals, and this frustrates her. "My mother indolent?" Miriam responds, "Never. Anyone who accomplishes as much as she does can't be indolent."

"Organization is not my forte either," says Eunice. "If I were organized, I'd have far more time to tackle some of these things that I see need tackling." Miriam overrules this self-criticism. "That's not true either. She's always on top of things, and I think of that as being organized. I would rather say she is

---

"A prophet needs a strong stomach when it comes to trouble, but I need Maalox. Conflict is painful to me, and ugly."

---

unfocused: she's a very intense person, and she can sometimes focus all her energy on one idea, but at other times she flits. When she got married she had three bank accounts, none with much money in it. She just wasn't good at keeping track of the balance, so she was afraid she would overdraw. Instead of sorting it out, she simply started a new bank account. That's what I mean by unfocused."

Eunice also recalls some memories that carry a sting. She remembers in particular the huge task of attempting to set up Christian high schools in two of the places Jim had pastorates. One school thrives, and one is closed. Many people have been hurt. Eunice grieves for the financial losses some people suffered, but she grieves even more deeply that hopes were dashed.

Perhaps it is her willingness to be aware of anguish that makes Eunice's prophetic vocation such a rich and poignant calling. Her husband says, "She is more of a prophet than I, if a prophet is one who sees trouble and is bothered by it and is forced to speak." Eunice herself hesitates to own a prophetic

---

There has been some crying in the Vanderlaan parsonage, but the most frequent sound heard there is laughter.

---

calling, saying, "A prophet needs a strong stomach when it comes to trouble, but I need Maalox. Conflict is painful to me, and ugly."

She refuses even to idealize the prophetic calling. "The prophet has an impatient temperament. Impatience can get you into a lot of trouble. You look like a troublemaker so easily. The very act of trying to bring about change may tear the social fabric that holds us together. Precisely here is the frightening part of it all," Eunice explains. "You have to rip the fabric to expose, but if you rip it too much, the very people you're trying to help will lose the support they need."

Given their role, all prophets must expect criticism and times of loneliness. Sometimes, Eunice explains, she can accept those things as part of the lot of a pastor's wife. At other times, the hurt is too great, and she struggles. Peace returns to her only when she is able, finally, to acknowledge, "He is the Lord." Church members have sometimes accused her of overdoing her Right to Life involvement. Some people believe that parenting seven children takes Jim's attention away from his pastoral duties. The Vanderlaans' conviction that eligibility for church office should not be based on gender and Jim's position on Calvin College's board of trustees during a time of controversy have alienated some people and resulted in transfers of church membership. All these things bring pain. "In the parsonage, however," Eunice adds, "you can cry, but you can't keep on crying."

There has been some crying in the Vanderlaan parsonage, but the most frequent sound heard there is laughter. Both Jim and Eunice love to joke. Sometimes Eunice comes up with absolutely ridiculous word sequences for Jim. "Just plain non-sense," Eunice admits. "I love to play word tricks on him because he's got to take the time to run the pieces of junk through his marvelous mental machinery."

Sometimes, though, it's Jim who laughs last.

An example: Eunice had a particularly modest nightgown that Jim had never liked. Flannel nightgowns, he was certain, belonged only in convents. One night he said to Eunice, "With all you wear to bed you might as well wear boots!" The next night, lying in bed in her big snowboots, Eunice could hardly wait for Jim to come to bed. Finally she heard him begin his nightly ritual of checking locks and stove knobs and children and then brushing his teeth. As he crawled into bed, his leg scraped against the heel of Euny's boot. There was a pregnant pause. Then Jim said to her, "Euny, do you think you could cut your toenails?"

Humor, action, intensity, dedication, and celebration. No wonder the children of Eunice Vanderlaan "arise and call her blessed; her husband also, and he praises her" (Prov. 31:28).

Barthie Knoppers Boon

Ingenuity and Independence

Some thought it nice that Nico would allow his wife to behave in certain ways considered "inappropriate" for a minister's wife, but Barthie did not need or ask permission. She identified her own needs and tried to meet them, even if it meant going against popular opinion. This sense of separate identity, a special gift, she gave to her daughters.

Barthie Knoppers Boon broke many stereotypes of ministers' wives and full-time homemakers. A feminist before the feminist movement began, she passed on to her sons and to her daughters the gifts of caring for others and of steadfast faith, independence, critical thinking, and concern for the status of women. Through "outrageous acts and everyday rebellions," she worked to empower her daughters — one of whom is me, the author of this story — and the daughters in the church.

Barthie Boon was born on July 10, 1918, in Amsterdam, the oldest child of a schoolteacher, Elizabeth Neeltje Wateler, and Jacob Boon, owner of a construction company. Elizabeth taught school, and she lived in a town some distance from her parental home, a rare circumstance for women in those days. For Jacob and Elizabeth Boon and for Barthie's namesake grandmother, Barthie's birth was a dream come true. Barthie was adored; she felt secure and loved.

When Barthie was in the first grade of the Atheneum (the equivalent of sixth grade in American middle school), her parents decided she needed some help with Latin. That tutor — thirteen-year-old Nico Knoppers — would one day become her husband. Her parents soon realized that the only Latin being taught was *amo, amas, amat!* The tutoring stopped, but the friendship did not.

Barthie's childhood home was Christian in both theory and practice. When Barthie was fifteen years old, Miekie, her thirteen-year-old sister, died after a long progressive illness from a brain tumor. Her death had a harsh impact on all. "It was hard for my parents," says Barthie, "but their strong Christian faith and Miekie's expressions of faith helped them to take up their life again after her death."

To Barthie's astonishment, on the day Miekie died streetcars continued to roll and people walked and biked on the streets as usual. The world went on as before. It was then that Barthie realized that life does not stop for anyone or anything — a lesson she has never forgotten.

When Barthie was eighteen and Nico was nineteen, the

two professed their faith in Jesus Christ. "It was the 'normal' thing to do at that age, after six years of catechism classes," Barthie notes. "Also, my future father-in-law was our minister. His explanation of making profession of faith was very simple: If I was glad and thankful that my parents had me baptized, then my profession of faith was saying 'yes' to that baptism. Our text was Romans 8:31-39, and since then that has been a favorite passage for me."

Barthie attended the Free University in Amsterdam, where she received a bachelor of arts degree. Included in her studies were Latin, Greek, and Hebrew. "I could not become a nurse because I was engaged to be married," Barthie says. "It was assumed that married women would focus on their husbands rather than on their patients. I chose these subjects [classical languages] because they interested me. And they might be useful if Nico and I realized our plans of being missionaries in Indonesia."

While at the Free University, Barthie noticed only one sorority for women. Outrageous, she thought. Barthie wanted an alternative. She, along with two others, started a new sorority called Phoenix.

Marriage and World War II interfered with Barthie's plans to continue her theological studies beyond the level of the bachelor's degree. Nico received his bachelor of divinity degree in January 1942, and in July he received a call to a *Gereformeed* church (sister to a Christian Reformed Church) in Lollum, a small Frisian village. In those days engaged couples married when the man had a job. Barthie and Nico had been engaged since 1936, when Barthie was eighteen, and now that Nico had the call, they could marry.

In Lollum, Barthie tried to resume her graduate studies, but being a homemaker and a minister's wife — and living in a country occupied by the Germans — consumed her time and energy. Besides, the closing of the Free University due to the war halted formal study for everyone. But, on the positive side, many people found food, shelter, and safety from persecution in the Lollum parsonage.

Thus began Barthie's career as a homemaker. For this she had little training. "One of the biggest adjustments in my life was getting married and being in charge of a household," she admits. Added to this was the difficult reality of living in an enemy-occupied country. Food and fuel were scarce. And Barthie also knew fear, because people who were hiding from the Nazis often stayed with the Knoppers. "Those war years were good for the soul, since I learned to live day by day and to thank God for each day I was alive," she says.

Barthie's preparation for the career of "minister's wife" was as limited as that for being a homemaker — and she was unpredictable in that role, to put it mildly. For example, in many Dutch congregations the minister's wife was expected to fill numerous leadership positions. But that was not for Barthie. She was outrageous: she refused the presidency of the Young Women's Society. She pointed out to the astonished members that she, at age twenty-four, had much less experience and ability to preside than did the current leader, an elementary schoolteacher.

Barthie and Nico had many dreams, one of which was to be missionaries in Indonesia. But a number of events dashed this particular dream: the war years; the birth of a son, Jacob, in 1945, and the following year the birth of a daughter, Annelies (me), who suffered from severe eczema; Indonesia's fight for independence. And Barthie and Nico soon faced another challenge: they were needed — in Canada. Many Dutch people had emigrated there immediately after World War II, and many ministers were needed to shepherd new congregations.

In 1955 our family — Barthie, Nico, and five children ranging in age from one to ten (Bastian, Bartha, and Nick, in addition to Jake and me) — emigrated to Edmonton. We ventured into the unknown with only our faith in God and our love for each other to sustain us.

My family traveled from Rotterdam to New York by boat, and from New York to Edmonton by plane. We were beset by delays, seasickness, apprehension. We children knew no En-

glish. On the day our plane neared Edmonton, we were several
hours late. Would anyone meet us? As our plane approached
the airport, Barthie noticed a crowd. "What famous person is
arriving the same time as we are?" she wondered. "For whom
are all those people waiting?" As it turned out, they were waiting
for us. Almost the whole congregation had come to the airport,
either by bicycle or by car, to greet us. Together they sang Psalm

---

*As someone who had come from the Gereformeed
church in Lollum, Barthie was shocked by the CRC
practices she encountered as an immigrant to
Canada. She had, it seemed to her, stepped
backward in time twenty-five years. Among the
practices that seemed regressive was the CRC's
treatment of women. In the Netherlands, the move
to ordain women as deacons, elders, and ministers
was already underway. In North America in the
1950s, the idea was too radical to discuss in public.*

---

134 in Dutch to welcome our family.

The warm welcome helped to cushion the shock of reality.
Barthie had to adjust not only to a new language and a different
culture but also to the absence of running water, indoor toilets,
and paved roads. The Young People's Club gave our family half
a pig as a Christmas present, and a member of the congregation
carved the pig into usable portions. With no refrigerator — and,
of course, no freezer — Barthie put the packages of meat in
huge ice-filled barrels standing outside the house. As a prairie
dweller she learned to be very creative.

The practices of the Christian Reformed Church shocked
Barthie. It seemed to her that she had stepped backward in time
twenty-five years. Among the practices that seemed regressive
was the CRC's treatment of women. In the Netherlands the

41

move to ordain women as deacons, elders, and ministers was already underway. In North America the idea was too radical to discuss in public.

The next years were busy for Barthie. After a sixth child, Gary, was born, Barthie decided to alter her dream of having eight children. "Six are enough," she said. Both she and Nico were shocked by the childbirth practices in their adopted land. Their first five children had been born at home. A doctor had assisted, and the family dog lying under the bed had felt comforting. The nurse's aide had stayed for two weeks to care for the new baby, Barthie, and the rest of the family. In contrast, Gary was born in an Edmonton hospital at a time convenient for the doctor. The birth was not a family affair: the children could only stand outside in the parking lot and wave to a window on the floor where Barthie and the baby were. After the birth, no midwife or nurse's aide helped Barthie adjust to the new baby or her increased workload.

During the "Edmonton period," I became aware that Barthie was a *different* kind of mother. As an adolescent, I compared her with other mothers I knew, and Barthie fell short. She didn't even try to be like other mothers and homemakers. For one thing, she made her own clothes and dressed in avant-garde style. She also loved flamboyant hats. When she wore them to church, my brothers and sisters and I tried to pretend Barthie wasn't our mother.

Other mothers, especially Canadian mothers, seemed much nicer, sweeter, and more orthodox than mine. Canadian mothers seemed to place very few demands on their children, but my mother never minded placing demands on us. Canadian mothers tried to smooth the way for their children. Not my mother. It's not that she didn't give us certain opportunities — we could take music or swimming lessons, for example. But Barthie made us fend for ourselves much of the time. Once we knew how to get where we had to go, for instance, we went by ourselves by bus. And we walked the two miles to school. Only when the temperature dipped to ten degrees below freezing did we get a ride.

Canadian mothers seemed to serve their children. Not Barthie. At our house those roles were reversed. Because we were required to help with the housework, we felt we were treated more like slaves. Most unfair, we thought, was that during summer vacations we had to take turns being Barthie's personal assistant. She explained that if children could have holidays, so could she. How unreasonable! After all, *good* mothers were supposed to work all of the time. We toyed with the idea of picketing the church on Sunday morning with signs reading "Minister's wife unfair to children" or "Mrs. Knoppers practices slave labor." Much later I realized that by constantly refusing to make life easier for us or to entertain us, Barthie was training us to be independent.

With this kind of independence and strength of character in mind, Barthie taught us to work for what we wanted and to accept what could not be. She and Nico also taught us to be willing to go against mass opinion when necessary. Other children had a list of "do nots" for Sunday dress and behavior. Our parents, however, allowed us to choose whether we wanted to go to the second church service. They also allowed us to bicycle

---

She stimulated her friends, children, and grandchildren to be sensitive to gender issues and to value women and their activities. Granddaughters soon realized they would never get Barbie dolls or make-up sets from this Oma.

---

or skate on Sunday — even wear shorts after church if we wished. Although Barthie and Nico were criticized for their parental permissiveness, they did not succumb to external pressure in raising us.

Barthie gave our family special traditions and inspired us with a love of life. We celebrated birthdays, weddings, anniversaries, and holidays in festive, fun-filled ways. She and Nico also encouraged us to write rhymes and songs and to produce skits and dramas. (They may have regretted this when we began to charge admission to our skits.)

Although Barthie taught us to amuse ourselves, she also sometimes joined in our fun. Sometimes on Sunday afternoons she stayed home with us six rambunctious children while Nico preached. The church was just a stone's throw away. Even so, Barthie put martial music on the record player. We kids marched through the house, clanging rhythmically on pots and pans. We may have been extra enthusiastic because we knew our young friends were sitting quietly nearby in church.

Both Barthie and Nico worked to instill in us a dynamic faith. Not, however, by formalizing religion or by constantly giving testimonies, but by engaging us in activities that made us think and question. Mealtimes especially were occasions for learning. We spoke few memorized prayers; instead, Barthie and Nico encouraged us to formulate our own. We children all shared in the Bible reading, and we often sang. We chose songs systematically — either because they fit with the Bible passage being read or because we were singing our way through the *Psalter Hymnal.*

Barthie was also a special partner, a woman in love with her husband — and he with her. She came first with him, and he would show her special consideration. For instance, he would patrol the house while Barthie took her daily nap. Woe be to the child who was noisy during that time! (Barthie later told me that she did not need those naps as much as she needed the hour for time for herself.)

Although Barthie did not conform to the description of a typical "minister's wife," she did justice to the role. She coped well with the code of should-nots for a minister's wife: she did not ride a bike, she was not a public feminist, she did not go camping with a female friend at age fifty, and so on. She was also a very dedicated and involved minister's wife. With Nico she visited every family of the congregations he served. She served many terms as president of the Women's Bible Society, sent her children to Christian schools even though funds were very tight, hostessed social gatherings of ministers and church councils, and more. She quickly befriended people on the margins of the congregation and visited them loyally.

We often glimpsed the depth of Barthie's strength and spirit as well as her loyalty to and love for Nico. She defended him (and he her). Her resilience to the pettiness of people amazed us. When members of a congregation once made life very difficult for Nico, Barthie fought fiercely for him. Years later, when those same people asked for forgiveness for the pain and hurt they had caused, she was quick to grant it. "You cannot live your life hating people," she explains.

Some thought it nice that Nico would *allow* his wife to behave in certain ways considered "inappropriate" for a minister's wife, but Barthie did not need or ask permission. She identified her own needs and tried to meet them, even if it meant going against popular opinion. This sense of separate identity, a special gift, she gave to her daughters. And her concern for others she passed on to her sons as well as her daughters. As we grew older, we began to try to incorporate her qualities into our own lives.

As we children gradually left home, Barthie had more time for other activities. She became active in Meals-on-Wheels. She volunteered weekly in a senior citizens' home. Because she loved to sing, she sang in the choir — and she knew this was one place where she would not be expected to take a leadership position. Today she works with M2W2, a program that provides support for the spouses of prisoners.

In addition, she gradually became more vocal and involved in feminist causes. In *The Feminine Mystique* Betty Friedan put into words ideas that Barthie had long had but had not been able to name. After becoming familiar with Friedan's work, Barthie began to look at her church through new glasses. In a letter to her church council she protested what she saw as its dishonesty: "New members are told they will have all the rights and privileges of membership, and yet women do not have all those rights and privileges since they cannot be elders or ministers." She signed her letter "a second-class member."

Her protest caused an uproar. Church members could not believe that Barthie would write such a letter. Nor that Nico

---

She challenged anyone who would listen about one of her pet peeves: the mistaken belief that those who do not work for pay or wages, such as homemakers, do not "work." She herself refused to be called a housewife. "I did not marry a house!" she fumed.

---

would have given Barthie permission to do so! Certainly Nico had read the letter before she sent it? No, he hadn't. Furor resulted. But the letter and the resulting upheaval awakened people to the issue Barthie raised. They began to think and talk about it. But the indignation her outspokenness had caused amazed Barthie. She realized that as much as she had thought herself to be a person independent and separate from her husband, many parishioners did not see her that way. Consequently, she continued to make her concerns about gender issues visible, but in a much more low-key way. She stimulated her friends, children, and grandchildren to be sensitive to gender issues and to value women and their activities. Granddaughters soon realized they would never get Barbie dolls or make-up sets from this *Oma* (grandmother).

Barthie also challenged sexist actions and remarks. She challenged anyone who would listen about one of her pet peeves: the mistaken belief that those who do not work for pay or wages, such as homemakers, do not "work." She herself refused to be called a housewife. "I did not marry a house!" she fumed.

Full-time homemakers who assist their husbands in their careers often pay a huge price for their devotion. Their self-esteem and contentment tend to be lower than that of married men, single women, and single men. What's more, as full-time homemakers age, their self-esteem tends to decrease (a fact documented by those who, like Virginia Sapiro, study the relationship of women and society). Barthie was no exception. Now that she had time to think about it, she shied away from leadership opportunities. All the years of being a minister's wife and keeping busy with its demands and being a full-time homemaker had taken their toll. Unexpectedly and contrary to research patterns, however, her self-confidence gradually began to rise again as her daughters made her aware of the strong impact she had had on their lives. She had given them a sense of separate identity, a feeling of self-worth.

By the time Nico officially retired in 1983, the children had all established their own homes. Now Barthie was free to become more active publicly — and she did so. As a member of the church worship committee, she encouraged the use of inclusive language in songs and liturgies. In Barthie's opinion, the church was dragging its feet on the matter of adopting inclusive language as official policy. On went the delay. Long enough, thought Barthie. One day she and a friend took all the songbooks from the church (all seventy-five of them). Together the two women changed many exclusive words to inclusive words: *men* to *all* or *people*, *sons* to *children*, and so on. At the next service, when parishioners opened their books to certain songs, they realized immediately what had happened! Now the terms of the debate shifted: if people wanted to overrule what Barthie and her cohort had done, they had to argue for *exclusive* language — difficult for her congregation to do.

This was one of the ways in which Nico's retirement gave Barthie more freedom to express herself. The balance between supporting him and supporting her own interests publicly could now change. Before, that balance had always tipped toward Nico's work and image. Now Barthie had more freedom to support issues that compelled her — like feminist causes. She writes occasionally to the editor of *The Banner* and the *Calvinist*

47

Contact, two CRC-related publications. She has challenged their one-sided approach to the abortion question and their relative silence on the "women-in-office" issue.

Although she had been a member of the Committee for Women of the Christian Reformed Church (CW-CRC) for many years, she now began to take a more active role in it. In 1982, when Barthie was sixty-four, she and a woman half her age started a CW-CRC chapter in Edmonton. Barthie inspired younger women. She disproved the myth that the feminist movement is something in which only "career women" are interested.

Barthie was at her best when confronting obstacles. She accepted all challenges. Tirelessly she promoted Christian feminism. According to a friend, Ann Castaing, "She never gives up when one avenue is closed. She doesn't bewail the fact but tries — and usually finds — another one. She encourages others and inspires them not to give up."

Barthie did not strengthen her self-identity, however, at the expense of nurturing her family or jeopardizing her relationship

---

In 1982, when Barthie was 64, she and a woman half her age started a CW-CRC chapter in Edmonton. Barthie inspired younger women. She disproved the myth that the feminist movement is something in which only "career women" are interested.

---

with her husband. This meant foregoing certain dreams. Instead of returning to school, as she would have liked, Barthie chose not to undertake anything that would require a great deal of time and energy. Instead, she saved much time and energy for Nico. From the moment their first child was born until the last one left home, Barthie and Nico had had little time for each other. His ministry and her homemaking had been 24-hour-a-day jobs. When it was just the two of them again, Barthie devoted much of her attention to Nico.

But Barthie has managed to raise her own voice and pursue her own interests successfully. In 1990 Barthie became an elder in the Fellowship Christian Reformed Church of Edmonton. She was one of the first CRC women in the Edmonton area to be chosen as elder. Barthie shares this position with Edith Sinnema. This unique arrangement, which the two women suggested, permits both to continue other volunteer activities.

Barthie has been a pioneer, a trailblazer. The basic belief that motivates her feminist crusade is simple. She believes that in Christ Jesus "there is neither Jew nor Greek, slave nor free, male nor female" (Gal. 3:28). She believes in making the best of what she has, and trusts that God will sustain her in anything she does for his glory. Her level-headedness and strong faith have marked her approach to life. That faith, although strong, has changed over time. "When I made profession of faith," she comments, "my faith was very simple. I didn't see as many 'why's' as I do now. But my trust in God is still the same."

Now seventy-three years old, Barthie still champions women, especially full-time homemakers. She is a vision of strength and inspiration to all who feel called to be more than the daughter of X, the wife of Y, and the mother of Z.

Dora Hofstra and
Marie Vander Weide

Mothers of Many

*Marie has already graduated to glory, and when our Lord
opens that final door to heaven to welcome Dora, he will
say to each of them, "Inasmuch as you have done it for at
least two thousand of my little ones in the land of Native
Americans, you have also done it for me."*

Together they touched the lives of more than two thousand Navajo children. As 24-hours-a-day, 7-days-a-week dorm mothers at Rehoboth (New Mexico) Christian Boarding School, they cared for sixty girls and sixty boys every year for thirty-six school years.

Dora Hofstra, 84, who cared for the girls, now lives in a retirement home in South Holland, Illinois. On the walls of her room are several oils, self-painted; a few Navajo rugs; and a small, framed plaque that reads "My grace is sufficient for thee." Marie Vander Weide, who mothered the boys, retired in 1953. She died in Ontario, California, in 1982. "Her crowning glory of silvery gray hair was symbolic of the aura of graciousness about her," according to an obituary published in *The Christian Indian*, a monthly news magazine for the Christian Indians of New Mexico.

"I didn't think I'd ever be a missionary," says Dora, "because I didn't have the education." Born in May 1907 into a family of nine children, Dora was the only girl. She graduated from the eighth grade and spent her teen years helping at home and caring for her mother, who was often ill, and pinch-hitting in her father's bakery. "My mother often said she regretted that I couldn't go to high school. At that time going to high school wasn't so common. My oldest brother, Richard, did go on because he wanted to become a medical missionary. Eventually he went to China, where he served for thirty-eight years."

The Hofstras were a missionary-loving family. "In our home missionaries came and went often," Dora recalls. "We'd often get them from the train, bring them home, and take them to the meetings where they would speak." Dora's mother, Lolkje (Lucy) vander Woude Hofstra, had wanted to be a missionary. "Ma prayed that the Lord would put a love of missions in the hearts of her children," says Dora. "When I went to Rehoboth, my father said, 'How your mother would have rejoiced that you have this opportunity to serve the Lord on the mission field!'"

Lucy and Dora were close. Lucy was often ill, and when she thought she might die soon, she talked with Dora about it;

it was Dora's twentieth birthday. "I may not be here very long, Dora," Lucy said. "I have prayed the Lord will lead and guide you. God's way is always the best way. I hope that you'll love and serve him and find your place in his plan. Pray, Dora, pray much."

"Yes, Ma, I know you pray as though you're talking to your best friend, but I don't feel that way. I can't talk to God like he's my best friend," Dora replied.

"Go to the piano, please, and get me the hymnbook," Lucy instructed. "Read aloud the song 'All the Way My Savior Leads Me.' That's my birthday wish for you today — and for all the years the Lord will give you. He will see you through."

"How do you know, Ma?"

"Because I have prayed for this," her mother responded quietly.

Lucy died the following month, in June of 1927. Dora grieved quietly, deeply. During her period of mourning a radio message brought her to her knees. A woman Bible teacher was speaking about how God through a cloud led the Israelites through the desert, just as he leads his children today. "That's it, Dora, you're just resentful," Dora said to herself. She fell on her knees and prayed, "Lord, please take over."

He did. And Dora found peace.

Several years later, in October 1936, Dr. Henry Beets, a family friend and secretary of the Christian Reformed Board of Foreign Missions (which later was divided into World Missions and Home Missions), visited the Hofstra home.

Dr. Beets spoke directly to Dora. "We need a housemother for sixty girls at Rehoboth. Did you see the ad in *The Banner?* What did you think about it?"

"Well, it would be kind of nice, but I don't think I could cope with sixty girls!"

"Maybe you're looking too much at doing this in your own strength. You have to look at what God can work through you," Dr. Beets replied. To John, Dora's father, he said, "Now, you pray about it, I will pray about it, and Dora will pray about it."

52

To Dora he said, "I want to know in two weeks if you'll take that position. We need someone there permanently."

---

*Dora arrived in Rehoboth on December 12, 1936.
Later she learned that Dr. Richard Pousma, a
medical missionary working there, saw her walking
to the dormitory. He prayed quietly, "Lord, help that
lady! She doesn't know what she's getting into!"*

"He had such a way about him," Dora remembers. For two weeks she and her father prayed about the matter. Dora realized that she was free to leave because her father had remarried. But what did God want her to do? She returned again and again to her favorite Bible verse: "Trust in the Lord with all thine heart, and lean not unto thine own understanding. In all thy ways acknowledge him, and he shall direct thy paths" (Prov. 3:5-6, KJV).

The two weeks passed. Dora wrote to Dr. Beets that she felt inadequate for the challenge and yet wanted to do God's will; she would help out until the end of the school year. The board set her salary at thirty-four dollars a month. Her task? To mother sixty girls, twenty-four hours a day, seven days a week.

Dora arrived in Rehoboth on December 12, 1936. Later she learned that Dr. Richard Pousma, a medical missionary working there, saw her walking to the dormitory. He prayed quietly, "Lord, help that lady! She doesn't know what she's getting into!"

Indeed she didn't.

As Dora walked down the sidewalk, she was scared. She prayed, "Lord, help me!" Her heart jumped. "What am I doing here?" A sea of girls greeted her — girls with shiny black hair, tawny complexions, and brownish-black eyes. But these were not "Indian girls" as Dora had pictured them: these girls were wearing gingham dresses! She soon learned that in September, at the beginning of the school year, the girls had exchanged their usual velvet blouses and bright silk skirts for the cotton dresses they were wearing now. They knew very little English — some of them knew no English at all — and they were only comfortable speaking in their native tongue, Navajo. Dora took in the range of girls she was expected to care for. She saw little eight-year-olds who in September had left their hogans on the reservation for the first time. She also saw middle-sized and big girls up to twenty years old. All were curious to see the white stranger who was to be their new "mother." It did not take Dora long to learn from them that they carried bitterness in their hearts for the white man who long ago had taken their land. This was a difficult issue. Over time Dora and Marie won the hearts of many — but not all — of the children.

All the way my Savior leads me? Dora wondered often. Had he really led her here? Whatever had made her think she, a "foreigner," could mother these sixty strangers! The girls did not make her feel welcome. "I remember, for example, asking a couple of them to please steady the rickety ladder I was using to reach a high shelf to get clothes or stockings that had been donated for them," Dora recalls. "'Oh, shut up,' they said. 'Do it yourself.'"

One evening, after an especially bad day and after the younger children were finally in bed, the director, Jacob Bosscher, dropped in at the girls' dormitory. "How are things going, Dora?" he asked cheerily. Dora looked at him and burst into tears. "Ah, not so good, I see," he said.

"No, the girls are unkind," Dora explained. "They tell me to shut up. I was reared to respect my parents. Must I tolerate this?"

"Absolutely not," Mr. Bosscher replied. He instructed Dora to get all the girls together in the playroom, even the little ones who were already in bed. After they had gathered — wide-eyed and wondering, a bit frightened, perhaps — he said to them, "This cannot go on. Miss Hofstra is your mother here. We've been praying that God would send us someone. In this dormitory Miss Hofstra is your mother, and you will respect her. If you who are leaders of this trouble continue in this way, you will have no place here. And I don't mean maybe. Now get to bed, everyone. This dormitory will be dark in one half hour." Then he left.

In a little while Dora went to what functioned as her room. "In the early days," she explains, "I did not have a room of my own. I slept on the studio couch in the girls' sitting room." She had no privacy. Feeling beleaguered, she wept. She prayed for patience and wisdom.

Dora leaned heavily on Marie, who had been dorm mother in the boys' dormitory since 1920 and had gained a treasure trove of experience with Navajo children. "Miss Van," as she was known, supported Dora unstintingly.

To cope, Dora leaned heavily on Marie Vander Weide, who had been dorm mother in the boys' dormitory since 1920 and had gained a treasure trove of experience with Navajo boys ranging in age from six to twenty. "Miss Van," as she was known, supported Dora unstintingly. The two women talked together daily. Dora often recalled her mother's saying, "God's way is the best way," and thanked God for including Marie's help as part of his way.

Information about Marie's early life is not plentiful. According to Georgia Jonkman, her niece by marriage, Marie was born in Chicago, the daughter of an immigrant housepainter. She went to Rehoboth in 1920. There she buried herself in the lives of the boys entrusted to her. She took only an occasional day off, and her vacations were few and short. But, said *The Christian Indian*, "dedication to her Lord and assurance that he had called her to this task helped her survive. Not only did she survive; she flourished."

She believed in her calling wholeheartedly and defended it against misperception. A popular stereotype was — and often still is — that missionaries wore dowdy clothes and were not quite "with it." On one occasion a male visitor to Rehoboth,

---

A popular stereotype was that missionaries wore dowdy clothes and were not quite "with it." On one occasion a male visitor to Rehoboth, noting Marie's lovely dress, commented, "I see no eligible men here. Yet all of you are so well dressed and well groomed. I thought women made themselves attractive for men." Marie, slender and stylish, drew herself up to her rather imposing height and said, "Of course we dress well. We are the King's daughters."

---

noting Marie's lovely dress, commented, "I see no eligible men here. Yet all of you are so well dressed and well groomed. I thought women made themselves attractive for men." Marie, slender and stylish, drew herself up to her rather imposing height and said, "Of course we dress well. We are the King's daughters."

"One had to respect Marie," says Dora. "She helped me work out schedules for the girls. Older girls helped with the little ones. Each morning we had devotions. Seventh and eighth graders went to school in the morning, while fifth and sixth graders did assigned tasks. We switched the groups in the afternoon. It was up to us to teach them what our mothers usually taught us at home."

Marie was strong and secure in her belief that her life was always and totally in God's hands; often she could laugh at what other people worried about, according to Dorothy Dykhuizen Vellenga, a former colleague of both Marie and Dora. "Marie's keen sense of humor, her story-telling ability, and her hearty laughter made her a welcome addition to any gathering," Dorothy added. Marie could also be resourceful. Dorothy recalls an incident that Marie handled particularly well. "One night Marie heard one of her little boys crying from an earache. 'Oh, Davey,' she soothed. 'I'll get the eardrops.'

"As she looked for the medicine, she saw a mop, just washed and freshly clean, now hanging dry on the radiator. 'I know what we'll do, Davey,' she said. 'We'll just give you this nice warm mop for a pillow. It will make your ear feel good.' And it did."

Marie retired in 1953, but until 1974 she remained at Rehoboth, serving as hostess to the many people who visited there. The "Indian field," as it was known to the Christian Reformed Church, was located on Highway 66, then the main route between Chicago and Los Angeles. Many supporters dropped in to see the field and the "Indian cousins," as they were called on the "Children's Page" in *The Banner.* In addition, "her boys" often brought their families to visit her at Rehoboth. Their visits continued, even during the last two years of Marie's life, when she was in a nursing home.

In 1974 Marie moved to California to live with two sisters. In 1980, two years before she died, she entered the Artesia Christian Home for the Aged. Julia Ensink, a colleague and friend who knew her well, said of her, "If she could come back

---

Marie was strong and secure in her belief that her life was always and totally in God's hands; often she could laugh at what other people worried about.

---

and say something to the many boys she had in her care, I think it would be something like this: 'Heaven is so beautiful. Won't you give your heart and life to Jesus, and accept his gift of eternal life? He died for you too.'"

It was from Marie that Dora gained both knowledge and confidence. Dora had harbored thoughts that her education had left her woefully unprepared for her task, but actually, she realized under Marie's influence, she was well equipped. Years of experience running a busy household, serving in various capacities in Chicago missions, and taking night classes in cooking, sewing, home economics, church history, and Reformed doctrine had prepared her well. At the end of her first six months at Rehoboth, she evaluated her performance. True, she had not accomplished all the goals that she had set for herself. Still, after visiting with her family for a month, she returned to Rehoboth.

The tasks at Rehoboth took all Dora's time and energy; at night she fell into bed exhausted. Sometimes one of the little girls, feeling homesick, would cry in the evening. "I'd say, 'Come with me,' because I knew if one girl cried I could soon have everyone homesick and crying. I usually took the little one to my room and gave her a peppermint or two and a picture book. Then I left because I had forty or fifty others to get to bed at three different bedtimes."

The children liked the pre-bedtime hour. Like all children, they found ways to avoid going to sleep right away. "We'd have a story, then we'd kneel down to pray. After they were in bed they'd say, 'Sing a song, Miss Hofstra. Sing a Dutch song.'

"'Okay,' I'd say, 'I'll sing you a Dutch song. It talks about going to sleep, so when I'm through all you little girls should be sleeping . . .'"

Today Dora wonders how she did it all. "Saturdays and Sundays were the busiest of all because there was no school. On Saturdays we'd have all sorts of special jobs and activities — baths, shampoos, shoes to polish, cleaning to do, games, hikes in the desert, and more.

"On Sunday mornings we'd take a walk to the cemetery (about three-quarters of a mile south) and repeat the 'golden text' until all the children knew it. The kids played on the big red rocks. Afterwards we changed into Sunday clothes and went to church, walking two by two. Miss Van and her boys sat on the right, and my girls and I sat on the left."

Both Dora and Marie quickly tended any child who felt sick. Not only were they troubled about the child who was ill, but they were also apprehensive about the sickness spreading, as it sometimes did. At times ten, twenty, even thirty children could be ill at once, and rest became impossible. On one occasion, when one of Dora's girls had measles, Dr. Louis Bos, a doctor at Rehoboth, came to the dorm to check on her. He didn't like to take patients with measles to the hospital, but this time he said, "I'm going to find a way to isolate her because you shouldn't sit up all night with her." He picked up eight-year-old Bessie gently and carried her to the hospital.

Dr. Pousma also kept a tender eye on Dora; he noticed when she was overwrought, overworked, and overtired. On one such occasion he gave her a much-needed prescription: "You go to the hospital. Take along some books and a radio, and rest there until Monday." Dora took his advice; one of the hospital nurses substituted for her in the dorm. On Monday, refreshed, Dora returned to her girls.

Clearly Dora's life at Rehoboth was perpetually challenging — and sometimes wearying. Still, when 1972 came and with it time for Dora to retire, her love for Rehoboth encouraged her to stay.

Dora's home in Chicago was gone: her father and stepmother were no longer alive, and her brothers were scattered. "Rehoboth is home to me," she told David Bosscher, a board representative, "and I would like to stay on as hostess, just as Marie did."

The Home Mission Board agreed, and Dora remained at Rehoboth for ten years, welcoming and hostessing many visitors. During this decade she often found time to call on some of the women who had been "her girls" while she was dorm mother.

When Classis Red Mesa of the Christian Reformed Church met in Crown Point one year, Dora went to visit two of her former girls who were serving food to the delegates. They laughed as they greeted her. "We were just talking about you, Miss Hofstra."

"Oh? Good or bad?"

"Well, we were here promptly at 8:00 a.m., but the other ladies of the committee didn't get here until after 9:00 a.m. We said, 'Well, why are we on time? Because of Miss Hofstra! She was always after us to be prompt.'"

Dora speaks modestly about having affected many girls' lives. Many write to "Mom" and tell her of her "grandchildren."

They laughed together, sat together, and enjoyed Navajo food together. Dora felt one with them. But during her years as dorm mother at Rehoboth, that had not always been true. "Sometimes I felt so inadequate. I would think, 'Oh, Dora, that wasn't right. You didn't handle that very well.'" She still remembers how inadequate she felt at the end of her first six months at Rehoboth when she returned to Chicago to visit. "And now to think that I stayed thirty-five years!"

She speaks modestly about having affected many girls' lives. Many write to "Mom" and tell her of her "grandchildren." She picks up a letter from the table and recalls, a bit sadly, one of her girls who, having lived through tragedy, is now torn between Christianity and her native religion. "I can't tell you what I know you would like to hear," she wrote, "but Miss Hofstra, don't give up on me. Keep praying for me." Which Dora does.

"Maybe I won't ever hear from her again," says Dora. "I'm old now. But she has been taught about the Lord. I love to hear from her and others, and especially of their love for the Lord."

Dora recalls one girl whose mother insisted, before bringing her daughter to Rehoboth, that she not stray from her native religion. She warned her not to take seriously anything about

Christianity that was taught at Rehoboth. But after graduation and several years of suffering with tuberculosis, this young woman returned to Rehoboth to profess her faith in Christ Jesus. She challenged the students to listen to the Gospel and urged them to follow in the Lord's way the rest of their lives.

Dora knows, of course, that not all "her girls" have given their lives to Christ. But she has learned not to lean on her own understanding but to trust in the Lord with all her heart.

Dora's mind drifts back to her twentieth birthday. "I remember my mother saying, 'I have prayed the Lord will lead and guide you.' All I can say now is that God has done exceedingly abundantly, above all that I could ask or think."

Miss Van has already graduated to glory, and when our Lord opens that final door to heaven to welcome Dora, he will say to each of them, "Inasmuch as you have done it for at least two thousand of my little ones in the land of Native Americans, you have also done it for me."

III

It was he who gave some to be
. . . teachers, to prepare
God's people for works of service,
so that the body of Christ may be built up
until we all . . . become mature,
attaining to the whole measure
of the fullness of Christ.

Ephesians 4:11-13

Nelle VanderArk

Compassionate Critic

"If you were a VanderArk, you were expected to become a teacher. And I didn't want to be a teacher." . . . In the end she did become a teacher — and a nurturer of souls.

She could have become a farmer. Her father was a farmer in Manhattan, Montana. Nelle (pronounced "Nell") VanderArk was a "skinny 11-year-old" when she learned farming firsthand. Bert Van Dyken, her brother-in-law, then in his first year of farming, had been devastated by a hailstorm that had destroyed his entire crop. He came to Dad VanderArk for advice and help.

Albert VanderArk listened compassionately to Bert's troubles and said, "I don't know just how to help you, Bert. The boys are all hired out." Then, looking toward Nelle, he said, "But there is Nelle. She has a lot to learn. She doesn't know anything about machinery, but she can handle horses. If she's willing and you can use her services, I'll take her over in the morning."

"Wow!" thought Nelle. "Bert needs me, and my father trusts me." Her heart was full; she didn't sleep all night. "By the end of the summer," she remembers, "I was doing everything that needed to be done, except the heavy lifting. I was especially proud of being able to do the plowing with six horses, driving with two sets of reins."

In the home of Albert VanderArk and his wife, Agnes Bouma, the four daughters had the same opportunities as the four sons. And mother and father were in many ways equal leaders of the family. "Mother was as much a spiritual leader as Dad," Nelle explains. "She was a natural teacher and a fine public speaker. She also led in family devotions. So many people of my generation, I feel, were impoverished because they never heard their mothers pray."

Nelle, born on November 5, 1920, was the seventh child of Albert and Agnes. Four of Nelle's siblings became teachers. "If you were a VanderArk," Nelle says, "you were expected to become a teacher. And I didn't want to be a teacher." She told her father that she wanted to go to seminary. "I really wish you could," he told her. But a woman in seminary was unheard of at that time. Although Nelle never studied formally at a seminary, her Bible study has been lifelong and deep. In the end she did become a teacher — and a nurturer of souls.

In 1988, synod, the ruling body of the Christian Reformed Church, appointed her to a committee mandated to examine again the meaning of "headship" as it related to the place of women in the church. The committee reported to Synod 1990, that historic synod which declared that churches may use their discretion in appointing women as elders or ministers.

"You know," Nelle says, "life is full of ironies. I became a

"In a sense, I've been ordained from birth; I just can't wait for the church to catch up."

---

teacher. There were delegates at Synod 1990 [where Nelle had the unusual privilege of addressing the delegates] whom I had taught to interpret the Scriptures. Some of them used to sit around in the lounge at the Reformed Bible College and debate whether women should have authority. Well, I was their teacher, and there is no such thing as teaching without authority. In a sense, I've been ordained from birth; I just can't wait for the church to catch up."

Synod's action, however, did surprise Nelle. "I think it's going to be a good thing. Our report served as the launching pad for the rocket. I like to joke that I am the only 'headless' person to speak on the subject of headship. . . . On Tuesday morning, when synod was discussing the proposal to open all church offices to women, I gave a personal testimony. What has spared me as a woman from becoming either embittered by the church or radically feminist was my home background. My father, from the earliest day I can remember, believed that women had as much a place in the home and church as men did, and this equality was practiced in our home. This model caused me to believe that God is fair. If he gives any person abilities, that person has the freedom and the responsibility to use them."

Nelle's parents recognized early on that Nelle was a "special child" — precocious, some might say. But she was also extremely sensitive. At the age of four Nelle was reading. Reading, however, became a stumbling block when she first went to school. Her teacher didn't know what to do with the little girl who was so far ahead of her peers in reading. Consequently, he "promoted" Nelle to the second grade. "A sorry mistake," says Nelle now. "I was very uncomfortable because I had no idea of what was going on and suffered much from jealous, pestering peers."

It was a hard year. And a worse summer. Nelle's parents consulted a doctor. "A nervous breakdown," Nelle overheard the doctor say. That diagnosis was unusual for so young a child. Albert and Agnes cared for their hurting daughter tenderly. "I had very special care, not only that summer but also throughout my childhood. My parents did it without spoiling me, I think. They understood my vulnerability and sensitiveness. I was extremely sensitive then — and I still am."

Eventually, Nelle became a teacher — a brilliant teacher, one who guided and inspired students in and out of school. Countless study groups — both women and men — increased their love and knowledge of God's Word through her spirited teaching.

To become a teacher, however, was not Nelle's original career goal. Defying the VanderArk tradition, Nelle decided to major in business when she began college at Montana State in 1936 — but her enthusiasm for that choice was short-lived. "I soon hated that field," she remembers. "And I would have made a lousy business manager!" After a year, she transferred to Montana State Teachers' College.

Upon graduating from high school, Nelle had won a four-year, tuition-free scholarship to any college in Montana. This was an immense help — but eventually not enough of one. When she was a junior, all Nelle needed to stay in college was fifteen dollars a month to pay the remainder of her board — but, despite her scholarship and her part-time job, she couldn't scrape together the money. Yes, tuition was free, and working helped, but there was no way she could raise the amount needed — a hefty sum in Nelle's day.

It was 1938, and Nelle's parents were struggling financially during the waning years of the Great Depression. They simply couldn't squeeze an additional fifteen dollars a month from the family budget. Her financial options thus exhausted, Nelle gave up the scholarship and applied for a teaching position.

She was now eighteen years old, the fifth VanderArk in her family to join the ranks of the teaching profession. She began in Manhattan, Montana, in a one-room country school with six students in grades four through eight. Although young and inexperienced, Nelle immediately felt at ease. "I realized then that my gifts lay in the field of teaching. I loved it!" Nelle exclaims. During this time she attended evening classes and earned another year toward her college degree.

"My father, from the earliest day I can remember, believed that women had as much a place in the home and church as men did, and this equality was practiced in our home. This model caused me to believe that God is fair. If he gives any person abilities, that person has the freedom and the responsibility to use them."

After three years, Nelle moved to the newly formed Manhattan Christian High School. For the first four years she taught all subjects of all grades to the eighteen students enrolled. During her last two years there, she taught "only" freshmen and sophomores.

All this while Nelle had been teaching with a certificate but without a degree, which was becoming increasingly necessary. So after her stint at the Montana high school, she went back to college to complete her education. Traveling to Grand Rapids, Michigan, Nelle earned her bachelor of arts in education at Calvin College, where she maintained her academic excellence. Because she hadn't spent all four years at Calvin, she was an alternate in line for an all-expenses-paid graduate scholarship in English teaching offered at the University of Michigan in Ann Arbor. When the first candidate accepted the scholarship, Nelle was crushed. "And the person who got it has never taught a day!" she notes ruefully. "That was a terribly hard pill for me to swallow."

Nelle pauses for a moment, then continues her story. "So I had to go back to teaching immediately. But I wouldn't trade it for anything. I don't always see this truth right away, but God's way, I have learned again and again, is always the best way."

In 1946, Nelle began teaching ninth-grade English and music at Oakdale Christian School in Grand Rapids, Michigan, where she remained for fifteen years. On one Sunday morning during that time, she became severely ill. Perhaps a ruptured appendix, her sister Gertrude thought. She called a family friend and cousin, Dr. Henry Holkeboer. "It's not your appendix," the doctor said after examining Nelle, "but you have a severely cramped bowel. All I can do is put you out for twenty-four hours. But before I do so, I want to tell you something about yourself. And it may help you to live well.

"Both the VanderArks and the Boumas are high-strung people, and somehow you have a double portion in your genes. You are a delicately tuned instrument. You will not have an easy life, but you will have a much richer life than many," he concluded.

"His advice helped me very much, especially through times of trouble," Nelle comments. "I visited with Dr. Holkeboer some thirty years later and thanked him for his kind, helpful words. He quipped, 'I didn't know I was that smart.'"

Nelle's loyalty to her Savior rules her life. She has remained single by choice. Following World War II, Nelle felt somewhat committed to marry a certain young man who had returned from service — and yet God's will led her away from this commitment. "The summer of 1946 was one of tremendous struggle for me," she recalls. "I could not escape the pressure of God's hand upon my life. I simply was not free to marry and settle on a farm in Montana. Not that there's anything wrong with that way of life. It simply was not God's will for me. But what pressures were laid on me by the church and the community! Marriage seems to be considered to be the most biblical state and singleness rather pitiable.

"The people who understood me best were my parents. They never made me feel that I should have married. My father always told me to 'stand tall.' I am tall, and sometimes he reminded me of my posture. He would say, 'Stand tall. Don't hide.' Dad was right; I learned the lesson well."

That summer's decision was a crucial turning point in Nelle's life. "I literally knelt and cried out in surrender, 'Oh, God, if you would rather that I do not marry, then I will be what you want me to be and I will do what you want me to do . . . but don't ever leave me.'"

For Nelle, surrender is the first step of faith. "All that I am I owe to God. I am very kingdom-oriented, though I confess I do not always live it out. I must steadily give up my self-centeredness and plunge into the task at hand with God-given resources. 'The Lord is my strength and my song, and he has become my salvation.' That's my text."

Today, looking back at the decision she made some forty years earlier, Nelle says, "Something in our religion militates against singleness. Contrary to our Calvinist profession that God comes first, we teach — even today — that marriage is the pre-ferred state. It is easier to work for God when you're single, but singleness makes many of us second-class citizens in the church."

She points to certain "singles" groups in churches today. "To separate singles from couples is a big mistake and very hurtful to many. Singles groups see themselves as rejects," she says animatedly. "The question each of us must ask is not 'Should I marry or not?' The question is 'How can I most fully be the person the Lord intended me to be?'"

Nelle, now retired, recalls visits from church leaders. They often asked, "What can our church do for you?" She replied, "I know your intentions are good, but such a question comes across to me as a subtle form of pity and patronage. The bigger question is 'What can I do for my church?' I don't want the church to decide what category I belong in. I will decide for myself with God's direction who I am and how I will do my work. Ask me what gifts I have and give me opportunity to use them freely!"

Nelle's study of and teaching about the book of Exodus,

"Something in our religion militates against singleness. Contrary to our Calvinist profession that God comes first, we teach — even today — that marriage is the preferred state. It is easier to work for God when you're single, but singleness makes many of us second-class citizens in the church."

---

among other subjects, undergirds her point. She comments, "The book of Exodus speaks clearly of how God freed his people for *service*. No, it's not what the church can do for people. It's how can each one's gifts be used cooperatively and completely to advance his kingdom."

Nelle still stands tall. Not only was she an outstanding teacher, but she was also a prophet with a convincing voice who spoke courageously about problems that needed attention, be they in church or school or elsewhere.

While teaching at Oakdale Christian School in Grand Rapids, Nelle learned that a serious discrepancy existed between the salaries of the men and the women who taught there. She and Dorothy Westra, a friend and colleague, studied the differential and called it to the attention of the education committee. This marked the beginning of serious salary study by the board as well as the National Union of Christian Schools (now Christian Schools International), which subsequently directed its efforts toward correcting this inequity.

"I guess I've always been a critic," Nelle says, "but that's the work of a prophet, isn't it?" Her perceptive criticism springs from close observation of disguised problems and her deep concern for people. A critic, however, seldom remains unscathed, and in the past when Nelle tackled a problem, her sensitive nature was often crushed.

In fact, this was what occurred in 1964 when Nelle left Oakdale to become the first curriculum coordinator for the National Union of Christian Schools. NUCS had paid her tuition at the University of Chicago (but not given her a salary) so that she could study curriculum development there. Excited and eager to apply what she had learned, she undertook the challenge at NUCS only to experience the sad reality that her expertise would be ignored. During her two years at NUCS she was given little opportunity to make basic decisions. It was an untenable position for her, but she succeeded in it nonetheless. "Very difficult years," she says, looking back, "but through struggle the time became productive. I laid the groundwork for a basic program in composition in grades K through 12."

In 1966 she returned to high-school teaching, this time taking a position at South Christian High School in Cutlerville, Michigan, for three years.

For most of the years that Nelle taught, women were not given significant committee appointments, and rarely were they appointed chairperson. However, in 1969, Nelle left South Christian High and her final high-school position to accept an appointment to teach English at Covenant College in Lookout Mountain, Tennessee. There a new world opened for her. She was appointed chair of the curriculum committee of the college and was placed on the faculty-board committee — both important positions in a college community. She was particularly pleased with her appointment to the curriculum committee; her studies in curriculum would be useful now.

Her closest colleague, Dr. Nick Barker, an English professor who later became dean, recognized her abilities and experience; he drew out her skills. He was the one who told the faculty,

"Nelle should represent us at the board meeting. She best understands Christian education as a whole and faculty needs in particular."

Nelle felt greatly honored but also a bit scared. The college president wanted to put up more buildings; the faculty supported strengthening the academic offerings. "I felt a little like Esther: 'Here I go. If I perish, I perish.' I spoke to the board of trustees — a significant first — and there was a breakthrough. No more buildings of brick for awhile but more building of minds."

For five years Nelle enjoyed Covenant College. Always eager to serve, she embraced unstintingly the opportunities presented to her. Says Dr. Barker, "She has been one of the most cheering influences in my life, in all of my professional life." Although Nelle thoroughly enjoyed her work at Covenant, she missed family and friends up north, so she returned to Grand Rapids in 1974.

For the next eleven years until her retirement in 1985, Nelle taught at the Reformed Bible College in Grand Rapids. Her penchant for recognizing problems and suggesting needed improvements was evident here too. It hurt her "to prepare women for jobs that didn't exist, a condition which was the fault of RBC mainly," she says. But she rejoiced in seeing that many RBC students became missionaries.

"Sometimes I had to ask God to make me a little blind so I didn't see everything," she says frankly. "I prayed that he would help me remember that my place was to teach. I loved the classroom, and I relied heavily on humor in some of the tough places."

Retirement hasn't halted Nelle's use of her critical gifts. At Raybrook Nursing Home in Grand Rapids, where her beloved sister Gertrude is a patient, Nelle serves as a chaplain's assistant. Self-described sensitive person that she is, she is also keenly sensitive of others. She has objected to the sometimes thoughtless treatment of the patients. Whenever an occasion presents itself, she tells caregivers, "Now listen, listen to the person." To

Nelle it seems that nurses and attendants sometimes assume their patients know nothing. "I see it so often — younger people assuming that older people don't have all their senses. This is the gravest indignity anyone can inflict on another; it is brutal."

Dorothy Westra, her dear friend, agrees. Today they share a home. "It's a joy to live with Nelle," Dorothy says. "Early in the morning I often hear her singing psalms (which she loves) or a hymn. She is deeply concerned about things that aren't right."

For Nelle there is no choice: things that are wrong need to be corrected, and usually correction is possible. In her zeal she can be impulsive and perhaps sometimes makes decisions or judgments a bit too rapidly, according to Dorothy. "At least she makes them much faster than I do," Dorothy notes. "She says I help her by listening and by being a quieting, stabilizing influence on her." Nelle admits she is impetuous and impulsive, and she appreciates her friend's help.

"But," adds Dorothy, "she often softens her criticism with her light touch and frequent witty or funny remarks." When it comes to humor and cheer, Nelle remembers her Aunt Annie, who had a good sense of humor she shared with others; she was a woman who was always joyful. "In many ways, she was my role model," Nelle says. "To me she personified the joy of salvation. She sang every day, was never pretentious, and possessed the gift of hospitality, which she shared with everyone."

"I guess I've always been a critic. But that's the work of a prophet, isn't it?"

Yes, Nelle loves teaching Bible and English, and she loves people. But she doesn't like to keep house or do any manual work. Her sister Gertrude once commented on Nelle's aversion to sewing: "Nelle is allergic to the needle. If there is a way between doing it yourself or escaping it, she'll find that way."

Even in retirement, Nelle still tries to avoid ironing, another household task she dislikes. "Someone else often does that for her," says Dorothy.

Although Nelle resists doing domestic tasks, she serves in numerous other ways. Whatever the need, she tries to fill it. Alyce Boender, one of Nelle's friends, told her of the need to form an interdenominational Bible study group for women in her community. The group needed a teacher, one who could explain the lesson. "We've had it with discussions among ourselves before we know anything about the subject," explained Alyce.

Nelle began teaching the Psalms "because I was living the Psalms at that time," she recalls. "I knew what it was to cry to the Lord day and night. I knew what it was to wait on God. The people I taught told me, 'The Psalms seem so real.' And I replied, 'You know why? I am in the Psalms.'" She taught the group for several seasons. Although she eventually became too busy for the task, the group continued.

Nelle's studies have also led her to write three books: *Praise from the Psalms* as well as *Inspiration from Isaiah* and *Devotionals for Teachers*. All have been published.

Today, even though Nelle is retired, her week is as busy as ever: from speaking to adult-education classes at various churches on Sunday, to addressing the elderly folks at Raybrook Manor on Monday, to teaching women's classes on the Psalms, to entertaining with her Yankee Dutch humor at weddings.

When Nelle left Covenant College, she was given a plaque. Part of the inscription, composed by Dr. Paul Hesselink, professor of English at Covenant, aptly describes her service there:

> She has shown herself a tireless (but sometimes tired) co-worker, . . . a perceptive, helpful, and when necessary, critical observer of Covenant's faculty, administration, and trustees. . . . With a confidently salty faith she has shared with the college community her special gift for worshipping our Lord . . . in fresh, vital ways.

Countless others agree with his tribute.

Mary Stewart Van Leeuwen

Scholar and Psychologist

*By the time she was in her early teens, Mary was
well-acquainted with the attitude that "there are just some
things you don't talk about. Society stressed looking nice,
seeming to be nice, being apparently problem-free, and being at
least modestly successful. And that always troubled me. So I
guess when I found that there was a discipline that allowed me
to escape this attitude legitimately, I fastened onto it."*

Verna Mary Stewart Van Leeuwen's mother, Verna, wanted her children to fit in with the upwardly mobile. Consequently, Mary attended a high school that tended toward the upper middle class, even though Mary's family was "barely middle class." "I always felt out of place there," recalls Mary, "in terms of my clothing, how much money I had to spend, and so on."

Mary remembers too that her mother didn't want her children "growing up particularly interested in a fully-orbed Christianity." When fundamentalist Baptist neighbors started a Bible club, Mary was allowed to go. But her mother, concerned that the Baptists were "a little bit manipulative," later found activities for Mary that directly conflicted with the Bible-study time.

Verna Mary Stewart, born in London, Ontario, on May 29, 1943, was the third child of Verna Walker and Harvey Stewart. Her father taught physical education and geography at a local high school. Because of World War II, he wasn't around much during the first few years of Mary's life; instead, he was busy coaching all the school's teams and working with the army cadets. When Mary turned eight, her mother returned to teaching. Later, after the Russians sent *Sputnik* into space, Canadian government and education hierarchies envied Russia's progress, and recognized the importance of good teachers in achieving such progress. Accordingly, Canadian teachers began to earn somewhat better salaries. "I can remember the difference," Mary says. "I got new shoes rather than hand-me-downs."

Mary's maternal grandparents had lost their farm to one of her grandfather's colleagues. "My grandfather was so crushed by the fact that a so-called friend would have cheated him out of his farm that he never worked again." The loss of the farm and the father's subsequent despair deeply influenced the lives of all the Walker children. The four sons married, but of the five daughters, only Verna, the youngest, married. Mary's mother had her older brothers as strong male role models and so apparently wasn't as leery of men and marriage as her older sisters. "The theory in our family," Mary explains, "is that the older girls in the family were so disillusioned with their father

for having lost the farm and having become a sort of parasite
. . . they figured you didn't gain anything by marrying males."

These aunts provided Mary with strong female role models.
Mary recalls her aunts as being "very prim and proper" but also
"adventurous." They traveled to Europe every few years and
brought back "wonderful souvenirs and photos." For Mary,
whose family could barely afford to vacation for two weeks at
a cottage by Lake Huron, "it was quite clear that you didn't
have to get married to do well and to have a very interesting
life."

By the beginning of the eighth grade, Mary had her heart set
on studying psychology. In psychology she found a way to understand herself and her community. By the time she was in her early
teens, she was well-acquainted with the attitude that "there are
just some things you don't talk about. Society stressed looking
nice, seeming to be nice, being apparently problem-free, and being
at least modestly successful. And that always troubled me. So I

---

*"As a Christian I see life holistically. I think
Christian scholars have the responsibility to say
things that are useful to all kinds of people, not
simply to each other."*

---

guess when I found that there was a discipline that allowed me
to escape this attitude legitimately, I fastened onto it."

She was more interested in the theoretical study of psychology than in its application. Still, she occasionally thinks about
one day becoming a therapist. "As a Christian I see life holistically," she explains. "I think Christian scholars have the responsibility to say things that are useful to all kinds of people,
not simply to each other."

Mary's original reasons for choosing psychology, however,
were not related to Christianity. Her father, a Scotch-Presby-
terian, and her mother, a Methodist, joined the United Church

of Canada (U.C.C.) when it first organized in the 1920s. Her parents did not join this new denomination out of strong conviction, Mary believes, but for "reasons of respectability." The U.C.C. was an upwardly mobile church that Mary describes as a "social club with some ethical and moral and religious overtones."

When Mary entered Queen's University in Kingston, Ontario, she put her religious questions on the back burner. Yet here, among a largely secular student body, Mary found "community and commitment." Queen's became her "home." The university had a "casualness about life" that she embraced. She enjoyed her many friends, whom she describes as "very intellectually inclined young women." Together, they read and discussed Betty Friedan's *The Feminine Mystique* and Simone de Beauvoir's *The Second Sex*.

In 1965 Mary graduated from Queen's with a psychology major and a biology minor. She joined the Canadian University Service Overseas (CUSO), an organization similar to the U.S. Peace Corps. She was assigned to teach high school in Zambia (formerly Northern Rhodesia). Her father supported her decision, but her mother was worried, partly because she was afraid that Mary would be "trampled by an elephant or killed by an African nationalist," and partly because she was afraid that Mary was "on the road to becoming an 'old maid.'" Her mother was somewhat relieved when she learned that Mary would be working for the Salvation Army in a safe location, teaching English and French at a boarding school.

It was during her two years in Zambia that Mary first noticed "the gender aspects of religion." In the lower ranks of the Salvation Army, either husband or wife could preach. The Salvationists had built their movement on the idea that a man and a woman of the same rank should marry and then move up in the ranks together. But the upper ranks were dominated by men; although "their wives had the same rank," Mary notes, "it was always *Mrs.* So-and-so."

Despite these flaws and despite her skepticism about some

aspects of Salvationist theology, Mary agreed to attend church each Sunday and to set a good example for students. Living on a boarding-school campus kept Mary "busy-busy-busy." She taught classes, supervised homework, and patroled the dining rooms and dorms. During her stay Mary asked her Salvationist friends many questions about their faith. None of their answers, she says, were "enough to have me make a commitment at the time."

In 1967 Mary returned to North America. Her stay in Africa influenced her to change her scholastic emphasis from "very standard behavioral psychology" to cross-cultural psychology and African studies. Since Northwestern University in Chicago specialized in African studies and granted foundation money for overseas research, Mary enrolled there in the spring of 1968. In October 1970 she returned to Zambia for six months to do doctoral research.

Looking back on her decision to return to Zambia, Mary reflects, "Maybe the Lord sent me there. Maybe he was saying, 'You didn't quite finish what I sent you there to do.'" She made more friends, including Gordon and Anne Bland. Their house was open to "Americans and Canadians and expatriate kids who were wandering around Africa in search of their souls . . . doing it on a shoestring." When these young travelers ran out of money or "picked up a parasite," they dropped in at the Blands and stayed there until they recovered.

Mary was financially secure, and she didn't feel she was "searching for her soul," yet she enjoyed the hospitality of the Blands. They didn't see Christianity as something "that meant you had to put your mind in cold storage," Mary recalls.

On New Year's Eve of 1970, Mary and a couple of friends spent the night with the Blands. Gordon, having decided that "Mary Stewart was hungry after the things of the Lord," told of a massive eastern African revival which had begun during the 1940s and 1950s. When he and Anne had first arrived in Africa in the sixties, the revival had still been moving through Zambia. It had involved many miracles, including healings that had not been prayed for. Gordon had witnessed one such healing at a prayer meeting. An old woman who was blind in one eye suddenly stood up and took turns holding one hand in front of each eye and shouting, "I can see! I can see out of both eyes!"

As Mary listened to Gordon's story, she felt as if her own

Mary appreciates the worldview of the CRC because, she says, "if you want to try to integrate faith and learning, it's one of the best traditions you can hook into. It provides a coherent way to undergird your Christian scholarship with a world-and-life view."

---

eyes were being opened in similar fashion. She was converted "from seeing the world as being kind of chaotic, one that I had to figure out by myself, to suddenly seeing it as the territory of a loving God who was patiently waiting for me to respond to him." Throughout the rest of the evening, Gordon and Mary discussed Christ and Christianity. Mary felt God's presence in that room — so real, she said, that she could almost "take a handful of it."

When she returned to Northwestern, the Christian community there embraced her. She later wrote in the *Journal of Psychology and Theology* (1973), "My first and biggest surprise on returning to North America as a young Christian was that, far from being told by fellow-Christians to take second place as a woman, I was being hustled from pulpit to podium almost before I had the baptismal water shaken out of my ears." Although Mary explained to her friends how one could be a Christian feminist, she herself had to work through the relationship of Christianity to psychology and feminism. She began with the task of reconciling psychology and Christianity. Even as a student at Queen's University, Mary had been uneasy with the determinism of behavioral psychology.

82

During the summer of 1973, Mary traveled to Regent College in Vancouver, B.C., to learn how other Christians had integrated their faith with their academic disciplines. Later she studied philosophy as an intermediate field between psychology and religion. Philosophy enabled her to explore various questions, including this one: What is it about the brain that makes humans morally accountable for their actions in a way that animals are not accountable and cannot be held accountable? Although many of her questions remained unanswered, in 1982 she completed a book entitled *The Sorcerer's Apprentice*, in which she focuses on the integration of psychology and Christianity. In 1985 she published a second book, *The Person in Psychology*, in which she argues for a fundamental shift in psychology that will provide a more realistic and humane understanding of *the person*, not merely "the subject," in psychology.

As Mary worked through her new faith, she also wrote for Christian publications. Over time her articles have appeared in *Christianity Today*, *The Banner*, *The Reformed Journal*, and *Radix*. "Something in me always knew that I could be a writer," she says, "but that side of me didn't get developed until I became a Christian."

In 1971 Mary began teaching at York University in Toronto. In May 1974 she met Ray Van Leeuwen. He was finishing a master's degree at the University of Toronto when he read one of her articles. He became interested in meeting the author. The two got together and were soon dating — and soon facing the reality of diverging paths. That fall Ray intended to pursue a Master of Divinity degree at Calvin Theological Seminary in Grand Rapids, Michigan. He and Mary quickly realized the alternatives facing them: "Either we escalate this relationship very fast or we forget about it." The couple decided on escalation. "We became engaged about two months after we met," says Mary.

The two were "engaged at a distance" for a year — Mary stayed at York while Ray went to Calvin — until they married on May 31, 1975. Since Ray still had to finish studying for his degree, Mary took a leave of absence from York and taught psychology at Calvin that year. Simultaneously, she took a course in Dutch, adding it to her language repertoire of French (in which she is fluent), Latin, Russian, and Swahili.

When Mary and Ray married, Mary joined the Christian Reformed Church, of which Ray was a member. She appreciates the worldview of the CRC because, she says, "if you want to try to integrate faith and learning, it's one of the best traditions you can hook into. It provides a coherent way to undergird your Christian scholarship with a world-and-life view."

Mary is committed to the Reformed tradition but doesn't feel as though it has an "emotional hold" on her as it has on many CRC members. "It can produce a very good kind of solidarity that comes from being raised together. If there is agreement on a certain program, then everybody supports it. But it can make things very parochial! It can make it difficult to rock the boat; for example, your opponent on the faculty may also be the person who was in kindergarten with you." She calls herself a "participant observer in the CRC."

Becoming part of the CRC community didn't mean letting go of her Scottish heritage. As a child, Mary had learned many Scottish country dances in after-school groups. As an adult, she earned a teaching certificate in Highland and Scottish Country Dancing. Using this certificate, she formed a Scottish dance group on Calvin's campus shortly after the Christian Reformed synod allowed dancing in the CRC. The group still exists, although it is no longer affiliated with Calvin.

Following Ray's graduation from Calvin Theological Seminary in 1976, the Van Leeuwens returned to Ontario. That same year Kenneth Dirk ("Dirk") was born, followed by David Stewart Neil ("Neil") in 1978. Because Mary, the primary bread-winner, was teaching again at York and Ray was working toward his doctorate at the University of Toronto, the kids were "very much co-parented," Mary says. Although Mary doesn't claim to be a "super-mom," she and Ray continue to spend a lot of time with their sons and with each other. "During the summer

Ray and I are usually both at home working at our word processors, and if one of us needs to go to school the other will say, 'Okay, I'll be responsible for the kids this morning, and you do it this afternoon.'"

"There are times when I get this feeling that I have to do it all. But the Christian in me won't let me do that. When I feel I'm being overworked or taken for granted, I say to my husband or kids, 'Remember, I'm a human being made in the image of God just like you. And I have needs.' That kind of stops us short."

She devotes a lot of energy to her marriage as well as to her children. "Marriage takes constant work — in spite of your commitment to each other — because people are always developing," Mary points out. "We are not the people we were when we first married." Being an academic married to another academic, she explains, is not without its disadvantages. "There can be tensions over whose project is the most urgent, and therefore who should have the most time to work on it." And despite their attempts to break down gender barriers, "there are times when I get this feeling that I have to do it all," Mary says. "But the Christian in me won't let me do that. When I feel I'm being overworked or taken for granted, I say to my husband or kids, 'Remember, I'm a human being made in the image of God just like you. And I have needs.' That kind of stops us short."

Mary served on the 1981-82 team of the Calvin Center for Christian Scholarship (CCCS) that studied the nature and role of the behavioral sciences. During that time, Ray became a professor of Old Testament at Calvin. After Mary's year on the team, she worked part-time teaching at Calvin and spent the rest of her time writing. In 1985 the college offered her a permanent reduced-load position in psychology and philosophy.

Mary enjoys working with Christian academics, but some-times she feels like a minority at Calvin, both as a "token woman" and as an adult convert. "When I find another academic woman who's also an adult convert, I'm in seventh heaven."

During the 1989-90 academic year, Mary organized a CCCS team to undertake a study entitled "Gender Roles: Stability and Change within the Context of a Christian Worldview." Working on the team allowed Mary for the first time in her life to be surrounded by more female academics than male. The idea for this CCCS team stemmed from Mary's personal integration of feminism and Christianity. Mary discovered that most Reformed doctrine is easily reconciled with feminism. She does recognize, however, that scholarship isn't neutral: "Your world-and-life view has to undergird your scholarship, whether it is Marxist or feminist or Christian."

Mary believes that the Christian Reformed Church needs to continue to discuss gender issues. "People have to examine their own fears" about gender, she says, and "stop treating it as a taboo subject." She is much less concerned about ordination for women than about the fundamental groundwork of gender reconciliation.

Mary believes the Christian Reformed Church needs to continue to discuss gender issues. "People have to examine their own fears" about gender and "stop treating it as a taboo subject."

As she worked through the issues of feminism and Christianity, she decided to write another book. In 1976 Inter-Varsity Press had asked her to write a book on gender and the social sciences. Initially, albeit reluctantly, Mary had agreed to write such a book, but she quickly realized that she hadn't fully worked out her own philosophical and social-science questions

— much less her theological questions. "I was still a young Christian in 1976 — I had only really fully become a Christian in 1971," she explains. "I was still becoming biblically literate at that time." So Mary asked to be released from the contract. In 1985, feeling that she was now able to deal with those questions, Mary re-contacted Inter-Varsity Press and offered to write the book, which was published in 1990 under the title *Gender and Grace: Love, Work, and Parenting in a Changing World*.

Because of her involvement on the CCCS team that studied gender roles, Mary has also been asked to serve on Calvin's Gender Concerns Task Force and on the synodical committee appointed to study physical, sexual, and emotional abuse. In 1990 she became co-editor of "Partnership," a newsletter published by the Committee for Women in the Christian Reformed Church (CW-CRC). "Sometimes I feel as if I'm on a merry-go-round," she says frankly, "and I'm starting to feel a little hemmed in by all these obligations."

She isn't totally comfortable with her strong focus on women's rights. "If I were really a prophet, it seems to me I would be doing as much about race as I am doing about gender." In an effort to become more active in issues of racial justice, Mary recently accepted an appointment to the board of Jordan College in Grand Rapids, a junior college that particularly serves minority students.

Above all, Mary likes to "enable" others. She deeply admires "people who have survived with dignity — Christians with a working-class background or women who have come from abusive backgrounds. They are living testimonies that you don't have to be highly educated in order to be wise." Out of this admiration and concern, Mary works hard to make sure "space gets widened for other women," not only for promising young women in college but also for women in their thirties or forties who are just now re-entering school or the paid work force.

Mary anticipates a time when the "period for consciousness-raising and being angry" will finally end. That will be the day when, among other things, people in the Christian Reformed Church embrace the dialogue of Christianity with psychology, and of Christianity with feminism.

IV

I will sing and make music
with all my soul.
Awake, harp and lyre!
I will awaken the dawn.
I will praise you, O Lord,
. . . I will sing of you.

Psalm 108:1-3

Emily Ruth Brink

Note Worthy

"*My faith has grown and has been strengthened by working with the revision committee on the Psalter Hymnal. This work made me look at worship from the inside. We worked with the words of songs, especially those written by God's inspired psalmists. We learned how some hymns grew out of the life and faith struggles of Christians. I am much more aware of how wonderful God is.*"

Even though in 1959 she had no idea what "music theory" was, Emily Ruth Brink, college sophomore, chose music theory as an elective. "Others told me I wouldn't have trouble with it, and I might even enjoy it," she remembers. "Howard Slenk was the professor. I fell in love with music theory the first day."

That was it for Emily. "I knew my interest lay there. I always did my theory assignments first. The class met before eight o'clock in the morning — including Saturdays. I still loved it.

"Professor Slenk also taught organ. Because he did and because he had inspired my love for music, I asked him the next semester if I could begin taking organ lessons — from him," she specifies. Professor Slenk recalls the day: "She sat in the front seat. Her ability to understand music was outstanding. I asked her to stay after class and I suggested to her that she should major in music. I told her she should take organ lessons — from me, I added. She went out the door, down the hall. I left my room just a minute later, and I saw her jumping down the hall with glee."

However, Emily Brink, college junior, began to wonder where a music major would take her. "What can I do with music?" she asked herself. Becoming a teacher seemed like a safer option, but education courses didn't interest her. Music content courses, on the other hand, intrigued her. So she opted for courses in music history and theory, and squelched career thoughts — at least for a while.

Little did she realize that these decisions would eventually lead to a day in 1988 when an all-male synod of the Christian Reformed Church would spontaneously give her a standing ovation as editor of the just completed, comprehensive revision of the *Psalter Hymnal,* the official song and worship book of the Christian Reformed Church in North America. This capped the task that Emily had undertaken more than a decade earlier.

In 1977 Emily was appointed to the *Psalter Hymnal* Revision Committee. The church's official songbook was thirty years old. Part of the committee's mandate was to pay close attention to the church's growing cultural and ethnic diversity as well as to women's and children's issues, and to reflect that attention in the hymnbook's revision. It became Emily's biggest challenge — and reward. The revised *Psalter Hymnal* embraces many cultures and traditions, updates language, is gender sensitive, and includes some songs for children.

> *"If anything about my parents contributed to what I am, it is my father's servant character. He was mild, gentle. He was an ordinary man, yet extraordinary. . . . I could always go to him with questions."*

Emily does not attribute her deep love for music directly to her childhood interests; she was not a child prodigy in music. But there were some factors that may have influenced her early on. For one thing, her parents, Ralph and Minnie Brink, both loved music. "My Dad is eighty-six years old and still plays the piano daily," says Emily. "It's his one hobby. My parents met when they sang in the Calvin Oratorio Society. Dad continued singing in it until he was in his late seventies." All six Brink children were given music lessons — even though this worked something of a hardship on their parents. "I didn't realize until much later that Mother cleaned people's houses so that I could take piano lessons," Emily explains.

Emily was born on October 21, 1940. Her childhood had its trials. Her father's sunup-to-sundown hours in a succession of small grocery stores frustrated her sometimes because she didn't see him much. "And even though he worked long hours, Dad never made much money. He was more interested in giving people good deals than he was in making a good living. Sometimes I was jealous of my friends who seemed rich." The only time at all that he had for his children — or himself, really — was on Wednesday, his "afternoon off," and "that didn't begin until three or four o'clock in the afternoon," Emily says. Despite such frustrations, Emily's assessment of her early years is basically positive. "My childhood was mainly trouble free," she sums up. "I have mostly good memories."

From her parents and the examples they set, Emily learned to love Christ. "If anything about my parents contributed to what I am, it is my father's servant character. He was mild, gentle. He was an ordinary man, yet extraordinary. Every morning he read his Greek New Testament, which always lay open on his dresser while he got dressed. Even though he had little free time for us kids, I could always go to him with questions. He would keep on with what he was doing, but he listened at the same time."

Perhaps it was from her mother that Emily learned to see challenges as opportunities. Minnie Brink *looked for* new opportunities and challenges — even though she had plenty of them at home. Besides raising the three children born to Ralph and her, she had the difficult challenge of raising three of Ralph's children by his first wife, who had died when the children were very young. Minnie also helped Ralph in the store, but even that didn't use all her energy. So she started her own delicatessen. She made bread, pies, and potato salad to sell in Ralph's stores, and eventually her income surpassed his. Later she became a realtor.

With parents like Ralph and Minnie, Emily heard theological and denominational discussions early in life. "I loved those discussions," she says. "I couldn't always understand them, of course. But they sent my roots deep into the Christian Reformed Church; I have always loved it."

Sunday was a very special day for the family of Ralph and Minnie Brink. They were very interested in visitors worshipping in their church. Ralph made a beeline to them immediately after the service. "Come on over for coffee," he would say, and Minnie would also urge them to stay for Sunday dinner. With this hospitality the strangers became friends.

With parents like Ralph and Minnie, Emily heard theological and denominational discussions early in life. "I loved those discussions," she says. "I couldn't always understand them, of course. But they sent my roots deep into the Christian Reformed Church; I have always loved it."

The decision Emily had made to forego education courses for music studies caught up with her when she became a senior. "I was so young, so immature. Without education courses I couldn't get a teaching certificate." What to do? She decided to go to the University of Michigan; there she earned a master's degree in organ and church music in 1964.

With no teaching experience but with a master's degree in music, Emily decided she wanted to teach at the college level. Bob Jones University wanted her to consider joining the faculty. She declined. A Baptist church invited her to become their music director. She declined. The position "didn't feel right at all" to the young Christian so steeped in Reformed Calvinism and so committed to her own church.

At this juncture she was puzzled but not daunted. Something would happen, she was sure — and it did. Later that same year Emily was offered a position teaching in the Christian school in Manhattan, Montana. She signed the contract; at least she would get her teaching feet wet there, she thought. Besides teaching music and directing the junior-high and high-school choirs, she taught spelling, speech, English literature, art, and girls' physical education. "It turned out to be a ball." She chuckles as she recalls her first career challenge, pushing back her glasses to the perch on her nose from which they frequently stray.

Like her mother, Emily loves challenges: she greets them as opportunities — most of the time. Her gait underscores her determination. She walks in rapid four/four time, steadily and firmly, to her destination. She is tall. Her hair, heavy and dark gray, hugs her face, and its short curliness suggests a style chosen for convenience. The warmth of her eyes matches her easy smile and quick laugh. Behind her wayward glasses her eyes are inquisitive, searching. When she is puzzled or uncertain, the slight creases in her forehead deepen, accentuating her thoughts and questions.

Steeped in music and, to her surprise, enjoying teaching, Emily became concerned about teaching methods. "I was operating by the seat of my pants, doing all kinds of things that were fun. But I wanted to be sure that I was teaching rightly," Emily explains. She didn't realize that when students *learn*, the teaching is usually "right."

She activated her placement file at the University of Michigan in 1966, and "it just turned out" that the State University of New York (SUNY) at New Paltz that year was looking for a person with training in elementary education, organ, and music theory. Emily accepted the position and moved to New York.

Ah, college teaching. Easy street! Seven hours a week in the classroom, a private office, small classes, a small music department. "I've arrived," Emily thought. But her "arrival" was short-lived. She taught, studied, and performed all the duties required of college professors. In addition, she became the organist and choir director at Christ Episcopal Church in Poughkeepsie, and she started a choir for evening services at Immanuel Christian Reformed Church in Wappinger Falls.

"It was my first ecumenical experience," Emily notes. "My thoughts and outlook about Christianity and church for the first time reached beyond the Christian Reformed Church." How important this experience was she would learn much later.

Before Emily had time to think about a second year at SUNY, Trinity Christian College in Palos Heights, Illinois, invited her to join their staff. Reduced rank. Reduced salary. Doubled workload. Yet so exciting. Forgotten were the ecumenical experiments. Gone were any thoughts of staying at SUNY. Wouldn't she be going back to the Christian education she cherished and to the church she loved? She moved to Palos Heights in 1967.

Emily never married. Twice she could have become serious about marriage. Both times she chose to stay single. While in her twenties, she worried somewhat, she admits: "Why not me? All my friends and other young women seemed to be getting married. But I did not want to marry just to be married. I never met the right person."

A very important friend in Emily's life is Edna Sikkema, with whom she lives. She met Edna at Trinity Christian College, where, as colleagues, they roomed together. They found they had much in common.

"Edna became and still is very important to me," Emily says. "I have learned much from her. Perhaps the greatest lesson I learned is one that has helped me immeasurably in my work as editor of the *Psalter Hymnal*. She taught me how to separate the issue from the person. It was a hard lesson for me to learn, but it has paid rich dividends." Attacking an idea differs from attacking the person who has it, Edna taught her, and someone could differ with Emily's ideas and still be a friend.

Like Jonathan and David, Edna and Emily value their close friendship. "We are very different, and we are good for each other," Edna says. "Emily is always cheerful; she always hangs in there, no matter what." This has been a particular help to Edna since she has learned she has cancer. Emily has given unstintingly of her time to care for Edna during Edna's illness.

Emily did not stay long at Trinity. But she was not flighty: each step she took was solid, confident. "That," explains Edna, "is how she takes life. She keeps life in perspective, and lives by an unswerving, uncomplicated faith. A strong faith. Nothing shakes her. Oh, yes, she has questions at times, but they do not affect her faith; they interest and challenge her. She was blessed with a cheerful personality and an optimistic outlook."

"I really haven't had difficulty with my faith," Emily agrees. "Sure, questions and minor struggles pop up now and then, but I have always felt secure. I have always felt that no matter what happens, I am in God's care. No, I have never struggled with doubt, although sometimes my faith is stronger than at other times.

"One thing, though: my faith has grown and has been strengthened by working with the revision committee on the *Psalter Hymnal*. This work made me look at worship from the inside. We worked with the words of songs, especially those written by God's inspired psalmists. We learned how some hymns grew out of the life and faith struggles of Christians. I am much more aware of how wonderful God is." Looking back, Emily sees how her past work and study had prepared her for this biggest challenge of her career.

Her work at Trinity had reminded her of teaching in Montana. At both places she taught "all kinds of things." Before she had been at Trinity very long, she realized she would need a doctorate in music if she were to continue college teaching. Accordingly, in 1972 she enrolled in Northwestern University in Evanston, Illinois, to study music theory. At the end of her second year of study there, she learned that the University of Illinois in Champaign needed a professor in music theory — quickly! It was a one-year appointment. "The professor who called me said, 'If you're interested, jump, because there are other names being recommended too.' I jumped, all right — right to the church yearbook. Was there a Christian Reformed church in that town? Imagine, the Hessel Park CRC was in Champaign."

She accepted the position, and two weeks later began teaching at the University of Illinois. She commuted to Chicago on weekends. The next year the position was opened to other candidates and advertised, "but I had my foot in the door and got the job," Emily says. Meanwhile, Edna had accepted a position as consultant with a corporation that ran nursing homes and hospitals, a corporation whose headquarters were located near Champaign. At this juncture the two women moved to that city.

Emily spent nine years — from 1974 to 1983 — at the University of Illinois. It was during her stay there that she was appointed to the *Psalter Hymnal* Revision Committee of the CRC. She traveled to Grand Rapids several times in conjunction with the committee work, and in 1983 she was invited to apply for the editorship of the new edition.

She didn't jump.

She had finished her dissertation. She had just settled in her professional field and had found her niche — heading the undergraduate program in music theory. She was in charge of the teaching assistants and taught music theory.

Should she just walk away? Emily wondered.

This was a difficult decision for her. In the end, however, the tug of love for her church tipped the scales in favor of the editorship. She moved to Grand Rapids and became the Chris-

---

Bringing a book from idea to hard cover is something like nurturing a baby from embryo to birth. It becomes your child long before it is ready to be born. With the help of a committee of dedicated Christian poets, ministers, and musicians, Emily nurtured the Psalter Hymnal from synodical mandate to its place in the pew.

---

tian Reformed prophet of music. (Edna, tired of the extensive travel necessitated by her consulting position, decided to move to Grand Rapids, where she managed real estate.)

The challenge proved to be a much larger task than Emily had expected but not greater than she could handle. "For Emily," says Edna, "it was a labor of love and dedication." Bringing a book from idea to hard cover is something like nurturing a baby from embryo to birth. It becomes your child long before it is ready to be born. With the help of a committee of dedicated Christian poets, ministers, and musicians, Emily nurtured the *Psalter Hymnal* from synodical mandate to its place in the pew.

The issues surrounding language use and the decisions made to change language were the most difficult part of the task, Emily admits. Resistance to changes in traditional songs, interpretation, and comparison of familiar words, phrases, and ideas with current, more understandable words and phrases and concepts with more scriptural accuracy accounted for only some of the dynamics involved. Dr. Bert Polman, a member of the committee, prepared a statement of principles as a guide. After much discussion, the committee adopted the statement as its policy. It was on this basis that certain changes were made. *Thee, thou,* and *thine* became *you* and *your.* Phrases, even whole sentences, were rewritten.

"I spent more time on text revision, more than I ever expected to," Emily comments. "It is not really settled yet. Perhaps it never can be because language changes constantly."

As editor of the *Psalter Hymnal,* Emily has answered hundreds of questions, explained how the committee made its choices of both music and words, and defended the changes made. Her knowledge of and deep love for the church and the Reformed faith have made her a dedicated defender of the texts and tunes the revision committee chose. Her vast knowledge and self-effacing demeanor have enabled her to respond — politely and gently, without rancor — to the disagreements and complaints she has encountered in presenting the *Psalter Hymnal* to the church throughout Canada and the United States. The "greatest lesson" Edna had taught her now became particularly important: she was glad that she had learned to distinguish criticism of her work from criticism of herself. She traveled tirelessly, visiting any congregation that called her to introduce the new book. She sang new tunes, explained changes, demonstrated rhythms, answered questions, and directed singing.

Yes, the *Psalter Hymnal* was a challenge — but a positive and rewarding one. "I've had more challenges than obstacles in my life," Emily notes. "My life has been easy in terms of vocation and employment, and I have been blessed with opportunities. I'm always game." Once in a while, however, her optimism exceeds her time and energy. She wants to take on everything and sometimes takes on too much. "I could easily use two days for every one to complete the things I want to do."

She, along with a committee, has also begun work on a new hymnal for children (in addition to *With Heart and Voice,* a spinoff of the *Psalter Hymnal*). The new hymnal is being coordinated with LIFE, a new church-school curriculum (for preschool through grade six) being prepared by the CRC education department for publication in the mid-nineties.

One task leads to another. During the introductory phase of the new *Psalter Hymnal,* people across the land kept asking for more sustained help in worship planning. This led to the publication of *Reformed Worship,* a quarterly, of which Emily is the editor.

In 1987 she began to lead the Calvin Theological Seminary choir. She concentrated on the new hymns in the *Psalter Hymnal* and added lectures on the history of hymnody. She opened the choir to students' spouses and to women in the seminary. "That assignment has proved to be pure joy," she says. In February 1990 she was appointed an adjunct faculty member.

Her outstanding work on hymnody has broadened and deepened her ecumenical outreach. In July 1990 she was installed as president of the Hymn Society in the United States and Canada. She has also been asked to speak on the subject of psalm singing in North America at the International Hymn Society meeting in Belgium in 1991. "I am very grateful for opportunities to meet and learn from those in other denominations," she comments. "The church of Christ is indeed much bigger than the CRC."

Emily has also faced challenges other than music. For her, they have been no trouble — not obstacles, she insists. For example, when she attended the chapel at the University of Michigan in Ann Arbor, she became a member of the steering committee. "According to my pastor, Rev. Don Postema, I am the first woman who ever served on a steering committee in the Christian Reformed Church." At Hessel Park Christian

Reformed Church in Champaign, she again served on the steering committee. Committee work was "divided into elderlike and deaconlike tasks," Emily explains, "and I was given elderlike tasks. We had some difficult years there, including being without a pastor. That was a challenge, but that I was a woman was not an obstacle."

The only time a challenge felt like an obstacle to Emily was when she was asked to be an associate elder at her present church. Her pastor, Rev. Leonard VanderZee, says, "She accepted this role at the same time she was prominent in the Christian Reformed Church. Others and I saw that some people might use that to undercut her work with the *Psalter Hymnal,* and some did try. But she was oblivious to this. She is very

---

"I am very grateful for opportunities to meet and learn from those in other denominations. The church of Christ is indeed much bigger than the CRC."

---

committed to principles and lives by them courageously."

Sometimes the position frustrated Emily. "When it came to voting, because I was an associate elder I could not open my mouth," she recalls. Still, to her that was not a *major* obstacle. "It did not prevent me from doing what I believed I ought to do."

Just as Emily has been touched by God's grace, so she believes Christians must touch others with his graciousness. To her, the question is, How can I, with the gifts I have, meet a need that confronts the Christian community and a hurting neighbor?

For Emily Ruth Brink, her life is her answer.

Joanne Haan De Jonge

Strings and Stories

Teaching [music] was God's idea for her life, Joanne believes. . . . Journalism was his gift. "With journalism, I bumped into a wide, wide world of nature and biology I had ignored."

"I came back from Malaysia a different person," says Joanne Haan DeJonge. "In Malaysia I lived outside of the Christian Reformed community. I lived among people of a different race and culture and discovered that Christians live in all parts of the world and that God is with me wherever I am."

For a woman who had a "typical Christian Reformed upbringing," as Joanne did, this discovery affected not only her outlook but also her decisions about her future lifestyle.

Joanne Haan DeJonge was born May 18, 1943, to Andrew and Johanna Haan. She joined three other children: Ralph, Margaret (Peg), and Louise. Like most CRC kids, Joanne attended a Christian elementary school and a Christian high school.

Religiously and traditionally, Joanne's upbringing can be labeled "typical" — but it was unusual in certain ways, too. Family dinner conversations in the Haan home were devoted to words, ideas, musical performances, and the arts — with almost no attention paid to sports. "Not that we were against sports," Joanne explains: "we were simply 'a-sports.'" Parents and children had equal opportunity to speak and to influence the table conversation. "Even I — the youngest — could say, 'This subject is no longer of general interest,' and the conversation would move into another area."

Andrew Haan was interested in music, and the children were encouraged to take music lessons, "but we were not pushed," says Joanne. Nor did Joanne take the privilege of lessons for granted. When she was in fourth grade, she approached her mother, who was reading the evening newspaper. "Mom, may I take music lessons just like Louise?" Her mother set aside the paper for a moment, then said yes. That simple affirmative made Joanne feel good — and marked the beginning of her journey from music student to music teacher.

Her love of mathematics and her "left-brainedness" she traces to her father. "Dad liked things just so — not picky-picky, but precise," she says. She treasures the mementos that reflect his precision: a clock he made in which "everything fits in

104

place," and the precise, clearly legible financial accounts, penned in black and red, which provide a model for Joanne's teaching plans. "He loved figures and had his own unique teaching tool for us to practice our multiplication tables — cards taped on the wall opposite the toilet," she chuckles.

She particularly remembers the nurturing, considerate, quiet side of her father. "When I was with him I didn't feel the rivalry I sometimes felt with others in the family," she says.

But she doesn't trace all her characteristics to her father. "I guess I'm really a combination of my parents," she explains. "Dad was precise, very left-brained. Mother was fast, but not precise. I want to do things fast, yet precisely."

During the last few years of her life, Joanne's mother became her role model for the way she would like to conduct herself when she is older. In 1987 doctors found that her mother had cancer. A few years later, in November 1989, the doctor told Joanne that her mother should no longer live alone, so Joanne moved her mother to a supportive care facility. "Mother was very accepting. She had a sweet smile," says Joanne. "Before this time I had seen her as a person imposing her will on others; now I saw her as more selfless. If I live until my eighties and need supportive or nursing care, I hope I can be as she was." Her mother died in August 1990.

As a nine-year-old fourth grader, Joanne was already thinking of the future. She had asked to take violin lessons, yes, but it was also about this time that she considered being a missionary — preferably in some faraway land. One evening as she and her mom were doing the dishes together, Joanne asked her what it would take to become a missionary. "At least a college degree," her mother replied, "and also seminary training."

"Since at that time women were not permitted to attend the Christian Reformed seminary, I figured I couldn't be a 'real' missionary," Joanne remembers.

What then? In junior high school she decided on a career in mathematics. "I was good with figures — like my Dad," she explains. It seemed to be a good choice; she would probably become a math teacher. But that plan changed when she was in high school. Joanne played in Calvin College's orchestra, and the director, Dr. Harold Geerdes, mentioned that the Christian schools needed strings teachers. For Joanne, "everything fell in place. I had to be a strings teacher. The schools needed strings teachers, not math teachers." She spent her freshman and sophomore years — from 1961 to 1963 — at Calvin College in Grand Rapids, Michigan, where she majored in both music and mathematics. In her junior year she transferred to the University of Michigan in Ann Arbor because of its excellent strings department.

During the spring term of her last year at the university, she wondered about her career again. "I had just finished reading an article in *Time* magazine about Dr. Thomas Carlson, a missionary who was killed by nationals in the Belgian Congo. It affected me deeply. So many people needing an education, I thought. I couldn't sleep." Immediately she wrote to the Peace Corps and to the Board of World Missions of the Christian Reformed Church. The Peace Corps answered first. In spring

---

The Joanne who returned to the United States was not the Joanne who had left the country two years earlier. God's marvelous creation of different lands and peoples, God's universal church — Christians everywhere — had awakened in her a keen sensitivity to all his gifts. Indeed, she was — and is — a different person: her serious wonder and commitment continue to mark her life.

---

of 1965, five days after graduation from the university, Joanne was in Hawaii, training in the Peace Corps.

She was assigned to Batu Lintang Training College for teachers in Kuching, a city in Sarawak, one of the Malaysian states found on the island of Borneo. On one wall of the living room in her current home hangs an 18″ × 36″ batik print that helps keep alive her memories of Sarawak and Malaysia. (As if she could forget!) The print, a gift that one of her students created with cloth, wax, and dye, depicts a panorama of the college campus. "My husband, Wayne, appreciates the batik as art," Joanne says, "but for me the cloth is heavily invested with memories of a time when I internalized the Malaysian culture."

The Joanne who returned to the United States was not the Joanne who had left the country two years earlier. God's marvelous creation of different lands and peoples, God's universal church — Christians everywhere — had awakened in her a keen sensitivity to all his gifts. Indeed, she was — and is — a different person: her serious wonder and commitment continue to mark her life.

She learned how to stand on her own two feet the hard way. She had to make important and far-reaching personal decisions. During her Peace Corps stint, she became engaged to another volunteer who was not a Christian. For several months, she hesitated. Should I? Shouldn't I? Yes? No? She thought about and prayed about all the ramifications. Then she decided that she could not marry a man who did not share her faith. "Nor could I raise a family with someone who wasn't committed to Christ," she adds.

At that point she didn't know that just a couple of months later her aunt, Gertrude Haan, then an assistant editor of *The Banner* (the weekly magazine of the Christian Reformed Church), would introduce her to a fine young man. Gertrude had always shown a special interest in Joanne. "She took me under her wing, but she also kind of pushed me," Joanne says. Gertrude pushed gently. She helped set up a blind date with Wayne DeJonge, the art director for *The Banner*. Wayne, the second son in a family of four boys, had been born and raised in New Era, Michigan. Gertrude's matchmaking was a success: Wayne and Joanne married the next year. Wayne, says Joanne, has always been her "main affirmer. He sometimes overdoes it. He thinks I can do anything."

They joined Immanuel Christian Reformed Church in Wy-

After two years in the Peace Corps and mingling with Christians of many denominations, Joanne wanted to be sure she was choosing the Christian Reformed Church for deeper reasons than that she had been born into it. So she and her husband Wayne scrutinized the denomination before joining it. "We consciously chose the CRC because of its tenets of faith and belief," Joanne says.

---

oming, Michigan. Both liked the preacher, and their choice was a compromise — a blend of Wayne's desire for a large, settled church and Joanne's preference for a smaller church with a more informal worship style and with fewer people in "the CRC mold." Their selection not only involved a choice of church but also reflected a conscious decision to remain in the Christian Reformed denomination. The Christian Reformed Church had been part of Joanne's upbringing: "It had been the tradition of our family to be CRC," she says. But after the two years she spent working in the Peace Corps and mingling with Christians of many denominations, Joanne wanted to be sure she was choosing the Christian Reformed Church for deeper reasons than that she had been born into it. So she and Wayne scrutinized the denomination before joining it. "We consciously chose the CRC because of its tenets of faith and belief," she explains.

Her Christianity and her doctrinal beliefs affect both her thoughts and her actions. "It's a marriage," she says. "It's just there, right off. So let's get on with it!" Joanne is a "deeply committed person with a rare strength of character, a person with a strong value system," says Esther Yff Prins, a close friend for more than twenty years. According to Trenda Vannette, a friend and teacher from Flagstaff, Arizona, "Joanne has done a beautiful job of making her personal life [a statement] of what she will do and won't do."

Joanne's strong commitment does not mean her life of faith has always been easy. For several years, from the late 1970s to the early 1980s, Joanne suffered much grief because of illness and death within her family. In 1978 her brother Ralph, 45, died of a heart attack. In 1980 her sister Margaret (Peggy), 45, died of amyotrophic lateral sclerosis (ALS), more commonly known as Lou Gehrig's disease. Six months later, Joanne's mother suffered a severe case of shingles, which lasted for two years. Then in 1982 her father died of complications from an aneurism; this pained her most deeply. Ralph's widow, Joan Haan Einfeld, who now lives in Bradenton, Florida, recalls Joanne's intense devotion to her father: during the seventeen weeks of his hospitalization, Joanne visited him daily.

Joanne remembers her anger, especially toward God. "It was not a struggle of the head, like you would have in your late teens and early twenties. It was emotional, heartbreaking," she says. She felt that "God was dumping on me. I always thought Louise and Mother had a rather close relationship, and I was especially close to my father. I remember thinking that I could never again be affirmed in the way my father always affirmed me."

For six months Joanne struggled. "Finally, I saw there was no real answer — but faith. I felt that things that happen are okay, or God makes them okay," she says. She found peace again.

During this difficult time in their lives, Wayne and Joanne purchased a cabin and ten acres on a river as their May-to-October weekend retreat and future retirement home. Even more, adds Joanne, "we needed roots and family, a sense of permanence." Yet even now Joanne finds it necessary to justify this seeming "inconsistency" in her intentionally simple lifestyle. "We pray every year when we open it that we will use it rightly."

This concern for life and how it is to be lived is also evident in her writing. Writing became a vocation for Joanne soon after she returned from the Peace Corps. Aunt Gertrude had faithfully corresponded with her and had remained interested in her activities. When Joanne came home in 1968, Gertrude asked her to write an article on the Peace Corps for *The Banner*. Subsequently she asked Joanne to write a series of articles for "The Young Look," a children's page featured in the magazine. "I didn't want to do a complete series on the Peace Corps, so I thought, 'I'll write about ants. There must be something on ants,'" recalls Joanne with a smile. She wrote the articles and has been writing "The Young Look" ever since, in which she focuses on the infinite wonders of God's creation. Joanne will never run out of bugs and insects, fish and fowl, or plants and trees to write about!

One of her favorite little creatures is the spider. Like most people, she has an almost morbid fascination with and fear of spiders — that's why she wants to write and speak about them. She calls attention to their humorous habits and laughs along with her audiences when she gives "spider talks." "Notice," she says, pointing to the edges of the blue carpeting in her home: "no spiders in the corners. That's because I put them outside in nice weather instead of killing them."

Teaching (teaching stringed instruments) was God's idea for her life, Joanne believes. Since she returned from the Peace Corps she has been teaching strings in the Grand Rapids Christian schools. Journalism was God's gift to her. "With journalism, I bumped into a wide, wide world of nature and biology I had ignored," says Joanne. She not only "bumped into" biology but also began to study and research it. "Why didn't anyone ever tell me how exciting, how wonderful it is?" she remembers thinking. Besides teaching and writing, she studied further at Calvin College. She earned a master of arts in teaching science studies — "basically," she says, "to achieve credibility for my writing."

Since 1975 she has written more than six hundred articles for "The Young Look" in *The Banner*. At the magazine's office, this page is known as "Joanne's page." She has also written about ninety articles for *It's God's World*, a Christian weekly reader. Many of her articles have been compiled in booklet or book form. "I guess my style of writing is cast into a kind of mold, but I love nature subjects," she says. "And perhaps I'm bound by my own limitations. I haven't gone as far afield as I thought I would."

Modesty notwithstanding, Joanne has written several books "from scratch," ranging in topics from bats and bugs, snakes and slugs, to sexuality for young people. With Marjo Rouw, a former missionary to Africa, she has written stories about African missionaries and their children.

Joanne also has some manuscripts "looking for homes" — one about endangered species, and another on the Ten Com-

---

In 1968, Gertrude Haan asked Joanne to write a series of articles for "The Young Look," a children's page in The Banner. *. . . "I thought, 'I'll write about ants. There must be something on ants," says Joanne with a smile. She wrote the articles — and has been writing "The Young Look" ever since.*

---

mandments for young teenagers. "I always have dozens of ideas floating around," she explains. "It would be neat to have time to do that — to follow your own ideas."

Joanne is always wondering, and is vocal about her sense of wonder. Her early introduction to music and the arts and her belief that creativity is a crucial part of the imaging of God shape her other ways of speaking out. "The Christian school system is on the wrong track in their treatment of the arts," she says. "We do not give music and the arts enough time or enough emphasis. Instead, we thoughtlessly follow the world in its emphasis on the physical [sports]. My own life may be unbalanced towards the other extreme — with almost no attention to sports

— but we have to have people like me who are heavily into the arts to balance the emphasis on the physical. I wish I were more vocal; maybe then someone would hear me."

Joanne's schedule is full. Strict research and writing hours occupy two days each week. On the other three days she teaches orchestra at two Christian schools in Grand Rapids. She loves the combination of writing and teaching but does not mix the two disciplines. "I can't appear in the role of author or speaker on the days I teach," she says.

Even though Joanne has established a definite routine for writing, the actual process of writing is hardly routine. "I'm always in touch with children as I recall and visualize settings. I'm talking with kids, not just addressing a computer screen," she says.

Because of her writing and her teaching, it might be easy to assume that Joanne is a mother. She is not. And although she and Wayne feel they have a right to their privacy, she did share her thoughts about their decision not to have children. "At first," she recalls, "I fell into the traditional mold: we would start a family and I would stay home with the children. But after about a year of marriage, Wayne and I began to talk about choices and reasons why we would or would not have children."

At the time both Wayne and Joanne felt a definite calling: Joanne to teaching and Wayne to his work as art director. "We felt our talents, our minds should be developed to their fullest and used in Christ's name for others," Joanne says. According to Joanne, an interest in conserving the resources of a rapidly overpopulating earth also played a part in their decision. "We felt that the usual reasons to have children (desire, fulfillment, old-age insurance, or 'It's the thing to do') were essentially rather selfish, and we should 'regulate' ourselves by not having children. Instead of having children or grandchildren for our parents, our contribution would be ourselves," she says. Little doubt lingers for either Joanne or Wayne that they made the right decision.

As her writing and her wrestling with parenthood indicate,

Joanne is very concerned about the environment and the conservation of the earth's resources. In 1990 Wayne and Joanne
moved into a condominium, leaving a small apartment where
they had lived for nearly twenty-one years. Friends joked that
Wayne and Joanne had moved from their honeymoon apartment to a retirement home. Joanne smiles at this but explains
that she and Wayne have made their housing choices as part
of a consciously simple lifestyle. "Lifestyle — conservation and
stewardship — is a deep concern of mine. I pray about it often,"

---

*"Lifestyle — conservation and stewardship — is a
deep concern of mine. I pray about it often."*

---

she says. "My husband and I believed that the land we would
occupy and the resources we would use in a house could be
used more wisely than simply to give two people comfort and
an inordinate amount of space. I did not want to go into a *house*,
and I hope I can be a small voice about recycling and conservation in our small community, especially regarding the woods
and the flood plain behind our condo."

Her voice intensifies as she articulates her philosophy about
the environment. She senses that she must speak out and be a
prophetic voice within the Christian community, and she has
spoken out clearly in much of her writing. Still, she feels she
has not been aggressive enough. That haunting Calvinist con-
science still lingers. Her lack of aggressiveness she attributes to
her father's influence. "Dad's influence was always gentle: he
believed in keeping the peace." So she doesn't feel she functions
like a major force; she describes her influence as "drip, drip,
drip" — an approach she's not altogether happy with. "It takes
an awfully long time to make an impact," she explains.

"It's one thing to practice or talk or write about conservation but it's another to take personal responsibility for it,"
Joanne continues. She took on this responsibility after a supper

113

for Calvinettes and their fathers held one evening at Immanuel CRC. Her current pastor, Rev. Robert Tigchelaar, made a comment to Joanne about all the plastic and paper products being used. "And I hadn't even noticed!" exclaims Joanne. "I'm surprised you let this happen," Rev. Tigchelaar remarked.

Her pastor's comment kept Joanne awake all night. "I spent the time praying for forgiveness," she says. "And I made a commitment to conserve resources in my life and to try to be a voice within the community." Accordingly, she proposed to the deacons of her church a comprehensive plan to eliminate church use of any plastic, Styrofoam, or other non-recyclable materials, and to encourage conservation among church members as well. The church accepted her ideas, and today conservation is in full swing at Immanuel. The number of Joanne's speaking engagements about nature and environmental conservation also continues to grow.

Joanne DeJonge's strings, stories, and self — and her selfless concerns — are her continuing contributions on this earth. Because she uses her pen to paint the mystery and marvel of God's creatures, today's — and tomorrow's — children (and adults) will more thoughtfully praise God, the Creator of heaven and earth.

V

Each one should use
whatever gift [s]he has received
to serve others,
faithfully administering God's grace
in its various forms.

1 Peter 4:10

Jelske TenHove Talstra

Prairie Pioneer

Jelske's strength, which ebbed infrequently because of her trust in the God of Psalm 121, gave her a joyful demeanor that helped level rough spots for people lonely for the old country, for women wondering why they had ever consented to cross the sea, for frail ones who lacked the stamina required of first-generation immigrants in a foreign, almost virgin country.

March 21, 1929. It was their wedding day.

It was also the day on which they were scheduled to emigrate from Holland to Canada — but they almost didn't.

Jelske (pronounced "Yels-keh") Talstra and Harm Jan Ten-Hove had been married in the morning on that 21st day of March. Only a few minutes remained of the wedding-farewell dinner they had shared with their family just before boarding the train. Only the heart-hurting good-byes remained. Jelske, always the organizer, gave their various papers a final check. With a shock she noticed that the clerk in city hall had not indicated on the line provided that she, Jelske Talstra, was now Jelske TenHove.

Hailing a taxi as they ran, Harm Jan and his brother Jan raced to the city hall in the next town for the vital correction. Tense moments passed. The bride, facing the first crisis of her marriage, finally hurried toward the train depot with both sets of parents. Little Opa (Grandpa) TenHove jogged down the street, the big wedding Bible under his arm. The minutes ticked by. What if . . . ? No, that wouldn't happen!

What relief when the groom and his brother finally came into sight, both gasping for breath. The brothers were still wearing the wedding corsages, and as they came nearer, Jelske heard a passerby say, "Oh, oh. His bride must have taken off without him." Harm Jan explained the delay: a drawbridge, allowing a boat to pass through on the canal, had held up the taxi.

Good-byes were cried quickly. (Maybe it's better that way.) The newlyweds boarded the train to Antwerp, Belgium, where the *S. S. Vollendam* waited to carry them and many more immigrants to Canada.

Jelske TenHove Talstra never saw her parents again. But the spiritual heritage that her parents had given her she carried to Canada — for her children and for the hundreds of others whose lives she touched. She also brought with her a picture of Dutch theologian Abraham Kuyper, a picture that hung in the "front room" as long as her children can remember.

For Jelske, the decision to emigrate to Canada was not lightly made. All of life, she believed, had to be lived with one's heart lifted up to the Lord and one's eyes looking down upon his Word. She had believed that since she was a child.

Her childhood, although spent in a sturdy, believing family, had not been easy. After her father, Eebele Talstra, and Dieuke Douma had married and had two daughters, Dieuke died. Eebele then married Dieuke's sister, Baafke. Together they had

---

For Jelske, the decision to emigrate to Canada was not lightly made. All of life, she believed, had to be lived with one's heart lifted up to the Lord and one's eyes looking down upon his Word.

---

eight daughters and four sons. Jelske was their second daughter.

The family, a very large one, was poor. Jelske remembered the frequent arrival of new babies in the family and her mother, in a long black skirt, always at the sewing machine remaking clothes for the children. Eebele struggled to feed his ever-growing family.

Jelske completed the sixth grade; after that she began working, pulling her own weight. Babysitting. Delivering vegetables. Clerking in Mrs. Reitsma's grocery store. Much later, when Mrs. Reitsma died, she gave Jelske her hand sewing machine plus one hundred guilders (much to the disgust of rich relatives). Some years later, when Jelske and her new husband emigrated to Canada, she took the sewing machine with her. For twenty-eight years she made good use of it.

When Jelske was twenty she moved to Leeuwarden, the "big city," where her older sister, Sijke, already worked. Jelske got work as a clerk in a store. One day she received news that her sister Fokeltje was ill, so ill that her parents had had to call the doctor. Jelske was stricken. She had to go home, she decided; the family had to be together at a time like this. Jelske needed her family; her family needed her. Her boss said she could leave if she could find a replacement. Somewhere in that city, Jelske knew, was Maike, a girl from her hometown. But where did Maike live? It didn't make much sense to look for someone whose address you didn't know — at least not to anyone but Jelske. Up and down the streets and down by the canal, she ran. It was providential, Jelske later told her children, that there, on the opposite shore of the canal, sat Maike on her father's houseboat. Yes, she would take Jelske's place.

Both Jelske and Sijke went home and cared for their younger sisters and brothers during Fokeltje's illness. Fokeltje didn't live long. Her death at age sixteen was caused by a brain tumor. The trauma of losing her young sister affected Jelske greatly. For two years she stayed home and helped her mother.

Eventually, however, Jelske grew restless. She loved helping people, but there had to be better ways than cleaning someone's house day in and day out. Her mother encouraged her to pursue a career. Jelske took her mother's advice: she chose nursing and earned her diploma as a psychiatric nurse. She graduated in May 1928 and became the head nurse in a Christian mental hospital.

Harm Jan TenHove worked at the same hospital. When the two met, the attraction was mutual, but immediately there was a problem. According to regulations, male and female employees of the hospital were not allowed to associate with one another. Courtship was forbidden, on pain of discharge. But can one deny the heart because the rules are heartless? Harm Jan and Jelske attended lectures together. They sent love letters through an accomplice, Mr. Van Vliet, who lived on the hospital grounds. They became engaged.

Of course, the hospital authorities found out. It was customary to fire the female, but Jelske was an excellent head nurse, so they decided they couldn't lose *her*. They asked Harm Jan to leave, but he refused. Because the couple's wedding date was not too far off, the administrator relented: both Jelske and Harm Jan were allowed to remain. Together they planned their wedding and their emigration.

Both Jelske and Harm Jan had known that life in Canada would be hard, but the heady days of courtship had colored reality with the glamour of climbable mountains and conquerable plains. Jelske's optimism reached far beyond the shores of Holland and the waters of the Atlantic.

The couple's first taste of their new country encouraged them. After they spent fourteen days on the ship and several more days on the train crossing Canada, they arrived at Carnduff, Saskatchewan. Their sponsoring farmer, Frank Howe, picked them up in an open Ford, in which his chickens roosted nightly. Even Jelske thought the nine-mile ride to Mr. Howe's farm was the longest stretch of their journey. Fortunately, a warm welcome and a hot meal greeted them. Jelske always remembered the dessert — saskatoons, a delicious purple-black fruit that she had never tasted before. "You know," Jelske told her children many times, "Mr. Howe was dirty and needed a shave, but he sat straight and ate properly with a fork and knife — so *deftig* [with class] — like a king. He didn't bend over and slurp as many *boeren* [farmers] in Holland do." Jelske was impressed. Canada was a good country, she decided.

A small upstairs room in the Howe house became the first home for Jelske and Harm Jan. Learning to cook and bake, Jelske fed the farm hands — with whom, of course, she couldn't communicate because of the language barrier. Mrs. Howe spent her days in town during the week, so the Howe children could attend school there. Harm Jan worked on the farm. This was a lonely situation for Jelske: she missed her parents and her siblings. She also missed her church. Still, God is everywhere, she reasoned, and he didn't need a formal church on Sunday. The young newlyweds held their own worship service in their stuffy little room; Harm Jan read the message from a book of Dutch sermons.

Not much time passed before the glamour of immigration faded. Jelske dreamed of her former work as a nurse. How ironic! Here in her new country she was again doing housework — for others. She hung tenaciously onto her faith. There had to be something more in Canada for her and Harm Jan, she was sure.

121

When immigrants were dissatisfied with their placement and wanted a change, they had to correspond with a "fieldman" (appointed by the Christian Immigration Society to help immigrants make work arrangements with local farmers). Harm Jan and Jelske did this and got results. They made arrangements to move to Lacombe in Alberta, where Harm Jan found farm work and Jelske could actually have a house.

But their time in that house was short. The next year their first daughter, Jean, was born. It was 1930; times were getting hard. When the Great Depression set in, Harm Jan lost his job. Their sponsoring farmer gave them a cow and two pigs in lieu of wages he owed. With the little money they had managed to save, Harm Jan and Jelske put a small downpayment on 320 acres west of Lacombe. According to the sales agreement, Harm Jan had to clear ten acres each year.

Jelske helped Harm Jan with the work as much as she could and cared for their two children — by this time a son, Eb, had

---

Providing quiet and unnoticed background support did not come easily for the young Jelske. Hadn't she been a head nurse in Holland, a person with some authority? Hadn't she enjoyed the independence that springs from self-confidence? In this new land she sometimes felt confined. . . .

---

also arrived. In the evening she helped Harm Jan combine the oats and barley stalks and set them up in bundles of eight — "setting up the stooks," it was called. She worried about the children sleeping alone in the house. One day while helping Harm Jan pull thistles out of the barley, she had the children outside with her. She left Eb in a box at the end of the field, with little Jean nearby. When she heard Eb crying frantically, she hurried to him. Her heart thudded when she saw little Eb, red-faced, sweating, and squirming. Jean had thrown dirt and ants into his box and onto his face.

Jelske had learned early that her marriage would not be a biography of bliss. She loved her husband, and he loved her, but, based on her understanding of God's Word, she believed that a wife must be submissive. Accordingly, she provided the home support when her husband became active in building the Christian school in Lacombe, served on the boards of schools and associations, went to the synod of the Christian Reformed Church, and more. She took some satisfaction in knowing that Harm Jan couldn't have participated in all of these activities if she had not kept hearth and home for him and the children.

Providing quiet and unnoticed background support did not come easily for the young Jelske. Hadn't she been a head nurse in Holland, a person with some authority? Hadn't she enjoyed the independence that springs from self-confidence? In this new land she sometimes felt confined to her own house. Life was hard, and everything was inconvenient. Settling as pioneers was difficult.

But each day Jelske adjusted to marriage and became a bit more acclimated to her new country. Adjustment was important: she would spend six decades in the virgin territory of Alberta in western Canada.

Jelske understood that a farmer and his farm are very directly dependent on God, especially for weather. She never allowed her children to complain about weather, regardless of how it affected their comfort, their activities, or even their father's crops. "God knows better than we do what we need," she would say firmly.

She helped Harm Jan clear more land each year, and she also helped him stook grain, pick roots, and milk cows. She carried water up the hill from the well, and she carried cream down the hill to the well to keep the cream cool. Although the family had little, Jelske found enough to share. Her smile welcomed anyone who needed her. "Mom was a joyful person," her daughter Betty says. "Even when we did the dishes — and there were lots of them — she sang. She loved Psalm 121 ["The Lord watches over you"] and often sang it. Sometimes we sang hymns together, Mother in Dutch and I in English."

Jelske's feet found a way beyond her family to church, school, and community. Harm Jan's hired men enjoyed her hospitality and her cooking. Working men needed good food, she believed. Immigrant bachelors often needed a bed and a meal, and she would provide them. The feet of uncounted immigrants and needy people seemed always to know her door.

Harry Siebenga, a young immigrant who had just lost both arms in a railyard accident, lived with the TenHoves while he adjusted emotionally and physically to a life in which he would have to be dependent on hooks for arms. He was a determined young man. He tried to master every task a farmer must know. He even drove the wagon and horses, tying and twisting the reins around his hooks. But one day there was a bad accident. Harry was attempting to calm the horses when they bolted, dragging him and throwing him against the corner of the barn. Because Harry had the reins twirled around his hooks, he couldn't extricate himself. Eventually Harry was freed, and Harm Jan carried him, stunned and badly bruised, to the house. Jelske nursed him back to health.

Later, when Harm Jan became the official fieldman for Dutch immigrants to Lacombe, he met arriving families at the train depot — at all hours — and brought them home for a day or a week. Today, when people meet someone from Lacombe, they will say, "Oh, you're from Lacombe? We landed in Lacombe forty years ago, and we stayed at TenHoves."

Most of the time Jelske enjoyed the part she could play in her husband's management of the farm. She didn't need a lot of creature comforts; she delighted in small things. The red dustpan with the long wire handle, bought on a farmer's Saturday night in town, stayed with her until she had to leave her home to be cared for elsewhere.

She would never acquire earthly fame or honor, but that

was all right. God and life were teaching her that fame and honor are as transitory as life. God had assigned to her this behind-the-scenes duty. Faith and obedience — these were her hitching post and guidepost, her watchword and practice. "Trust and obey," she taught her children. (At her funeral her grand-daughters sang, "Trust and obey, for there's no other way to be happy in Jesus but to trust and obey.")

Jelske became the community nurse-doctor. Hospitals were expensive and for many people far away. She was the neighbor-hood's expert, available for emergencies. She wiped fevered brows, prescribed homemade remedies, and prepared bodies for burial.

Jelske also delivered babies; births in the area were frequent and often came at inconvenient times. One night she went to the Charles Butler home. Charlie had gone with his team of horses to meet the doctor, who couldn't get over the muddy

---

Although the family had little, Jelske found enough to share. Her smile welcomed anyone who needed her. "Mom was a joyful person," her daughter Betty said. "Even when we did the dishes — and there were lots of them — she sang. She loved Psalm 121 ["The Lord watches over you"] and often sang it. Sometimes we sang hymns together, Mother in Dutch and I in English."

---

road in his automobile. The baby was not yet due; nothing was ready. But the baby didn't wait. Jelske planned to put the new-born, with the cord attached, on the mother's stomach until the doctor arrived. But then Mrs. Butler yelled, "There's another one coming. I don't want it!" Jelske sprang into action. She grabbed a flour sack, ripped off a strip, boiled it, and used it to tie the first baby's cord. The second baby came feet first; Jelske pulled her into this world because the mother wouldn't

125

cooperate. Next Jelske emptied the woodbox, lined it with an old sweater, and laid the two little girls in it. Alta and Elsa survived and became strong, healthy farm women.

Jelske's days and part of her nights were full. Out of necessity she became a counselor. Her friend, Wieke VanderLeek, said, "If one felt weary or downhearted, she made a nice cup of tea or coffee and would sit down just to listen. She knew how to comfort and help a person see the brighter side." She comforted wives and mothers who had a hard time accepting the bare-bones existence of a small house with no electricity or running water and a "neighborhood" with no corner store. She calmed Harm Jan when he came home tired, down, and out of sorts after listening all day to immigrant complaints.

Her strength, which ebbed infrequently because of her trust in the God of Psalm 121, gave her a joyful demeanor that helped level rough spots for people lonely for the old country, for women wondering why they had ever consented to cross the sea, for frail ones who lacked the stamina required of first-generation immigrants in a foreign, almost virgin country.

Not that Jelske was immune to tragedy. Not at all. Both of her parents died before she had the time or money to return to Holland. She also experienced repeated tragedy in childbirth. After Jean and Eb came two more children, Dick and Betty. But Jelske's fifth child, a girl, was stillborn. Harm Jan buried little Altje under a spruce tree north of the house; Jelske grieved deeply. Two years later Jelske gave birth to twin boys, but each baby lived only a few hours. Both were buried under the spruce with Altje. Jelske bore her grief quietly, only occasionally voicing her sorrow.

Worship remained an important focus for Jelske. In the early thirties the settlers began to hold church services. They met in the public schools nearby. Once a month a visiting minister came; it was a special joy if he stayed two Sundays. Occasionally a student "sent by the seminary in Grand Rapids" would stay for the summer. For Jelske, that meant spiritual stimulation. It also meant putting the white cloth on the dinner table, making

126

up the guest bed with white, embroidered sheets — and keeping all of the linens ironed.

On land given to them, the settlers in 1935 built the First Lacombe Christian Reformed Church, which much later became the Woody Nook Christian Reformed Church.

Jelske had nearly reached her half-century birthday when illness struck. She couldn't know then, of course, that God would allow her to survive several more illnesses and offer forty more years of ministry before he would invite her home.

When Jelske was fifty-one, Harm Jan took her to Edmonton for diagnostic surgery. It revealed a malignant pancreatic growth which, the specialist said, was terminal. She did not have long to live, he added. When she was moved to the hospital in Lacombe, her family doctor rigged up a thin tube that Jelske had to swallow before every meal. Through this tube she was fed bile, which her body needed for digestion. To the doctor's amazement — he could find no reason for recovery — and her family's delight — it was a God-sent miracle! — Jelske's appetite returned, and her strength increased. God wanted her on earth, Jelske believed.

For sixteen more years, Jelske continued her mission to many. Then one day a violent seizure — which struck while she and Harm Jan were in a coffee shop — left her unconscious. "Multiple myeloma," the doctor said. Her bone marrow was producing too many white blood cells. But again she recovered, miraculously.

Once again Jelske picked up where she had left off — for another three years. Then a stroke stopped her cold. A second stroke soon after left her partially paralyzed, unable to talk, swallow, or walk. It was a tense time and a great trial for Jelske, Harm Jan, and their children. "Mother was very alert," her daughter Jean recalled, "and with her one good hand she tried desperately to tell us things that we never understood."

Those six weeks that Jelske was incapacitated were difficult. "Find a good nursing home," the doctor advised the family. "There's little hope for improvement." But he underestimated

God and Jelske. Her indomitable spirit surged once more. Her speech began to return, and her swallowing improved. She *would* walk again too — with a walker. She returned home to live with Harm Jan for another eight years. Although she couldn't go out much to minister, those who visited her became her ministry.

When Harm Jan died in 1976, Jelske's strength surprised her children again. When the time came, three years later, for

---

Faith and obedience — these were her hitching post and guidepost, her watchword and practice.

---

her to enter Lacombe's Senior Citizens' Home, Jelske had no regrets. Wasn't this another step closer to her destination?

Her slower speech made her cheerfulness more beautiful. For a year she lay on her back with a slowly mending broken hip. At the end of that year, with one of her legs three inches shorter than the other, she was confined to a wheelchair. For still another six years, she remained the "sweetheart" of the nursing home.

Jelske, pioneer prophet of trust and obedience, stayed alert until her death, even making her own decisions. "Mother always gave generously," said her daughter Betty, "and towards the end she doubled her giving — except once." That time she said, "A couple of dollars is enough for the church this week. The dominees can pay for their own holidays." Puzzled, Betty checked the church bulletin; the offering was for the Pastoral Institute, a Christian counseling service. Jelske thought the institute was a "retreat" for pastors. (She changed her mind about her tithe when Betty described the institute.)

Jelske died at age ninety-one. She had made her own decisions about her leave-taking too: "Write inside the cover of my Bible Psalm 25:4 and 5 ['Show me your ways, O Lord . . . ; guide me in your truth and teach me . . . my hope is in you all day long'], so that you don't forget to use this text for my funeral."

To her children, Jelske TenHove Talstra was God's child — obedient, trusting, joyful. Hundreds of Canadians remember her that way too.

Elvinah Spoelstra Zwier

Servant of the Poor

*After her fiancé's death, she knew she had to pick up the
pieces, but how? "Without God's everlasting arms
underneath me, I would have gone under. I struggled as
never before to know the Lord's plan for my life. . . . I
rededicated myself to the Lord, committing myself to go and
do his will anywhere, anytime."*

130

It happened in late 1968. The women had boarded the train in Taegu, Korea, and were traveling to Seoul. With them were two babies who would be adopted in Seoul. "Sh-sh." Mrs. Shim Hyun Sook touched her lip and tapped Elvinah's arm lightly. "Listen." Above the cacophony of train wheels clacking, people talking, and a baby crying, Mrs. Shim and Elvinah listened. Closely. Carefully. It was the voice of Mrs. Pak Che In (not her real name) talking on the radio about CAPOK — the Christian Adoption Program of Korea — in a land where adoption of children was just beginning to break the barriers of social taboo. The two women shuddered with delight. Elvinah Spoelstra was the director of CAPOK.

Elvinah has spent her life in service to others — first in Denver, next in Korea, then among the poor in Mississippi, and finally in retirement. God prepared her well for a life of sacrifice — with poverty, pain, perseverance, and compassion.

Elvinah was born in Douglas County, South Dakota, on February 26, 1925, the first child of Dick Spoelstra and Cora DeLange. She lived on the farm until she was fifteen years old.

During her childhood, times were difficult. Her father worked from sunup to sundown on his small farm. Drought, dust storms, grasshoppers, and the Great Depression denied him a full harvest for many years. But he wasn't consumed by his own struggles. He knew that the Depression affected his neighbors as well, and he had compassion for many. "Dad exemplified for me the love of God and love for your neighbor," Elvinah says. "Later, when we moved to Denver and Dad worked with blacks, he conveyed the idea that discrimination had no place in the life of Christians. He was wise.

"It was hard for my parents to keep their bills paid," Elvinah continues. "Dad probably worried most about not having enough for the family. He suffered with stomach ulcers for many years. Still, we always had enough to eat. Mom sold the eggs, counted the money, and knew just how much she could buy. We might have to split an apple five ways, but we never went hungry.

"I remember particularly a faded blue coat that Mom received from someone in Michigan. She took it all apart, washed it, turned it inside out, and made a coat for me — a coat I was very proud of."

The young Elvinah did not realize that God would use her Depression experience to prepare her for her lifework. Elvinah

---

"Dad exemplified for me the love of God and love for your neighbor. Later, when we moved to Denver and Dad worked with blacks, he conveyed the idea that discrimination had no place in the life of Christians. He was wise."

---

thought that she "would marry and have eight children and a quiet house." (She didn't know then that a house with eight children is never quiet.)

Looking back, Elvinah sees how her early experiences affected her later perspectives. "Being poor definitely affected my evaluation of hunger and poverty. I believe one can be poor and still be responsible. Poverty is relative. In Korea I saw women and children who literally did not have enough to eat. In our country, in Mississippi — which is almost Third World in a sense — I never saw acute hunger. People could always get food if they needed it."

Issues related to food and hunger came up frequently in Elvinah's work. She remembers an incident that occurred when she was working for Mississippi Christian Family Services. "I recall the time another agency had a fund-raising drive for food. Some supporters of MCFS inquired whether we also needed funds for food. Our staff reviewed all the information available and decided we could better begin a service offering a money-management program than to supply food for our clients. Client response far exceeded our expectations. It turned out to be a very successful program.

"I struggle with some existing feeding programs," she says frankly. "It isn't the best way to help people preserve their dignity when they need food. Living through poverty has helped me see that.

"Mom's ability to make do — how she made my coat, for example — also influenced me when I was in administration and developing programs to help the poor. I had to think of ways for people to use the resources they did have, as limited as they were, and make the most of them."

Elvinah's parents had both completed the eighth grade. Her mother often talked about her dream that her children would complete high school. Part of that dream came true when the pastor of the Harrison Christian Reformed Church invited Elvinah to live at the parsonage, with free room and board, so that she could attend the ninth grade in Harrison. Elvinah accepted the invitation.

Many people left Harrison around 1940, including the Spoelstras. They moved to Denver, where Elvinah completed high school. She dreamed of becoming a teacher or maybe a social worker. Many of her friends were planning to get married; a few went to college. Elvinah went to the candy factory and dipped chocolate for a year, saving her earnings to go to business school. She did, and graduated as a secretary; subsequently she served various employers for sixteen years.

But secretarial work simply did not satisfy Elvinah. "Why, Elvinah?" her employer asked. He sketched her future if she pursued her dream and got a degree in social work: "You'll go to school four years; then you'll be a social worker, and you'll earn less money than you're making now." This didn't discourage Elvinah, even though her employer's prediction did come true: Elvinah quit her job, went to school, became a social worker, and earned less than she did as a secretary.

But she *was* a social worker! She spent half of her time preparing budgets and the rest of her time carrying a full-time case load for the Denver Welfare Department. Her supervisor, a caring person, encouraged Elvinah to transfer to the child welfare department and apply for a work-study grant. Elvinah did, and she was granted the transfer. In that situation she divided her time between work and school and was paid for full-time work.

During this time, Elvinah fell in love. What would that do to her plans? Should she quit school? Her fiancé, Les Swanson, urged her to get her master's degree: "This is something you always wanted to do. If anything should happen to me, you'll at least be equipped to do the work you've always dreamed of." She stayed in school, and she and Les began a three-year engagement. Eventually she reached her goal, earning a master of arts in social work. She continued at the child welfare department, to which she had made a two-year commitment. The wedding date drew closer.

Les's work required that he travel frequently. One day he called Elvinah, as he often did, and said, "I have two job offers. I'll tell you about them when I get back."

But Les never came back. On September 8, 1964, he was killed in an automobile accident.

Elvinah was devastated.

Les's death was "the supreme test" of her life, Elvinah says. She asked the questions that plagued her heart: Why, God? Why me? What are you doing, Lord? Why do you allow such tragedy? She and Les had believed that the Lord had led them to each other, and they had dedicated their lives to him.

Elvinah struggled with her monumental loss. Loneliness enveloped her; grief overwhelmed her. What did God want of her life? She knew she had to pick up the pieces, but how? "Without God's everlasting arms underneath me, I would have gone under," she says. "I struggled as never before to know the Lord's plan for my life. Psalm 46:10 became meaningful: 'Be still, and know that I am God.' I rededicated myself to the Lord, committing myself to go and do his will anywhere, anytime."

In late 1965, Elvinah went to a slide program put on by the Christian Reformed World Relief Committee (CRWRC). She remembers only the last two minutes, the announcement made:

134

the CRWRC needed two social workers in Korea. Suddenly her mind flashed back to an evening when she was alone. "I was reading *The Banner* [the weekly magazine of the Christian Reformed Church] when an ad for a social worker in Korea jumped out at me. I said, 'Oh no, God. I'm committed to Denver Child Welfare, and I'm engaged to be married.' I put it out of my

---

Elvinah accepted the challenge of becoming a social worker for the CRWRC in Korea. When the Korean staff doctor left for the United States, Elvinah became the director of a proposed adoption program. "The program will never work in Korea," people told her, but Elvinah pressed ahead.

---

mind. But when I saw the CRWRC slide program, the need jumped out at me again."

She talked with a friend, prayed, and asked God for three signs: that family and friends would affirm her; that God would either open or close the door; and that the Spirit would confirm this call in her heart. Elvinah discussed the matter with her mother, with whom she lived. If Elvinah would go to Korea, her mother would be alone, because her father had died several years earlier, in 1959. But her mother did not resist the prospect of Elvinah's leaving. "If that's what God wants of you," she said, "that's what I want you to do."

"That's not the answer I expected, Mom," Elvinah replied.

"I can't explain it," her mother assured her, "but when you told me about your possible plans, I thought of the text that says, 'He that loveth father or mother more than me is not worthy of me,' and I knew that had to be my response." Through her mother's reply, Elvinah received many of the signs she had been seeking.

She went to Grand Rapids for an interview with the CRWRC. "I'm basically shy," she explains, "and when I was questioned by a roomful of men, I was scared. I remember one board member had been in Nigeria, and it seemed to me he asked the pertinent questions."

She passed the interview. God had opened wide the door. Confident that she was doing God's will, Elvinah went to Korea. "I liked it from Day One," she says. The staff was small: besides her, there was an administrator, an agriculturalist, and a medical doctor. She started slowly. She became familiar with the culture, and her ability to adapt surprised her.

When the Korean staff doctor left for the United States, Elvinah became the director of a proposed adoption program. "The program will never work in Korea," people told her. But Elvinah pressed ahead.

The skepticism with which people greeted the idea of such a program was understandable: adoption was a foreign concept to Koreans. Only children with family blood flowing through their veins were adoptable. If a couple did not have a child, the husband would take a concubine in order to have a child with his blood flowing through its veins. True, the law sanctioning that restrictive view of adoption had been repealed, but the taboo remained significant. The few people who did adopt, did so secretly. "I remember one woman who padded herself," Elvinah recalls, "and everyone thought she was really pregnant."

The Christian Adoption Program of Korea — CAPOK — began slowly. At first it processed one or two adoptions per month. Guided by Elvinah's caution and confidence, it expanded gradually to include a relinquishment-counseling program (for mothers giving up their babies) and a foster-home program. CAPOK was the first program in Korea to be licensed as an in-country adoption agency. Gradually its number of clients grew, and CAPOK began to process twenty or more in-country adoptions per month. The program won several governmental awards for excellent community service.

Elvinah recalls the story of Mrs. Pak Che In, the woman who was instrumental in getting the news of CAPOK on the air. Regularly Elvinah and Mrs. Shim, the program director, visited the Municipal Babies Home in Seoul. "The first time I walked into the room of abandoned babies, my impulse was to leave immediately," Elvinah admits. " 'Lord,' I said, 'you're going to have to give me grace to love these children.' The room was hot, very hot, and humid. Rows of tiny, tiny cribs were pushed so close together they touched each other. Little babies, some crying, others listless, were little bodies barely covered with skin and bones. Sores covered much of their tiny bodies. I couldn't bear it.

"I remember one visit especially. The nurse said to us, 'Here, take this one. If he doesn't go into a foster home today, he's going to die.' Mrs. Shim and I looked at each other. Our foster homes were full. But we couldn't say no. We picked up the fragile, dying child and took him to Mrs. Pak Che In, who was a foster mother.

"Mrs. Pak looked at the baby, shook her head sadly, and said, 'I can't take him. I don't want a dead baby tomorrow morning.' " But when Elvinah pleaded — "Give the baby a chance at least," she begged — Mrs. Pak relented. The baby lived through the night, and Mrs. Pak nursed him back to health. Later he was adopted.

"That foster mother," says Elvinah, "became a very strong

"The first time I walked into the room of abandoned babies, my impulse was to leave immediately. 'Lord,' I said, 'you're going to have to give me grace to love these children.' "

---

and vocal advocate of CAPOK. She spent much time and energy getting CAPOK's story on radio and television. Hearing her speak on the radio has been a highlight of my life."

After spending nearly six years in Korea, Elvinah returned to the States. After many speaking engagements and a rest, she went to Cary, Mississippi, to work with the Luke Society there. "The first year was very difficult," she recalls. "In Korea I could expect certain behaviors and policies from a culture where over 90 percent of the people do not know Christ. Now here I was in my own country, a Christian among people who generally identify themselves as Christians. But it didn't *feel* like a Chris-

---

Elvinah worked for the Luke Society in Cary, Mississippi, which was poor and racially troubled. "I saw poverty, yes, but then I saw that poverty was a symptom of deeper needs. Long-term scars of discrimination could not be corrected by quick fixes. . . . I was experiencing the truth that God had his remnant among both the black and the white cultures of the Mississippi Delta."

---

tian environment. I hadn't realized that such poverty existed in parts of the United States. Pat responses came rather easily for me from past conditioning.

"But I dug in and worked hard," she continues. "I saw poverty, yes, but then I saw that poverty was a symptom of deeper needs. Long-term scars of discrimination could not be corrected by quick fixes. I saw too that both the black and the white cultures were scarred. There was much talk. Among black people, anti-white talk. Among white people, anti-black talk. I had to fight to avoid becoming involved in that. I was experiencing the truth that God had his remnant among both the black and the white cultures of the Mississippi Delta, sinners saved by grace, struggling as I was to be conformed [obedient] to the image of Christ in me.

"It took about a year before I finally realized what God was saying to me. He was saying, 'Look, Elvinah, I've called you to work with *everybody* in this area.'"

It was a crucial awakening, a stunning eye-opener, an experience that comes rarely in a lifetime. Elvinah saw with her heart, soul, strength, and mind that *all people, without exception, are God's people.* With God there is no distinction. "It was another highlight of my life," Elvinah says. "It helped me to go forward with a new vision."

After Elvinah had spent three years in Mississippi, God opened the door for her to begin a ministry under the sponsorship of the CRWRC: Mississippi Christian Family Services. Susie Smith Evans, a local black Christian who was gifted and committed, decided to join Elvinah. Together they built a ministry to individuals with disabilities and their families. Frequently the work overwhelmed them. But one thing helped tremendously, Elvinah explains: the CRWRC's decision to allow MCFS at its inception to be incorporated with a local bi-racial board of directors. "I don't think I could have endured thirteen years without this board," Elvinah says frankly. "The members were unusual, and they opened the door for God to work many miracles."

Elvinah recalls a particularly gracious miracle that occurred when the work had outgrown the space and MCFS required more facilities. "At the board meeting, a member said, 'I think we should move out in faith, get a piece of property, and build our own facility.' My jaw dropped. We were having a difficult time just making ends meet!

"The board member said later, 'What I said surprised me too, but I had prayed much about it.' Amazingly, the board didn't question her or object. They just accepted her idea, which was strictly a faith venture.

"Only a few days later, Kathleen, one of our advisory committee members, came into the office to talk. We discussed the needs of MCFS. After a bit she said, 'Elvinah, can you wait a few minutes? I have something I want to discuss with my husband and brother.'"

She returned soon with a stunning offer, Elvinah recalls. "'Elvinah,' she announced, 'we would like to give you $100,000 to develop a group home project.' I couldn't believe it. I guess

139

I said thank you. Later that afternoon I called her. 'Kathleen,' I asked, 'you said $10,000, not $100,000, didn't you?'

" 'No,' Kathleen replied, 'and if we hadn't talked today, the money would have gone elsewhere tomorrow.'" Kathleen's father had died recently, and he had stipulated in his will that a certain amount of his money be given to charity. Kathleen,

---

"If I am to be remembered at all after I'm gone, I hope that memory will be of a Christian who believes that every person is of equal and much value in God's eyes."

---

along with her husband and her brother, decided to give the money for the new facilities that MCFS needed.

Yes, God still does work miracles.

The MCFS board, with the help of an additional grant from HUD, built the necessary group homes and also bought a five-acre plot with an old building on it. CRWRC volunteers then renovated the building completely. "We paid to install a fire alarm system," Elvinah says. "That's all. The grants paid the balance of the project, appraised at $489,500."

It was another highlight of her life.

Although she regretted having to consider leaving her work, Elvinah began to think about her retirement, which had tentatively been set for summer 1990. Did the Lord have anything particular in mind for her retirement? she wondered. She didn't wonder too long.

On November 2, 1987, a group of volunteers from Michigan came to Rolling Fork, a small town about six miles from Cary. Among them was Don Zwier, the recently retired business secretary of Christian Reformed World Missions. Like Elvinah, Don knew grief: he had lost three wives, one to a heart problem and the other two to cancer. To Elvinah this gentleman seemed different somehow — just how, she couldn't say. "When he first

140

came into my office I felt this man eyeballing me," she recalls, "and I thought, 'Is he never going to take his eyes off me?'" But Don didn't have romance on his mind: he had decided never to marry again. He almost hadn't made it to MCFS; it had taken him three days to come from Michigan to Rolling Fork. The last night en route he lay awake struggling with his thoughts, wondering whether he should turn around and go back or go on. He went on.

The two had a casual acquaintance until that Saturday when Elvinah and a couple from the CRWRC office went sightseeing. About ten miles outside of Natchez, Elvinah's car broke down. It was towed to a local garage for repairs. Later, when it was fixed, a volunteer — Don Zwier — went with her to pick up her car. "Well," she says, "it went pretty fast after that. We were married on October 1, 1988." It was yet another lovely highlight.

Elvinah moved to Jenison, Michigan, enjoying greatly the gift of marriage. She remains busy for the Lord and concerned for others: she visits her mother in Denver, serves on the Committee on Disability Concerns of the Christian Reformed Church, and helps whenever she sees that help is needed — regardless of race, color, class, or creed.

"If I am to be remembered at all after I'm gone," she says, "I hope that memory will be of a Christian who believes that every person is of equal and much value in God's eyes."

And that is just how the people who were touched by Elvinah Spoelstra Zwier do remember her.

VI

We have different gifts,
according to the grace given us. . . .
If [her gift] is leadership,
let [her] govern diligently.

Romans 12:6, 8

Sheri Dunham Haan

Executive in Education

"One day my fifth-grade teacher filled the chalkboard with a list of many things people could do with their lives, and then explained how these were all opportunities for us to be God's people — no matter where we went. It all came together for me in that dingy fifth-grade classroom: that I was to serve God in his world, and that I could inspire kids to see themselves as God's creatures — just as my teacher had done for me."

145

A painting displayed on the wall in Sheri Dunham Haan's office at CSI (Christian Schools International) in Grand Rapids, Michigan, describes this ambitious woman of fifty years more precisely than any words could. The painting shows a young girl of six or seven sitting at a table with a book in her hands and a faraway look in her eyes. She has pushed aside the dolls and knitting needles with obvious disinterest and is dreaming about reading, learning, and imagining.

Sheri, born December 19, 1940, remembers when she was that little girl whose desire for knowledge seemed unquenchable. And stronger still was her desire to share that knowledge. "Even before I went to school I wanted to be a teacher," she says. "I remember foraging through the wastebasket each day to find school papers my older sister had discarded, and then I would play school using a makeshift desk."

Throughout her years in school, her desire to teach was strengthened. But just as the little girl in the picture disregarded tradition and focused on expanding her horizons, Sheri too let her dreams, her ambitions, and most of all her God lead her down a career path that few women have traveled.

At age thirty she joined Christian Schools International as curriculum consultant; later she became the director of operations; and in 1989 she assumed the role of executive director. She now leads an organization that serves 441 Christian schools throughout North America.

Sheri minimizes her accomplishments. "I really haven't done anything more significant than my mother, for instance, who worked as a secretary for forty years and raised four children," she says. "I'm just an ordinary person doing my job." The word "ordinary" hardly captures the essence of either Sheri or her mother, even though Sheri's childhood years were not extraordinary in any obvious way.

The child of a young Dutch woman, Alice Scholten, and an English "farming gent," Glen Dunham, Sheri grew up in Battle Creek, Michigan. Her parents worked diligently for their moderate income. Sheri inherited her "drive" from her mother, who is "a master of planning and scheduling," according to Sheri. "When we were growing up, she made sure we fit everything into the cracks and crevices: piano, catechism, chores. Around Mother we would feel guilty just walking the beach or lying down with a book." While Sheri's mother was not "heavy-handed or negative," her innate drive to achieve impressed and inevitably affected her daughter.

Glen Dunham played an equally important role in Sheri's attitudes about life and people. "I remember coming home early from school one day and hearing my father yodeling in the basement. I just stood there amazed and captivated — partly because it was so beautiful and partly because I never knew he could do it," recalls Sheri. "Often Daddy opened up for me the delight that could be found in every person."

Since Glen Dunham never had the opportunity to attend high school, he was determined that his four children would be well educated. There was never any question about *whether* the children would attend college, only *where*. And if they wanted financial help, Calvin College was the breadth of their choice.

When Sheri and her siblings were growing up, Christian education was not always a viable option for them (there were no nearby Christian schools), which partially explains their parents' insistence on a Christian college. Sheri attended the Battle Creek Public School for most of her grade-school years, with the exception of grades five through nine, which she spent at a small Christian school in Kalamazoo. "That five-year interlude [in a Christian school] had a dramatic effect on my life," says Sheri.

Sheri remembers thinking her parents had "flipped" when they took her out of the beautiful, modern public school she was attending and registered her at Comstock Christian — a wornout building with sagging wooden steps, a dark, musty cloakroom, and a stark, barren classroom in the basement. Everything was antique, including the library books, which were held together with electrical tape. Sheri's young fifth-grade

147

teacher was fresh out of Calvin College. Although the nervous young teacher did not hold Sheri's attention in any "spellbinding" way, she was instrumental in helping Sheri understand the key difference between Christian and public schools.

"It had nothing to do with the building, but it was to me a place where Christ was seen as central to everything that went on," says Sheri. "I felt mentally energized being guided by the mind and spirit of a Christian teacher who took her Christianity and her job very seriously."

That year Sheri decided that she wanted to be a teacher in a *Christian* school.

Some of her teachers in the public school had also strengthened Sheri's goal of being a teacher, but her Christian teacher helped put that goal into perspective. "One day she filled the chalkboard with a list of many things people could do

---

While Sheri genuinely entrusts matters to God in prayer, she also feels comfortable saying to the Lord, "I've been praying for some time and I feel no direction from you, so I'm going to do this. If it's not right, then let me know in a way that I'll understand."

---

with their lives, and then explained how these were all opportunities for us to be God's people — no matter where we went," recalls Sheri. "It all came together for me in that dingy fifth-grade classroom: that I was to serve God in his world, and that I could inspire kids to see themselves as God's creatures — just as my teacher had done for me."

Ironically, a transfer back to the public school a few years later did not diminish Sheri's desire to teach in a Christian school but instead affirmed it. Although she received a quality education at Battle Creek High School, Sheri remembers missing the "Christ" in learning. "I felt a part of me was pining for what might have been," says Sheri. "My education was not complete."

Sheri handled her secret disappointment by turning inward and searching the Bible and other books for answers to many of her questions. Her manner of handling that first real challenge as a teenager set a precedent for how she would handle difficulties as an adult. God was preparing her for the long journey ahead.

In 1962 Sheri graduated from Calvin College with a major in elementary education, with an emphasis in English and social studies. A dream fulfilled! She was now a teacher. Oakdale Christian School in Grand Rapids hired her to teach second and third grade, which she did for three years. While tackling her first teaching position, she also pursued a graduate degree in reading education from the University of Michigan.

In addition, she found time for a serious romance. Sheri had met her husband-to-be, Glen Haan, while attending Calvin College. They were married a year after Sheri began teaching. Among the couple's many shared goals was a desire to continue their education — in the field of education.

A few years after their wedding, the two moved to Kalamazoo for a year to enable Glen to attend Western Michigan University while Sheri taught first and second grades at Battle Creek Christian School. Sheri completed her master's degree the following summer. At this juncture the couple moved back to Grand Rapids, where jobs awaited them. For three years Sheri was an instructor in the education department at Calvin College.

"We were told early in our marriage that we might not have children, so I decided to pursue education as a career," Sheri explains. "But then — shock of my life — we had three children," she says with a gleam in her eyes. "It just goes to show who is really in control." In fact, Sheri and Glen had never given up hope that God would bless them with children. "I really loved teaching, so I didn't have the *craving* for being a mother that some people talk about, but I did pray about it faithfully for seven years," says Sheri.

149

In 1970 Sheri gave birth to Chad Allen, in 1971 to Shelly Ann, and in 1974 to Keith Michael. Sheri comments, "The Lord must have smiled when four years later I said, 'That's enough now, Lord.'"

She recalls that although she was thrilled at the prospect of becoming a mother, she did have some doubts about whether she would be content to "stay home all day and do diapers." Although raising children has been one of Sheri's greatest goals, she prayed for something that would "keep this deep love for education in my heart."

God again proved to her his sovereignty. While she was pregnant with Chad, Sheri wrote her first book for Baker Book House entitled *Good News for Children* (1970). That endeavor opened many new doors for her. "Once you publish a book, many people think you're an expert on religion, children, and writing," says Sheri, laughing. She accepted offers to write materials for Bible courses for Christian Schools International (CSI) and for the Christian Reformed Church's Board of Publications; both of these tasks she could work on at home. She also became a part-time language arts consultant for CSI.

Because Sheri and Glen had waited many years for a child, Sheri was apprehensive about leaving Chad in day care. She advertised and prayed for an appropriate day-care provider, and God's will became clear to her as she conducted interviews. "I found a beautiful Christian woman who ended up taking all three of my kids through the years," says Sheri. "Once again God cut through the red tape of life and showed me the way."

Sheri's search for a day-care provider exemplifies her manner of handling decisions. She prayed *and* advertised; she trusted in God *and* took action. "I always believe in taking some initiative," explains Sheri. While she genuinely entrusts matters to God in prayer, she also feels comfortable saying to the Lord, "I've been praying for some time and I feel no direction from you, so I'm going to do this. If it's not right, then let me know in a way that I'll understand."

The ultimate test of Sheri's — and Glen's — ability to place matters in God's hands — and to make a firm decision — came several years later. Their only daughter, Shelly, then seven years old, was diagnosed as having terminal leukemia. They had to choose whether or not to have Shelly undergo a bone-marrow transplant. The outlook appeared bleak: tests had revealed no perfect marrow match for a transplant; chances of success were

---

"When Shelly breathed her last breath, I felt unspeakable pain. My heart dropped into a chasm so big, so deep, so dark . . . and then suddenly I felt a certainty, an absoluteness as never before that God and heaven really are."

---

slim. But without the surgery, Shelly would probably die. "We had prayed and prayed for a perfect match, but there wasn't one," recalls Sheri in a calm, quiet voice. "So we were honest with ourselves and with the Lord and told him that we were not going to take Shelly [for the transplant] unless he'd show us that it was the wrong decision."

Sheri remembers clearly the day she first learned the "hard, cold facts" about Shelly's illness. "It's a rare form of leukemia — terminal — no chance of survival," the doctor told her. Sheri was alone at the time because Glen was out of town. "When I heard those words, I just prayed that God would bring us through this in such a way that Shelly's faith and our faith would not be tested beyond what we would be able to bear, and that we could maintain a vibrant, living testimony," Sheri says.

That was the first of many, many prayers. Christians from their church, school, community, and workplaces prayed for a miracle. Often Sheri could not find words but chose Romans 8:26 to speak for her: "We do not know what we ought to pray, but the Spirit himself intercedes for us with groans that words cannot express." Sheri knew that the Spirit "intercedes for the saints in accordance with God's will" (Rom. 8:27), and that God could choose *not* to work a miracle in Shelly's life.

"I wore out pages in the Book of Job the summer Shelly was in the hospital," says Sheri. "I was losing a daughter, but

---

"People ask me how one gets through things like that [the death of a child], and I really don't have a pat answer. I only know that I drew deeper into God's Word. People can't fill the inner void for you. They can walk alongside you, cry with you, talk with you, but they can't give you the spirit of peace that comes only from God himself and his Word."

---

look at Job: he loses *all* of his children, his belongings, his prestige, and his health. He wants desperately to talk to God. Finally God appears and Job wants some answers," continues Sheri in her expressive, story-telling voice. "So God — disregarding Job's intentions — takes him on a trip, pointing out the vast wonders of creation that show God's grandeur, power, and might. . . . And then it hits Job that God is *God* and he's sovereign and he doesn't need to give any answers."

So it was with Sheri. Shelly struggled with cancer for three years, and then — after a long, final summer in the hospital — went to be with Jesus. It was August 20, 1982; she was ten years old. "When Shelly breathed her last breath, I felt unspeakable pain," whispers Sheri. "My heart dropped into a chasm so big, so deep, so dark . . . and then suddenly I felt a certainty, an absoluteness as never before that God and heaven *really are.*

"People ask me how one gets through things like that, and I really don't have a pat answer. I only know that I drew deeper into God's Word," says Sheri. "People can't fill the inner void for you. They can walk alongside you, cry with you, talk with you, but they can't give you the spirit of peace that comes only from God himself and his Word."

152

No matter how difficult it seemed, Sheri and Glen had to proceed with their lives after Shelly's death. Their sons Chad, then eleven, and Keith, then seven, desperately needed their attention. "One of the difficult aspects of Shelly's illness was leaving our two boys for a long time without a real family life," Sheri recalls. "We don't have any relatives in town, so when the boys were not out of town staying with relatives, we relied totally on friends to care for them. I still thank the Lord for our friends."

Soon after Shelly was buried, the Haan family left town for a week-long vacation. "We needed immediately to rebuild our family, for the boys' sake and ours," explains Sheri. "If we had stayed home, that empty bedroom and seat at the table would have overwhelmed us. We wanted to be able to laugh and play without worrying about the appropriateness of our actions. It was important for us to go on." The months and years following Shelly's death were trying — yet strengthening — for Sheri. She grew closer to God and trusted his leading every step of the way.

Today Chad and Keith continue to bring their parents much joy. Chad, currently a student at Calvin College, may be following in his mother's footsteps with a career in education. Keith, now in high school, is setting his sights on the medical field.

Sheri is grateful for the way her children have often broken through the clutter in her busy life and helped her put things in perspective. "They'll say, 'Relax, Mom. You're not executive director at home.'"

During all but the last four months of Shelly's illness, Sheri had been able to continue her various writing projects and her part-time work as language arts consultant for CSI. Just two years after Shelly's death, Sheri was faced with new challenges and opportunities that once again tested her faith in God. Her position as consultant for CSI was eliminated as part of an overall restructuring effort within the organization. However, a new, executive-level position was created: director of operations. Was that a possibility for her?

Sheri didn't apply for the job immediately. "I had little training or experience in financial management," she explains.

"But the people who were applying for the position hadn't spent their lives in Christian education, and that really bothered me.

"When I began to consider applying, I talked to Glen about it. He pointed out the things I could do well and the reasons I should apply, but we also had to discuss the implications of full-time work for the family. Together we concluded that I should apply," says Sheri.

Glen's advice alone would not have been enough to convince Sheri, however. "I do consider his advice, but just as important are my convictions; sometimes they're stronger in another direction," she explains. "I believe that you can sense what God intends for you next." God's will became even more apparent when Sheri received the job of director of operations. She took her responsibilities seriously, and for the next five years the organization's efficiency increased to the extent that — once again — her position was eliminated.

Just prior to that time the executive director had announced his retirement, which prompted another evaluation of CSI operations. Many functions that had been performed by the director of operations were made part of the executive director's position, and others were given to a business manager. Sheri faced the choice of applying for the position of executive director or leaving CSI for other career pursuits.

While Sheri felt confident in her ability to manage CSI, she was concerned that some people might resist having a woman as the executive director and that such resistance might hinder the operation of CSI. "I wanted the urging of the Spirit in answer to my question, 'Lord, is this what you want me to pursue?' I asked God to let me know if this job was *not* right for me," says Sheri. "Finally I had to say, 'Unless you show me otherwise, Lord, I will apply.'" And she did.

In 1989 the CSI board appointed her as executive director. Occasionally Sheri has encountered people who she senses are uncomfortable with a woman being the director. "When that

154

happens, I focus on the job at hand and am sensitive not to offend them," she says.

Her ultimate goal is to use her gifts for the glory of God — not for herself or for women in general. "I would cringe at the thought that the CSI board chose me as director to make a statement. That would violate my person and the integrity of the board.

"I sometimes receive calls from people who want me to make sure a woman gets a job as school administrator because she's a woman. That's wrong," says Sheri. "It's also wrong when a man is chosen for a job in lieu of a more qualified woman." She hopes to incorporate a "justice" policy into CSI's newly developed *Strategic Plan for the 1990s* to assure that all people are treated equally, with no discrimination based on such factors as gender or race.

As much as Sheri enjoys working hard at CSI, her future doesn't necessarily end there. "I'm sure there will come a time when I'll have given all I can," she says with frank self-assess-

---

Her ultimate goal is to use her gifts for the glory of God — not for herself or for women in general. "I would cringe at the thought that the CSI board chose me as director to make a statement. That would violate my person and the integrity of the board."

---

ment. "I'll need to be alert to that and then have the resolve to realize that it's time to move on for the sake of CSI."

When her life on earth is finished, she doesn't want it to be measured in terms of accomplishments. "I don't want to be remembered as the executive director of CSI," she says. "I would rather that the words on my tombstone reflect how God sees me and state simply 'A child of God.'"

Katherine M. Vander Ziel Vandergrift

Politics and Perseverance

Kathy grew up in a Dutch Christian Reformed community in the Midwest, a community with a mission that was essentially restricted to church, home, and school. This view confined and restricted her. Her questioning spirit did not let her conform to family or community expectations. The conviction burned within her that the Gospel's good news must reach far beyond the sacred triumvirate of home, school, and church if Christians were to witness effectively in society.

From an isolated farm in southwest Minnesota to the mayor's office in Edmonton, Alberta — that's how far she's traveled over time. No, Katherine M. Vander Ziel Vandergrift is not the mayor. She is Mayor Jan Reimer's assistant. Working in the mayor's office, Kathy says, is not a permanent plateau. Rather, it's a stopping place for now: Mayor Reimer asked her for help, so for now Kathy gives herself to Edmonton.

In her position Kathy analyzes and evaluates reports, does research, and advises the mayor on public policy. She also works on special projects and acts as a community liaison. With almost two-thirds of a million people in some way affected by her work, Kathy needs to be composed, fair, thorough, and insightful. And that she is.

Over time, people, events, and circumstances have subtly equipped Kathy for work in the public arena. Her life developed in stages. The first stage was her childhood, spent on the family farm, and her subsequent experiences and associations at Calvin College in Grand Rapids, Michigan. Stage two involved marrying Larry Vandergrift and becoming a mother caring for small children. And stage three was her increasing involvement in myriads of personal and public justice issues, which led to her present work.

Kathy, born November 1, 1947, was the seventh of nine children born to George Vander Ziel and Bessie Fransen. Kathy's parents were part of the Dutch Christian Reformed wave of settlers who came to farm the Great Central Plains region of the United States during the 1940s and 1950s. Like other Christian Reformed families in the Edgerton area, the Vander Ziels regularly attended church and obeyed the community's social mores. Home, school, and church were inextricably linked, and for the most part the scope of the community's mission did not go beyond these three spheres. This view confined and restricted the young Kathy, who was emerging as an individual in her own right. Her questioning spirit did not let her conform to family or community expectations. The conviction burned within her that the Gospel's good news must reach

157

far beyond the sacred triumvirate of home, school, and church if Christians were to witness effectively in society.

Her upbringing was challenging in other ways too. "Ours was a typical family farm," she says. "The farm came first, and we did what had to be done to run it." For Kathy and her eight brothers and sisters, chores were not negotiable. And her father took his tasks as a farmer very seriously. "For Dad, his work on the farm reflected his deeper belief: he was a caretaker in God's creation." He maintained a prudent variety and balance of livestock and crops, and he believed in careful stewardship of his resources. Long after neighbors were using combines in their fields, Kathy remembers, "we were still using the threshing machine to harvest grain. We cooked on a wood stove and used corn cobs and wood for fuel." Her father's "lived-out" faith impressed Kathy deeply.

The labor-intensive, family-run farm had its drawbacks. Daily chores before and after school did not allow participation in school events. Although work was forbidden on Sunday, work sometimes did take precedence over school attendance. Opportunities to develop friendships suffered because outings, other than church meetings and catechism classes, were non-existent. "We really didn't even want friends over," Kathy says, "because our family was less modern than everyone else." For entertainment, Kathy made playing cards out of their unused tithing envelopes from church. "My Dad gave generously and regularly to the church, but he never used all the envelopes," Kathy explains. "So on the sneak we would use them to play card games — especially Rook." Growing up on the fringes of the community equipped Kathy with a keen sensitivity for the alienation that less advantaged people in society face today.

A bit of a tomboy, Kathy regularly worked next to her father on the farm. His deep fondness for her and her admiration for him characterized their relationship. Although he was busy, George took time to listen to his daughter's unending questions. They often discussed world news. "Dad was keenly interested in the outside world," Kathy says. "But he had no choice [other than farming]. Otherwise, I think he would have gone to school."

Kathy's relationship with her mother was at times distanced. Bessie was hardworking, resourceful, and strict. She prized a clean home, and she worked very hard to cope with the many challenges of farm life and raising a large family. These concerns left little or no room for reading, asking questions, seeking reasons, or examining causes — things Kathy instinctively valued.

At the same time, Kathy does take after her mother in some ways: her work drive rivals her mother's. "I'm probably a workaholic," she admits. Her husband, Larry, agrees that Kathy's focus on work is thoroughly ingrained. "If two or three things can be done at once, that's all the better for Kathy. She gets more done that way," he says. Her daughter Ellen, who is eighteen, comments, "'Work, work, work' — that's Mom's motto, and she gets impatient when people aren't as quick as she is." Her son, Michael, now twenty years old, worries about his mother's hectic pace. "Sometimes she gets up in the middle of the night and works too. I'm afraid she's going to drain herself." And daughter Andrea, who is eight, says of her mother's schedule, "It's too much work!"

"I've always had a strong sense of calling to Christian service, not a career."

Kathy's workaholic nature is complicated by her perfectionism. "Something in me will not let me settle for less than my best," she says. According to Larry, his wife's tendency to perfectionism is rooted in her childhood, when it was difficult to win parental approval. "There was little or no emotion shown or focus on the self in her family," he comments. Since her parents believed that "pride comes before a fall," they found it difficult to openly affirm Kathy's accomplishments.

159

At times Kathy's perfectionism is a drawback. Her questioning, analytical mind makes it hard for her to accept anything but the best from herself, her co-workers, her family, and her church. "Sometimes this makes it hard for people to live with me," she admits. Her children know the depth of her perfectionism. "Perfectionism is a mixed negative/positive characteristic," says Ellen. "On the one hand, my mom is hard to talk to because she sees the big picture and handles small problems in that way. But, on the other hand, she has taught me to rise above little problems and to be independent."

The "holy unrest" about reaching out that Kathy felt while growing up has remained an intense part of her nature. Today she pursues her vision as earnestly as the time when, against her parents' wishes, she left home to attend Calvin College in Grand Rapids, Michigan. Dad and Mom had wanted Kathy to go to Dordt College in Sioux Center, Iowa, if indeed she insisted on getting a higher education. Dordt College was conveniently close and actively established and enforced rules and practices *in loco parentis* (in the place of parents). Besides, Kathy could come home every weekend. But nothing was further from their daughter's aspirations. The key question to which Kathy sought an answer was this: Can one be a credible academic and remain a Christian? At Calvin College, she believed, she would have the freedom to ask any question, including this one, and still enjoy the support of a Christian academic community.

In September 1965, when she wasn't yet eighteen, Kathy left for Calvin. She received no financial or emotional support from home. Scholarships paid a sizeable chunk of her tuition, and she worked part-time. Given how dependent she was on scholarship money, she says, "I literally couldn't afford not to do well." Her painful "breaking out" was not made easier by the angry mail — mostly from home — that predicted her fall and failure. But Kathy persisted, determined to do what she believed to be right in spite of the odds. Little did she realize at the time that that same determination to do what is right would eventually make her a force to be reckoned with in situations in which determination and justice would be key elements.

Calvin College and its professors challenged Kathy. "Some professors dared us to question," she says. In pursuit of the truth she craved, she tasted honesty, integrity, and depth. "I was ready to throw Christianity overboard," she says, "but my Calvin experience changed that. Besides, I wasn't going to let my mother's predictions be right!"

Kathy didn't go to Calvin to find a husband, but that did happen. At that time Calvin had certain practices designed to prompt male/female relationships in keeping with traditional sexual mores. Kathy recalls the rituals critically. One of them required women to be seated first in the dining hall. They had to take every second seat. Men would then join the women, and usually a man chose to sit next to a woman he wanted to woo. "Once I missed supper for a whole week just to get rid of an unwanted dinner partner," she says frankly.

Ironically, assigned chapel seats introduced Kathy to her future husband, Larry, who was a Canadian. "This is where I will say providence was active," she laughs. "No amount of cold shoulder could put him off!" By the end of her sophomore year, this chapel-inspired relationship was solid. That she would marry a Canadian, something Kathy had told her father she would never do, became obvious. After graduation in 1969, Kathy and Larry were married.

Kathy now faced the prospect of becoming an immigrant, since Larry felt called to work in Christian education in Canada. But moving did not pose much of a problem for her. She believed she would find an opportunity to serve: "I've always had a strong sense of calling to Christian *service*, not a career," she says. "In my era girls were brought up to focus on serving, not on fulfillment or on pursuing our own goals."

In Edmonton, where Larry and Kathy settled, Kathy soon saw many needs and opportunities within the Christian community. She voluntarily set up the library at Edmonton Christian High School. When someone was needed to direct the school play, she volunteered. When a teacher became ill and couldn't complete the school year, Kathy took over.

Doing her duty took a new twist when the Vandergrift children were born. Michael, born in 1971, Ellen, born in 1973, and Andrea, born in 1982, required full-time mothering. This period proved extremely difficult for Kathy. With her energies

> *"The assumption that if you could give birth you could also take care of small children all day and every day almost killed me. The match of my abilities to homemaking was not a good fit. I kept thinking there had to be something more. I didn't expect to feel so trapped."*

directed toward becoming Supermom, she was distressed to discover that full-time homemaking was not personally fulfilling. "The assumption that if you could give birth you could also take care of small children all day and every day almost killed me," she says. "The match of my abilities to homemaking was not a good fit. I kept thinking there had to be something more. I didn't expect to feel so trapped."

Kathy's intense personal struggle and critical questioning were very difficult for her and for Larry. They both acknowledged the watershed nature of this period in their marriage. Together they worked out a pattern that would help them allow each other the room each needed for community involvement. "Though Kathy was a very good mother, it became quite clear that she needed interaction with others and a focus outside of the home," says Larry.

Issues related to politics and justice rapidly enveloped Kathy. The Canadian expression of Reformed thinking fascinated her. And the speeches about Christian vision and action by professors from the Institute for Christian Studies in Toronto challenged her. Theirs was not the traditional approach to

Christian mission. It was exciting! Challenging! These men thought they saw the big picture to which she had always been drawn. Although inspiring, her encounter with these Canadian Kuyperian thinkers was not all rosy. Their brash arrogance and harsh criticism of contemporary Reformed thinkers, especially Calvin's professors, upset and angered her. "I had to bite my tongue because of Larry's job," she says. "And at one point I wanted badly to move back to Grand Rapids."

Not easily deterred from her convictions, Kathy shared her vision, the big picture, with others. She saw needs and began to serve. Her mind — and her heart — were captured. Citizens for Public Justice (CPJ), a Christian action group based in Toronto, provided a natural niche for her. With its roots firmly embedded in Reformational thinking and its energy devoted to justice issues, CPJ fit Kathy's interests.

Before long, Kathy was the driving energy behind a CPJ chapter in Edmonton. In 1976 CPJ joined other groups in a campaign to stop a major pipeline from ruining Canada's virgin North, home for many native people. Kathy became the spokesperson for Edmonton.

"The way she handled the media and represented the coalition was impressive," remembers Gerald VandeZande, public affairs director for CPJ. "CPJ gained a great deal of credibility because of her." John Olthuis, legal counsel for CPJ, corroborates this assessment. "Because of her thorough, honest work, non-Christians have come to appreciate what Christians can do. As a Christian, she always tries to improve things for others."

From this experience Kathy's confidence grew. She began to pursue social-justice issues on many fronts. For five years — from 1977 to 1982 — she served as assistant to Bettie Hewes, a city alderman. "Bettie did not sell her soul for votes," says Kathy. "She was not afraid of the powerful forces in society, and she stood up for the 'little people' who had no clout. From her I learned strategy — how to be as clever as a fox — something that Christian witness needs to pay attention to."

163

According to Hewes, Kathy's effectiveness was enhanced by her compassion, integrity, and insight. "I think we grew together," says Hewes. "Her spirituality is a real strength and is well integrated in all she does. She champions not only the poor in spirit but also the poor in pocketbook." Both Bettie and Kathy see each other as significant role models.

While working for Hewes, Kathy chaired the Urban Reform Group of Edmonton (URGE), most members of which were not Christians. She lobbied hard for a humane city at a time when Edmonton seemed to be at the mercy of developers. With others, Kathy actively promoted building a park and constructing a bicycle path through a ravine rather than building a freeway. Massive road development? No. Kathy pushed for public transportation. Tear down the old? No. Kathy advocated preserving older neighborhoods and historical buildings. She argued for revitalizing Edmonton's downtown. Her efforts flowed out of her always-active sense of stewardship and her concern for the environment.

"This was a time of tremendous learning for me," recalls Kathy. "I learned how to organize public education events, how to analyze public policy, and how to propose public-policy alternatives." She didn't succeed in all her efforts, of course, but she soon became known in Edmonton as one whose persistence and integrity were not to be denied.

Later, in 1984, the Vandergrifts moved to Ottawa for a year, during which Larry pursued a master of arts degree at the University of Ottawa. Kathy reached out by volunteering. Soon she found employment on Parliament Hill as a research assistant for Lynn McDonald, a member of Parliament. McDonald remembers Kathy as a "calm, intelligent presence. Unlike some women who worked on the Hill," she remarks, "she did not dress for success, but few could have been as successful in getting the job done." In this position Kathy gained an even deeper sense of the possibilities for Christian witness within the system.

When Kathy and her family returned to Edmonton, Kathy

became the Edmonton director for Citizens for Public Justice. Operating CPJ on a meager budget was a constant drain on her energy. But the urgent importance of advocacy in public policies affecting people in need spurred her on. In her modest downtown office she spent long hours working for fellow citizens, most of whom were unable to find help for themselves. In addition, she researched poverty, pornography, and family issues. She combined principle and practice. Her work was widely respected and influential in the submissions that CPJ made to government.

According to John Olthuis, "Kathy is very practical. She is guided by her deep spiritual sensitivity to human need and the human condition. She understands Christian justice, and she has the ability to apply justice to a specific situation. Her work on the original CPJ abortion submission to the federal government demonstrated this ability."

Kathy's extensive research on the issues of poverty, the family, and the role of women in the community highlights painful examples of how distorted biblical teachings have perpetuated human suffering. "I value Reformed tradition," she says, "but we must openly acknowledge distortion where it has set in."

From her CPJ post, Kathy energized a recycling program for Edmonton. For eight years she and others worked on it. Then she became one of the founders of a recycling group that sought to combine job creation for the less advantaged with the recycling program. This project was a highlight for Kathy because it combined two goals important to her: pursuing stewardship and providing opportunities for the less privileged. "In many ways," she says, "this is the closest I have come to a contemporary model of God's way for care of creation and community." Because of Kathy's program, Edmonton today is on the cutting

165

edge of Canada's recycling movement. Dave Hubert, chairman of the Edmonton Recycling Society, calls Kathy "the mother of a whole new consciousness."

Stewardship is not the only challenge that faces Christians, Kathy believes. Her extensive research on the issues of poverty, the family, and the role of women in the community highlights painful examples of how distorted biblical teachings have perpetuated human suffering. "I value Reformed tradition," she says, "but we must openly acknowledge distortion where it has set in."

In 1988 Kathy was nominated — and selected as runner-up — for the "Outstanding Citizen of Edmonton" award. In the feature article about her that appeared in the *Edmonton Journal,* she explained how her faith and her work come together. "I guess my strongest motivation is my Christian commitment to the well-being of my neighbor."

Not only has Kathy worked on the organizational level within Edmonton, but she has also had a hand in filling the

---

Kathy still has a long agenda. Each step she takes brings her closer to the realization that Christians have no clear theory of social change. "Christians need to get into the system without accepting it as it is; then we can effect change."

---

mayor's chair. In 1989 she encouraged Jan Reimer, then a city council member, to run for mayor. "I encouraged her because her personal integrity and her vision for the city were generally consistent with what I understand to be the kind of just and caring community called for by the Bible," Kathy explains. After becoming mayor, Reimer selected Kathy as her personal assistant. "I don't know what I'd do without Kathy," Reimer says. "She always does her homework. She has a good background in environmental and social issues. She is an excellent community liaison. She's perfect for the position."

Although she is very busy with her responsibilities to the city, Kathy has not neglected home, school, or church. Her children talk of the special "Mom things" she has done with them. "I'll never forget Mom's reading me *Anne of Green Gables*," says Ellen. Michael recalls the hours his mother sat with him at the hospital when a knee operation sidelined his plans to attend Calvin College. And playing games and going bike-riding with Mom are special times for Andrea. "I've always spent time with the kids," Kathy explains. "What I've sacrificed is personal time."

Kathy is also active in Third Christian Reformed Church, where she and her family are members. When the church needs teachers, leaders, or committee members, Kathy is there. "Mom is a person who makes a difference," says Ellen. "Whatever needs to be done, she'll do it."

Kathy still has a long agenda. Each step she takes brings her closer to the realization that Christians have no clear theory of social change. "Christians need to get into the system without accepting it as it is," she says. "Then we can effect change." In a 1988 address to the Canadian Council of Christian Reformed Churches (CC-CRC), which she served from 1981 to 1987, she made a similar point: "A powerful Reformed witness would include both advocacy done outside the system and principled involvement within the system."

"For now I've chosen to work for change from the inside," she says. "It's a tough but rewarding situation."

Kathy Vandergrift lives intensely — she has to. So much remains to be done, and she has no choice but to do it.

Shirley Vande Kieft Van Zanten

Government without Guile

"Inequities, roadblocks, and frustrations — the evil of our world — upset and discourage me. The only thing that makes any sense is that I have a personal Savior and he controls this world. He guides me. The results, the management of the world is his, not mine."

Floodwaters ripped over western Washington state in the fall of 1990, leaving ruined property and angry people in their wake. The people were irate property owners who wanted answers from somebody, anybody: Why hadn't the river dikes been maintained? Why hadn't the river been dredged? Who would fix everything?

Shirley Van Zanten, the county executive of Whatcom County in the northwest corner of Washington, didn't have all the answers. But she did have the ability to hold a meeting to get some answers. She brought together angry citizens and heads of the appropriate government departments. She deflected the deluge of indignation by calmly chairing the public meeting and listening carefully to the people's complaints. In the end, she could do little to assist those who had lost property in the flooding, but people felt that she had heard them and honestly wanted to help them. That poised, caring, self-assured style is the hallmark of this top-level county politician.

On a more normal workday, that same air of capability prevails. If you walk into Shirley's office in the courthouse, you walk into a world of wood and flowers, a metaphor of competency and hospitality. Hanging and standing plants soften the wood paneling, the large wooden desk, and the highly polished wood conference table. Potted azaleas from Shirley's husband's nursery provide splashes of color. The office exudes professionalism and welcome, an ideal setting for the woman who works there.

Shirley Van Zanten's job as county executive is an administrative position to which she was elected in 1983 and reelected in 1987. The first woman to become county executive in Whatcom County, she is also the first and only woman to hold that office in Washington state. "County government has not been easily or readily accessible to women," she explains.

The political dimensions of the job make her the official representative of the county government and its people. She represents the county position to state and federal agencies, and she also serves as liaison to businesses, community organizations, and other cities. "There really should be about three of me," she laughs.

Sometimes she thinks there should be three of her to do all of the reading she'd like to do as well. Reading restores and renews her both personally and professionally. As far back as she can remember, she has read. "I read cereal boxes! Wherever I go, I take reading material with me," she says. Her favorite authors are Madeleine L'Engle and C. S. Lewis. "Both," she says, "have excellent insight into how human beings relate to the world and creation." She also enjoys novels, biographies, and mysteries. "I work in a world that is so complex and irrational that I like to read mysteries, where the world has more structure," she explains. "They're a little bit of a metaphor of what life is supposed to be like."

Shirley, one of the four children of William Vande Kieft and Henrietta Kneubel, was born on November 19, 1935, in Sioux Center, Iowa. Neither her father nor her mother had completed elementary school, and Shirley's excitement over reading and learning perplexed them at times. But they encouraged her interests to the extent that they could, she recalls.

In 1948 the Vande Kieft family moved to Washington state. Jobs were few in Sioux Center, and Shirley's father wanted a better future for his family. The family eventually landed in Lynden.

Shirley graduated from high school at age sixteen, and subsequently enrolled at Calvin College in Grand Rapids, Michigan. She was the first in both the Vande Kieft and the Kneubel families to go to college; to them it was "an absolutely novel idea," Shirley says.

In addition to her studies, the activities in which Shirley participated at Calvin helped her in her later political work. She was a member of Calvin's debate team, a team that took first place nationally, recalls Mari Vanderpol, Shirley's longtime friend. "That stood her in good stead in her political life," Mari says.

During her second year at Calvin, Shirley became engaged

to Paul Van Zanten, who was serving in the U. S. Army. Financially unable to continue attending Calvin, Shirley returned to Lynden.

That fall, a small two-room school in Mt. Vernon, Washington, a town about thirty miles south of Lynden, needed a teacher. The principal, Marvin Vanderpol, Mari's husband and friend of Paul and Shirley, asked her to apply. Shirley did so and accepted the position that was subsequently offered, teaching grades one through four for a year. In December she married Paul.

Shirley and Paul settled in Lynden and became the parents of three daughters: Susan, Sandra, and Barbara. "I have three very talented daughters," says Shirley proudly. Her daughters reciprocate that pride. "I remember election night," says Mari. "When Shirley won, the girls just hugged their mother."

Shirley isn't a "lovey-dovey" mother, Mari points out, "but she made her children feel how important they were to her. She read to them a lot, and they saw her read too. She made them see that pleasing God was the most important thing in life."

While raising her children, Shirley worked part-time doing accounting for Paul's nursery business, in which he shipped azaleas across the United States and to Canada. When a librarian position at Lynden Christian School opened up, however, Shirley applied. She got the job and spent eight years serving there.

Even though she was busy with work and children, Shirley returned to school. "I had a dream and a goal: to have a college degree," she says. She transferred her Calvin credits to Western Washington University in nearby Bellingham and began taking night courses. She accumulated an enormous number of credits because, she says, "I loved learning for its own sake as well as for the credits. Nineteen years after starting college, I finally graduated in August 1971."

As family demands decreased and Shirley had more time to use her gifts, she admits she "experienced a great level of frustration with the role of women in the Christian Reformed

171

Church." She knew she had abilities — to speak, to lead, and to analyze — that were not being used by or in the church. "The church delineated what my abilities were, and where I could use them," she says. She wrestled long with the problem and developed a way to handle it. "Fifteen years ago I emotionally divorced myself from the church," she says frankly, "but I did not divorce myself from Christ." She decided that God had called her to work in other areas.

Her pastor, Rev. Ken Koeman of Sonlight Christian Reformed Church, concurs. "Shirley has distanced herself from involvement in denominational, classical, and even local issues," he comments. "But she does whatever is necessary to be a member of our local congregation. On a Sunday morning, when it's her turn, she cares for babies in the nursery. Or she may help set up chairs in the local gym where our church worships." Ken views this as "a workable practice. We believe her role is better served in the public sector."

"Although professional and technical skills are desirable [for a political position], the main ingredient for success is some basic human skills. The basic qualifications needed to be a good parent or a good teacher or a good county executive are pretty much the same."

In the 1970s, Shirley's eyes turned toward government. During that time Paul was involved in the county planning commission, and she was on the library's board of trustees. Her interest in politics and government grew; here she found a niche in which to use her capabilities.

In 1977 she became involved in the drafting of a new county charter. After the charter was finished, Shirley was on her way.

The charter called for reorganization of the county government. A seven-member council, headed by a county executive, would make up the government. In 1978, Paul encouraged Shirley to run for one of the council openings. He was committed to good government but didn't have the time to participate. "Shirley, you're more capable than some of the people in elected office," he told her. She took Paul's advice, and in 1979 she became the first woman to win a county seat. Soon she was elected council chairperson. She worked hard to shape the new government, and in 1981 she was re-elected.

Two years later the current county executive chose not to run again for health reasons. He asked Shirley to run. "With a great deal of trepidation, I agreed to do so," she recalls.

She was elected County Executive Shirley Van Zanten.

Not everyone was happy about her election. "What does being a school librarian have to do with being a county executive?" some of her opponents asked. Shirley has a good answer: "Although professional and technical skills are desirable, the main ingredient for success is some basic human skills. The basic qualifications needed to be a good parent or a good teacher or a good county executive are pretty much the same.

"The parallels between positions in life are incredible," Shirley goes on. "Relationships, problems, people, and interactions are much the same in a family, in a ladies' society, or in politics. In fact, dealing with difficult people in my present position is just like dealing with some difficult adolescents."

The ability to see many facets of an issue and to explain them to others is one of Shirley's strengths. "She's very analytical and can see what types of questions have to be asked before an issue can be solved. She doesn't rest until she has the answers," says Marvin Vanderpol. He ought to know: currently he represents his district on the Whatcom County Council.

Although Shirley's logical mind is an asset, it can frustrate her. Often the world in which she works is not logical. Instead, it's filled with power trips, emotion, and manipulation. To survive this illogical world, Shirley does three things. First, she views the world as a "theater of the absurd." It helps her to remember that the world has been distorted by evil and that the presence of evil is a reality. Then she asks herself, "How do we as Christians redeem this?"

Second, she cuts through illusion. "I listen as much as I can and then try to decide what the reality actually is," she says. This facilitates decision-making and problem-solving.

Finally, she falls back on God again and again. "Inequities, roadblocks, and frustrations — the evil of our world — upset and discourage me," she says. "The only thing that makes any sense is that I have a personal Savior and he controls this world. He guides me. The results, the management of the world is his, not mine.

"Some people," she continues, "think only a good politician can get things done — a 'good' politician being one who compromises integrity in order to get ahead." This Shirley refuses to do — and she recognizes that this decision doesn't work to her advantage in all ways. "It limits how you wheel and deal," she says. "It means things don't get done as fast when you're not willing to throw people out when they're a little bit in the way."

But get things done she does. "She's good at setting goals and seeing that they're implemented," says Marvin. "She expects a great deal of herself. She works long hours, and she works closely with her staff."

Her persistence paid off recently. For fifteen years she tackled a project involving solid waste disposal and a recycling program. Developing the original proposal was no small feat. The county had to dismantle, rewrite, and reassemble the proposal again and again in order to conform to a seemingly unending stream of changing government guidelines. But Shirley persisted. Today, while other counties still talk about a good recycling and disposal program, Whatcom County has a program that's been approved.

Not only can Shirley see things logically and see things through; she can also articulate what she sees. "Even people who disagree with her respect her because she articulates concerns and her stand so well," says Marvin — although this articulateness can have a downside, he admits: "She doesn't waffle. Sometimes she can be curt and cutting when an issue needs to be spoken to. She's something of a no-nonsense person."

One of her opponents said Shirley was unopposed when she ran for re-election as county executive because she is intimidating. Shirley understands what prompts a comment like this. "I have a quick mind and can be extremely sarcastic and

---

Paul manages Shirley's election campaigns, a job he thoroughly enjoys. She hates campaigns; he loves them. "I ride in parades. He kisses the babies!" exclaims Shirley.

---

cutting, especially in the heat of battle. It can translate into arrogance," she says. This makes the motto hanging above her desk at home — "Silence cannot be quoted!" — particularly appropriate. "For a politician, that's useful to keep in mind," says Shirley with a smile.

At times her other strengths — persistence and attention to detail — can also be weaknesses. "The downside is perfectionism and placing too many demands on myself and on others. That can destroy relationships," she says. She thinks the best way to keep strengths from turning into weaknesses is to know yourself.

Besides the challenge of keeping her strengths working for her, not against her, Shirley also faces other challenges: a hectic pace, a fishbowl sort of life, and shifting pressures that come from being a woman in the workplace. "She works hard," says her friend Mari. "It's nothing for her to be in the courthouse at seven in the morning until ten at night." To help Shirley cope with her multiple roles as professional, wife, and mother, someone else does the household tasks in the Van Zanten household. "So at least Paul gets his laundry done," Shirley says. During one particularly hectic political time, Paul didn't. The couple had no household help then. At a rally, when Shirley was preparing to give a speech, Paul came to her and asked, "When are you going to be home?"

"Why?" she asked.

Paul explained that the family was running out of clean clothes because the laundry hadn't been done. "But he's an adult with above-average intelligence," observes Shirley, "and he easily learned how to do the laundry."

Besides balancing public and home life, balancing public life with personal privacy also looms as a challenge. "The constant public exposure can get exceedingly weary," says Shirley. "You're always on display. There's not much privacy."

The mixed signals she receives as a woman in public office also challenge her. She got to her present position because of slow, steady exposure to people as she worked on the reorganization of the county government. But despite the office she now holds, she sees that she still cannot access some of the service clubs open to men (such as the Rotary Club and the Lions' Club), and as a result, those sources of information are not available to her. "I try not to let that get in the way," she says.

Patronizing attitudes can also be obstructions. "I suspect some men have difficulty dealing with a woman in a position of authority," Shirley says frankly. "It takes extra effort on my part. Occasionally I get weary of this."

In order to get relief from the pressure cooker in which she works, Shirley sets aside time for herself and relies on people close to her for support. "My husband is my greatest promoter," she says. "He gives me freedom to do my work. At home, I show up when I show up. He doesn't expect to be waited on. I think this is critical. I don't think a person can be in public office without the full agreement and support of the spouse. I can see how disagreement on that wrecks marriages."

Paul manages Shirley's election campaigns, a job he thoroughly enjoys. She hates campaigns; he loves them. "I ride in parades. He kisses the babies!" exclaims Shirley.

176

Paul is also her chief confidant. She wishes she had more people to help her connect the challenges of being a woman, a Christian, and a politician. "One person who does help me sort out the challenges is my pastor," she says. "I do talk things over with Ken periodically."

"When Shirley campaigned for office, she freely stated that she sought office in order to serve. Politicians often say that, but to Shirley this was not a trite sentiment. Her high view of a public trust is that it is a place where one is to serve the King of Kings by executing the affairs of a local government efficiently, justly, and selflessly."

According to Mari, Shirley herself is an excellent friend. Mari should know: she and her husband Marvin have been friends with the Van Zantens for more than forty years. "She's a very caring person and has a lot of compassion," says Mari. "She always remembers special things."

Besides relying on people close to her for relief from her job pressures, Shirley relies on special blocks of time that she sets aside for herself. "My work consumes me one hundred percent, if not more. So I take select blocks of time that I must have for myself," she says. She spends some of this time with her husband, some with the authors and the books she loves, some with good music (perhaps a night at the symphony or opera), and some with herself, just getting away for a while. She often saves Sunday after-church time for herself, which she calls her "restoration time." Once she rented a cabin and stayed there for an entire week by herself.

Undergirding everything — her work in politics, her home and family life, her learning, her relaxation — is her unshakable faith in Jesus Christ. "My concept of a personal Savior is the absolute central core of what makes it possible for me to do what I'm doing," she says. Calvinist ideas about stewardship and about God controlling all of life are, she points out, "an enormously useful kind of grounding to have."

Shirley's faith, including the concept of servanthood, provides the focus for her politics. "When she campaigned for office, she freely stated that she sought office in order to serve," says Rev. Koeman. "Politicians often say that, but to Shirley this was not a trite sentiment. Her high view of a public trust is that it is a place where one is to serve the King of Kings by executing the affairs of a local government efficiently, justly, and selflessly."

Shirley works continually on this "servant" focus. It helps her work on the implications of political issues, helps her wield her political power. Just how much raw power is available to her still amazes her. She could move people around at will in order to advance her own career. She could manipulate and maneuver and control and direct — but she doesn't. She seeks ways to use her power to serve rather than to control. She points out that the servanthood view of power is neither well-defined nor easy. "Christ said, 'Don't manipulate; don't use people.' Sometimes that's in direct conflict to how you get things done in the political arena, and that's a struggle," she admits.

In the midst of the complexities of the office she bears, Shirley has found ways to distill the essence of her beliefs. "I don't know how many times I've driven to work and repeated the Twenty-Third Psalm — 'The Lord is my shepherd . . .' — because of things I knew I had to face that day," she says. Or she thinks of the phrase "thy kingdom come" from the Lord's Prayer. To her that means that when we live close to the Lord in even the smallest area, when we carry out his will, then his kingdom is a reality. "That's been something I go back to a great deal," she comments.

Says her pastor, "In Shirley we see a keen mind, a tough will, a tender heart, and a humble spirit — a woman determined to serve and unambitious for herself. Recently high winds and severe cold knocked out over half the county's power. Whose home was one of the last to have power restored? Shirley's. On a Friday she may be flying over the county with the governor,

---

"Christ said, 'Don't manipulate; don't use people.'
Sometimes that's in direct conflict to how you
get things done in the political arena, and
that's a struggle."

---

assessing a flood disaster. On a Sunday she may well be taking her turn in the Sonlight church nursery.

"She is an image of Christ among us — and more than an image," continues Rev. Koeman. "It's not her we see, but Christ in her, dressed as a servant, doing her duty with excellence."

VII

*How beautiful on the mountains
are the feet
of those who bring good news, . . .
who proclaim salvation.*

Isaiah 52:7

Neva VanderZee Evenhouse

Leader and Servant

At the end of her first year in seminary, Neva allowed herself to admit that she wanted to be ordained. More clearly than ever being led by God, endowed generously with the necessary gifts, deeply committed to serving God with all her gifts, and entering doors God had clearly opened, she believed herself called by God to the ministry.

"God made a mistake when he made me. I should have been a man or a dumb blonde." She was in a counselor's office, and the words stumbled out angrily. It seemed to Neva Evenhouse that her deepest desires conflicted directly with what the Bible had taught her from childhood. Why was it that what the Holy Spirit seemed to be saying to her contradicted what her church and its synod had said repeatedly and emphatically?

Neva VanderZee Evenhouse divides her life into two periods: before and after her mid-life crisis. It was during mid-life that Neva was forced to face and grapple with "unworked-through matters that had to be resolved." Working through these issues required that she unlearn some of the "truths" she had accepted in childhood, truths that contributed to the feelings of guilt with which she struggled often.

Born in Watkins Glen, New York, on September 26, 1933, Neva was the oldest of five children born to Leonard and Elizabeth (Betty) VanderZee. The family lived in Rochester, where her father worked at the Eastman Kodak Company as a skilled tinsmith. But eventually the family moved to Michigan. "Mother especially was concerned that we children go to a Christian high school," Neva explains, "so we moved to Grand Rapids when it was time for me to go to high school.

"It was a great sacrifice for Dad to move to Grand Rapids," Neva continues, "but Mother was convinced it was necessary, and she had a strong influence in our family. Frequently she exerted influence with her emotions."

One aspect of Neva's mid-life crisis involved working through her relationship with her mother. "One of the strongest memories I have of childhood in Watkins Glen is that I had a real temper," Neva recalls, "and when I got angry with Mother, I would say to her, 'I hate you,' and she would holler at me for my nasty temper and tell me it was a sin. I would run to my favorite tree two blocks away. I would climb up and sit on a branch, full of raging emotion. Then God would come to me and say, 'It's okay. I'm still with you.'

"I remember going home extremely repentant and apologetic. I would get on my knees before Mother and ask her for forgiveness. She would say, 'I can forgive you but I can't forget.' And for a couple of weeks she would let me know of her displeasure by cold hugs and bare pecks on my cheek. Gradually she would warm up."

Despite such experiences, Neva adds, "I loved God as a child and felt a personal relationship with him as long as I can remember. And I credit Mother with instilling that in me. She talked about God in personal ways, and she often prayed with me. I have more Bible knowledge from my Mother reading Catherine Vos's Bible stories over and over than I have from my Christian school education."

Mrs. VanderZee's devoutness instilled love for God in all her children, even though each child experienced and responded to her personality and behavior differently. Eventually Neva would become the third ordained minister in her family; her brothers Leonard and John had both been ordained in the Christian Reformed Church.

Clubs, social life, fun — these were not part of Neva's high-school experiences. Her parents insisted on Christian education for their children, but family money was tight. So Neva had to pay her own tuition, and that meant hours of work. Nevertheless, it was a rewarding time: Neva won the silver Bishop Memorial Bible award when she graduated from high school. Her love for study and books made high school worthwhile — and it thoroughly absorbed her. "Once while I was reading there was an accident in front of our house," Neva remembers. "I came out of the house much later and wondered what had happened. I hadn't heard a thing. 'How can you be that way?' my family asked."

All the while she was growing up, until she was about to start college, Neva had wanted to be a teacher. But that goal suddenly changed, she says. "Just as I was about to start college, I remember, I was sitting in the bathtub one day and calling out to my mother, 'I'd rather be a nurse than a teacher.' Just like that! Mother said, 'Well, you better make up your mind.' I had only ninth-grade general science, and nursing required much more. At that time it took about a year to get into nursing school. But I applied anyway. I know God had a hand in that! As I look back, I believe part of me possessed a gift for teaching. What needed to be developed in me was sensitivity to the needs of people. That's what nursing did for me." Neva graduated from the Calvin College/Blodgett Hospital nursing program in September 1954.

In October 1954 she married Robert Evenhouse.

In November 1954 she became pregnant.

"There went my big career in nursing," she says.

Bob, her husband, worked first as a salesman and eventually as a manager for Waste Management in Chicago, Illinois. Over time Bob and Neva had four sons. The oldest, Robbie, lived six years; he was severely retarded. Her other sons are now grown and on their own: Mark is a doctor, Keith works for U.S. Air, and Richard is a head mechanic in Alaska.

"I enjoyed motherhood very much," Neva recalls. "I worked a day or two a week. I needed an outlet, but I don't remember wanting to make a full-time career of nursing while the children were home." Her childhood love for reading and study continued during her years of homemaking — "I wasn't the Kaffeeklatsch type," she says.

In 1970, when her youngest son started kindergarten, questions that Neva had long submerged in the busyness of nurturing children began to surface. What would she do with her time now? What did the Lord want of her? She wanted to work for the church; the thought of nursing did not quiet her searching spirit.

"At that time Bob and I were charter members of Peace Christian Reformed Church in South Holland, Illinois," says Neva. "We wanted our church to be different. We wanted to minister in ways that other churches were not ministering at that time." About her personal ministry Neva prayed; she reflected; she cried. Her unfocused quest intensified. She talked with her minister, Rev. Al VanderGriend. One of his comments to her was "I see you as a *teacher* of women." Neva remembered her childhood dream of becoming a teacher, but up until now she had never taught a class of any kind. Nevertheless, Rev. VanderGriend's words impressed her deeply.

In 1970, when her youngest son started kindergarten, questions long submerged in the busyness of nurturing children began to surface. What would she do with her time now? What did the Lord want of her? Neva wanted to work for the church; the thought of nursing did not quiet her searching spirit.

From names she received from the Welcome Wagon, Neva began to call on newcomers to the area and build bridges of friendship to many women. She established many "good relationships," she says. "Then I invited several women to come to my house for Bible study. They knew me but didn't know each other. I was very excited and did an inordinate amount of preparation." The morning for the first group study came.

No one showed up.

What a stunning blow! What was God teaching her? What did God want of her? Where was he leading her?

Slowly she realized she knew nothing of group dynamics; she had pushed ahead into territory about which she had no knowledge. She had run ahead of herself — and ahead of the Holy Spirit, perhaps? Neva turned her energies toward one-to-one Bible study. And then, with the women with whom she had developed one-to-one Bible studies, Neva began her first Bible study group. It went well. Coffee Break, a Bible-study program designed particularly for women in the community, had begun.

It was 1970. Within a few years Coffee Break blossomed into a full-blown evangelism program that is still used by the

Christian Reformed Church today. "I always had the feeling that God was pulling us along," Neva says.

She began to write her own materials for the group. Meanwhile, other churches became interested in what was going on at Peace CRC. Would Neva permit others to use her materials? Of course. Would Neva be willing to pass on to leaders her comments, suggestions, and advice on how to use the materials? Gladly. And would Neva be willing to lead workshops on successful Coffee Break programs? She'd be delighted. Before long, the Home Missions agency in Grand Rapids, Michigan, heard of the popular Coffee Break study program in South Holland.

"The ten years with Coffee Break was a beautiful time in my life," Neva recalls. "I saw how God was working in women's lives." She watched women open up as they delved into God's Word. And they responded individually at appropriate times as she presented the Gospel. Little did she realize that some time later she would be severely criticized for leaving her Coffee Break ministry — and the church she loved.

It was also at this time that she and Rev. VanderGriend formed a corporation called "Discover Your Bible," of which Neva was the director. She and Rev. VanderGriend prepared

---

Within a few years Coffee Break blossomed into a full-blown evangelism program that is still used by the Christian Reformed Church today. "I always had the feeling that God was pulling us along," Neva says.

Bible-study lessons, group leaders' guides, and supplemental materials. Neva traveled to Grand Rapids frequently in connection with Coffee Break and the corporation — whose materials were eventually purchased by Home Missions.

As she traveled around leading workshops, Neva was increasingly bothered by a discovery she made: very few of these women joined Christian Reformed churches. "Why?" she grieved. "I began to think, 'If I were the minister . . . If I had something to say . . .' and these thoughts made me feel very guilty."

Neva's restlessness returned. She believed God had something else for her to do — but what? She couldn't suppress these thoughts.

In 1976, Bob "wanted out of Chicago — anywhere — even Hawaii or Alaska," says Neva. Since Neva was traveling to Grand Rapids frequently, they moved there, where Bob bought a small business. But the move did not lessen Neva's restlessness, guilt, and confusion. She concluded that she must be coping with mid-life crisis, the all-the-children-are-gone-now-what crisis that so many women struggle with, and which so often is misunderstood.

She visited Rev. Jim Kok, then a counselor at Pine Rest Christian Hospital in Grand Rapids. It was to him that she said, "God made a mistake when he made me. I should have been a man or a dumb blonde."

But God doesn't make mistakes.

At this point Neva was still involved with Coffee Break, feeling too guilty to leave. And, she told Rev. Kok, she didn't know what the next step was for her.

Neva ended up undergoing many, many hours of therapy. She became keenly aware of pride in her life, and it troubled her. She saw that it wasn't just one sin on a list of sins: "It was part of who I am." When she confessed it, God said, "But I love you anyway, Neva." Suddenly she understood: the God of her childhood — the God who said, "It's okay. I still love you" — was the God of unconditional love for her now as an adult. In that love she found rest.

She enrolled in an extended quarter of Pine Rest's Clinical Pastoral Education, which met one day a week. She loved it. Next she accepted an invitation to take the full-time spring-quarter course. Then she faced a critical question: Would she now be interested in a year's internship in clinical pastoral education at Pine Rest?

What an exciting, painful, difficult decision! Although it meant leaving Coffee Break, Neva accepted the internship. She

---

During her internship, her heretofore unspoken desire to enroll in the seminary finally surfaced. At last, she admitted it openly.

---

moved forward — to what she didn't know, but she was going ahead. During her internship, her heretofore unspoken desire to enroll in the seminary finally surfaced. At last she admitted it openly. It was a relief — of sorts. Merely admitting the desire, however, didn't solve any of the problems surrounding the thought.

Neva knew the Christian Reformed Church did not call or ordain female ministers. Still, she talked with Dr. Melvin Hugen, professor of pastoral care at Calvin Theological Seminary in Grand Rapids. His words, though gentle, did not encourage her: someone in Neva's situation would need three years of undergraduate work, plus three, maybe four years in seminary. Seven years of schooling sounded like a long time to a woman who had already reached her forty-eighth birthday.

Someone suggested that Neva see Dr. Gene Heideman, dean at Western Theological Seminary in Holland. She did. "We talked at length," Neva says, "and at the end of that time, he said to me, 'On the basis of your life's experience, I think we can take you right now on probation.'" Was she hearing Dr. Heideman correctly? Go to the seminary immediately? Clearly, God had flung the door open for her. In September she enrolled in the seminary of the Reformed Church of America.

Women were very welcome in the RCA seminary. The use of non-sexist language immediately impressed Neva, although occasionally sexism did surface. One professor, usually very aware of the pain of sexism, once talked to a class about min-isters who got too busy with tasks they shouldn't be doing. In that context he said, "I would get a woman to run the mimeo-graph." Neva was stunned and disappointed with the professor. In chapel she mentioned the incident to another professor, who said she should talk to the instructor. "I did," she says, "and he was glad I came to him. It pointed out once again to him — and to me — how difficult it is for men to get out of the sexist trap."

Neva did well in seminary. Her probation ended after the first quarter.

But the horizon was not without clouds — dark clouds. At the end of her first year in seminary, she allowed herself to admit that she wanted to be ordained. More clearly than ever being led by God, endowed generously with the necessary gifts, deeply committed to serving God with all her gifts, and entering doors God had clearly opened, she believed herself called by God to the ministry.

But . . . she was a woman.

The door to ministry in the Christian Reformed Church was closed. Neva saw no possibility of ever being ordained as a minister in her denomination. "By the time I would graduate from the Calvin Seminary, I would be 54 years old, and I didn't have that many more years to minister," she says. "Each year was important to me."

But it was terribly difficult to consider leaving the church in which her spiritual self had been raised. "The Christian Reformed Church had nurtured me since childhood," Neva explains. "It was the church to which I had given of myself." It was a time of pain. Of prayer. Of deep self-examination. After much soul-searching, Neva joined the Reformed Church of America. She wanted to slip away quietly, but others urged her to let the CRC know why she left. In "A Farewell Letter," which appeared in the January 31, 1983, issue of *The Banner* (the weekly magazine of the CRC), Neva said good-bye. She wrote frankly about her struggle:

191

My own life and growth were profoundly affected as I led Bible study groups, developed and led leadership training workshops, and perhaps most of all, wrote Bible study materials.

Yet, ironically, that very growth was bringing me to the point of intense inner conflict. On the one hand, I recognized that my gifts were being developed and used. And I was discovering that the gospel I studied and shared was fundamentally a gospel of freedom — freedom from sin and its effects and freedom for living fully.

On the other hand, I had a nagging feeling — something like guilt — about my leadership role and my desire to use my gifts more fully. . . .

. . . I know, in the most deeply profound sense of knowing, that after forty-eight years I'm free to be what God wants me to be: a woman, a wife, a mother — *and a minister.*" [italics added]

The pain of making her decisions regarding ministry, ordination, and leaving her denomination was intense, yet Neva emerged from her struggles with a "profound sense of well-being, purpose, peace, and joy."

Graduation from Western Theological Seminary was thrilling and heartwarming. "As I walked across the platform to receive my diploma, I trembled," Neva remembers. "Then I heard two male voices call out, 'Yea, Neva!' I wanted to sink through the floor." She wanted to chide her young adult sons for the exclamation, but she soon learned it came from her two "preaching" brothers, Leonard and John, welcoming her to their ministerial rank!

Neva declined her first call, which came from Anaheim, California. Again it was a painful time as she grappled with the reality of being a *woman* minister. Earlier she and her husband had agreed that Neva would not accept a call to a city unless in that city there were places for both of them to follow their callings. In Anaheim there was work for Neva but there was no work available for Bob.

It was a difficult situation for both of them. Bob grappled with the reality of being married to a woman minister. He had supported Neva through all her questionings, doubts, and discouragement. And now this new challenge confronted him. He had known that this could happen — but reality was different. At one time, several years earlier, a brother-in-law had

---

"I know, in the most deeply profound sense of knowing, that after forty-eight years I'm free to be what God wants me to be: a woman, a wife, a mother — and a minister."

---

asked Bob what he would do if his church had a woman minister. "I wouldn't be caught dead there," Bob had replied. Later, when Neva, at that point on the way to becoming a minister, asked him what had caused him to change his mind, he replied, "Living with you." He knew her struggle was real.

Giving up the call to Anaheim was extremely painful for Neva. She felt angry that Bob's call or job seemed to eclipse hers. But the decision she needed to make was plain: she and Bob had agreed on the conditions. She simply couldn't go to Anaheim.

Despite this crisis, Bob continued to support Neva. She applied to many Reformed churches, some of which were open to women ministers and some of which were not. What was in store for her?

In the interim she worked at a pastoral counseling center in Battle Creek but refused a full-time position there. She knew it wasn't the work to which God had called her. In January 1985 she heard that the position of "minister of small groups" was being created in Christ Memorial Church in Holland, and the church had her in mind for the position. "But it wasn't until September, after a thorough search process, that I became one of the final two being considered," she says. The position would require all the training, education, and experience she had. In the end the church called her.

In September 1985 she was installed as Minister of Counseling and Small Groups in the 2,500-member, still-growing church. A couple of years later, she, along with a committee, developed a unique plan for caring for members: ninety-two men and women were ordained as pastoral care elders. Neva, who is now Minister of Congregational Care, administers the program.

Neva VanderZee Evenhouse had listened long for God's voice. Now, in the sixth decade of her life, God was using her carefully honed talents — talents for caring, counseling, administering, teaching, and preaching. She was not the misfit she had once thought she was. Indeed, God had planned her work as minister — but according to his schedule.

Marchiene Vroon Rienstra

Ministry and Meditation

Marchiene faced a painful choice. She could remain Christian Reformed and continue to fight for women's ordination — and be denied the opportunity to use her gifts. Or she could leave the denomination and follow her call elsewhere. After many weeks of prayer and struggle, she and her family concluded that her call was to be a woman in ministry.

195

As the ship on which she was a passenger glided into New York harbor just before dawn one cool summer morning in 1955, Marchiene Vroon knew that the lady of freedom, with torch thrust proudly into the sky, was welcoming her to her own country. Marchiene was fourteen years old. Up until this time, Pakistan had been home to her. Born in Rangoon, Burma, in 1941, while her parents were traveling to their first missionary post in India, Marchiene until now had seen the United States only once.

For Marchiene, life in the States — specifically, in Grand Rapids, Michigan — brought both homesickness and excitement. She missed the beautiful dark-skinned people in brightly colored saris; the smells of curry, fragrant flowers, and citrus trees; the camel bells chiming softly as she fell asleep each night. But she was also excited about all that was foreign to her here.

One thing surprised her immediately: everyone she met at school and church identified strongly with the Christian Reformed Church. She knew, of course, that the CRC was her parents' home denomination, but she had never met anyone

---

Even as a little girl, her mother said, Marchiene couldn't wait to go to church. Already then Marchiene had insisted that someday she would be a minister. Was it still possible? she wondered.

---

else from this church before. With missionaries from many Christian denominations — Methodist, Church of the Brethren, Catholic, and others — Dr. Vroon had helped found the United Christian Hospital in Lahore. To Marchiene, her family and the other missionaries had simply been Christians in a sea of Muslims.

It was strange, she thought, that her new schoolmates in the States saw themselves as "Christian Reformed" rather than just as "Christian." But she managed, with a bit of struggle, to adjust to this and many other "strange" things in her not-quite-home-land.

Three years after she arrived in the States, Marchiene graduated from Grand Rapids Christian High School, and in 1958 she entered Calvin College in Grand Rapids. Her parents went to Nigeria; her father was one of the first doctors sent to Nigeria by the Christian Reformed Church. During those years, Marchiene struggled with what God might be calling her to do.

She had seen how the Gospel transformed people. Women *missionaries* were common to her, and the need for missionaries was so great. No one was concerned about the gender of those who brought relief. But she could see that in the Christian Reformed Church becoming a minister was not an option for women.

So she thought about teaching and hoped to major in Bible at Calvin, but a Bible major didn't exist. She settled for her second love — literature — and majored in speech as well. Her studies went well, but after two years at Calvin, Marchiene became restless, frustrated. She still had major questions about her future vocation and the Christian faith that remained unsettled. Was there really a loving God who cared for her personally and had a plan for her life? She prayed for guidance, for some kind of sign. Soon she received a call from Dr. Ralph Blocksma, her father's former colleague in Lahore.

"Marchiene, they could really use your help in Nigeria," he said. "Why don't you take a year off and go? Your way will be paid by the Henry Beets Missionary Society of LaGrave Avenue Christian Reformed Church." Within weeks, Marchiene was on a plane to Lupwe — the mission station founded by Johanna Veenstra (a pioneer missionary in Africa) — for a year she was to spend teaching, traveling to mission stations, and working in an orphanage. As it turned out, Marchiene's parents were in Takum, a village located just four miles from Lupwe.

During her year in Nigeria, Marchiene discovered that God had sent her Dr. Blocksma's phone call for many reasons — some of which she hadn't suspected. One of these "reasons" was John Rienstra. A young Christian Reformed medical student, John had received a scholarship to study overseas. Through phone calls and letters, he had been matched up with Dr. Vroon. John arrived in Nigeria for the summer of 1960, and before he returned home, he and Marchiene had fallen in love.

John returned to Wayne State Medical School in Detroit, Michigan, for his last year of study, and Marchiene remained in Africa until the following summer. Long months of prolific letter-writing passed. The two married in March 1962 and moved to Grand Rapids, where John would serve his residency.

After finishing her degree at Calvin, Marchiene considered enrolling at Calvin Theological Seminary, adjacent to the college, to study theology. A professor there explained that one should go to seminary only if one wanted to be ordained — and of course, Marchiene couldn't be ordained! Subsequently she accepted an offer from Calvin College to teach English part-time. She put the thought of theology out of her mind — at least for a while.

Marchiene and John's first child, Jonathan, came along in 1964. Eighteen months later, Ron arrived. At this juncture Marchiene quit teaching and concentrated on caring for her two sons. John, then in residency at Butterworth Hospital, had opted to defer his armed services requirement until he had finished that part of his training. In 1966, when he had completed his residency, he enlisted in the Air Force, and the family moved to Goldsboro, North Carolina. Their third child, Janelle, was born on the Air Force base in 1968.

At this point Marchiene was too busy to worry about education, theological or otherwise. Raising her family was exactly what she wanted to do; she was exactly where she belonged — at least for now. Still, something was missing. Something. What was it? Could it, perhaps, be a call to ministry?

Even as a little girl, her mother said, Marchiene couldn't wait to go to church. Already then Marchiene had insisted that someday she would be a minister. Was it still possible? she wondered.

Meaningful opportunities reawakened these buried thoughts. The Air Force chaplain on the base asked Marchiene and John to lead Bible study and outreach programs of ministry. Marchiene became president of the Protestant women's group; John led a Bible class. As the annual Layman's Sunday approached, the chaplain asked if Marchiene and the president of the Protestant men's group would lead the worship service and each preach a short sermon. Marchiene agreed. After the service, the general's wife, a Methodist, complimented her. "Marchiene, you should be a minister. For once my teenage boys listened in church!"

"You're very kind," Marchiene replied, "but of course I couldn't."

"Why not?"

"Because I'm a woman."

"What does that have to do with it?"

"Well, look around. Do you see any women chaplains here?"

"Oh, the Air Force just hasn't gotten around to it. We Methodists have ordained women for years. There's no reason why you shouldn't be a minister. You have the gifts. You've got to use them."

A few weeks later the local Methodist church called and asked Marchiene to preach. "I was scared, but also very excited," Marchiene recalls. "This was a *real* church. I felt nervous as I began to speak, but I soon felt very much at home in the pulpit. As if this were right, somehow. My old dreams just leaped back into life."

Marchiene had a lot to think about when she returned to Grand Rapids in 1969. Soon after that, Rachel was born, and John accepted an offer to go into practice in Grand Rapids.

Because of their mission experience, John and Marchiene soon got on the "Sunday evening circuit," speaking to various church groups and showing slides about missions. On one occasion, Marchiene's mother was scheduled to speak to the Ladies' Missionary Union at an annual event held that year at Calvin Christian Reformed Church. At the last minute, Mrs.

Vroon became ill. She asked Marchiene to step in, and Marchiene agreed. Afterward she received many requests to speak at Lenten luncheons, Bible study groups, and other fellowship events. Many men and women began to encourage Marchiene to consider becoming a minister.

"I finally became convinced that going to seminary was really and truly something God wanted me to do. What would be at the end of the road for me, I did not know. All I knew for sure was that I was supposed to go to seminary."

Meanwhile, several of the Rienstras' friends from their church, LaGrave Avenue Christian Reformed Church, and others were experimenting with a new kind of worship service. They held Sunday evening worship services designed to give young people — especially those confused in their spiritual lives — a vital, more intimate worship experience. Encouraged by the interest and participation of people of all ages, the group decided to launch a new congregation, which later became Church of the Servant Christian Reformed Church. Marchiene helped plan and lead worship services and helped wrestle with the problems of the infant congregation.

All her experiences seemed to her to point in one direction. She struggled to find some other way. But the call — as she began to think it might really be — would not go away.

In 1972 John and Marchiene went to Nigeria for three months. Away from the pressure of her daily life, she thought, prayed, and reflected. "I finally became convinced that going to seminary was really and truly something God wanted me to do," Marchiene explains. "What would be at the end of the road for me, I did not know. All I knew for sure was that I was supposed to go to seminary."

She entered Calvin Seminary in September 1972, the first

and only woman enrolled in any seminary program there. Strange looks greeted her. On her first day a young man approached her in the coffee shop, and in a friendly voice he asked, "Hi, whose wife are you?"

"Well, I'm John Rienstra's wife," she answered, "but he's a doctor. He's not here at the seminary."

"Oh. Well, why are you here?" the man pursued, a little confused.

"To study."

"Why do you want to do that?"

"Because I want to know more about the Bible and theology and Christianity."

The man looked at her as if to say, "Well, I can't argue with that," and then aimed straight at the heart of the matter: "What do you want to do when you get out?"

Marchiene looked at him in surprise. "Whatever God leads me to do! My word, it's my *first* day!"

By this time the Christian Reformed Church had begun to wrestle with the issue of women holding church office. A committee appointed to study the issue reported to Synod 1973 that it had concluded that excluding women from church office could not be defended on biblical grounds. Many delegates to the synod were upset with this report, and the issue began to trouble the church. During the next several years, more committees were appointed to study the issue further.

Marchiene received many requests to speak and write about the issue. She studied the various aspects in earnest, researching both Greek and Hebrew texts, and reading the studies of many other researchers. "People quoted the classic texts about women being silent in church, and I would think, 'But you don't believe that!' I saw women teaching at the Christian high school and in Sunday school. I saw women missionaries preach and teach and help establish churches — on their own or as missionaries' wives. I thought: If people really believe that, those verses should be obeyed literally; then none of this would be happening."

Meanwhile, tensions on the floor of the annual synods rose to fever pitch. Vehement letters began to appear in the CRC's weekly magazine, *The Banner*, and some of those letters aimed directly at Marchiene.

It was now the spring of 1978, and Marchiene believed even more strongly that God had called her to parish ministry. But she had a particularly formidable requirement to fulfill before she could graduate. To qualify for ordination, students had to preach ten sermons — a problem for Marchiene, since she was not allowed to preach in a Christian Reformed Church. Synod 1975 had declared that women could receive a degree from Calvin Seminary without fulfilling this requirement, but Marchiene refused to be an exception. Her problem was solved when nearby Presbyterian churches heard of her availability and invited her to preach — exactly ten times.

Providence had also helped Marchiene meet another difficult requirement earlier. Seminary students were also required to serve as interns during or after their senior year. Marchiene insisted she do this too. As of September 1, 1977, she had no internship. But on Labor Day Sunday she preached in a Presbyterian church, and a few days later the pastor of the church asked her if she would be interested in serving an internship there. Indeed she would.

"If those things hadn't fallen into my lap," Marchiene says, "I don't know how I would have fulfilled all the requirements for ordination. It was as though God just opened the doors."

Presbyterians she knew encouraged her to seek ordination in their denomination. She considered this possibility. She had almost made up her mind when some friends invited her to lunch. "Marchiene, you can't just quietly sneak away," they pleaded. "You've got to take a stand and speak for all those who believe that the time has come for women to be *full* partners in the CRC." Marchiene knew what she had to do. Her friends were right. Perhaps part of her call was to help prepare the way.

Accordingly, Marchiene submitted her file to the CRC candidacy committee. "We all knew each other, and some were very supportive personally, but officially they couldn't support me," she recalls. "No one said, 'Marchiene, don't do it. It's wrong.' Some encouraged me to try the process and see what would happen." She appealed to the Calvin Board of Trustees.

When Marchiene asked to speak to Synod 1978 about why she wanted to be ordained, her request was refused. "I could handle the bitter letters in The Banner. *I could handle the occasional hostile voices at church groups. But when the synod refused to face the issue on a personal level — not just a theological or hermeneutical level — I felt betrayed."*

When they turned her down, she appealed to the synod.

Certain friends, familiar with the workings of the synod, suggested that she request to be ordained as an exception; she might have a better chance of being accepted that way. Marchiene thought about it but decided against it. "I didn't want to suggest that women had to fulfill the additional requirement of being 'exceptional,'" she says.

In June 1978 Marchiene appeared at the meeting of an advisory committee of the synod. She summarized her reasons for her desire to be ordained. She asked permission to speak to synod. The committee received her courteously, asked a few questions, and reported her request to the synod. Her request was refused.

"The two things that hurt most," Marchiene remembers, "were, first, that most of my professors — who knew me and encouraged me privately — did not support me publicly; and second, that the synod denied me an opportunity to give my personal testimony. I could handle the bitter letters in *The Banner.* I could handle the occasional hostile voices at church groups. But when the synod refused to face the issue on a personal level — not just a theological or hermeneutical level — I felt betrayed."

What now? Marchiene faced yet another painful choice. She could remain Christian Reformed and continue to fight for women's ordination — and be denied the opportunity to use her gifts. Or she could leave the denomination and follow her call elsewhere. After many weeks of prayer and struggle, she and her family concluded that her call was to *be* a woman in ministry.

Wyoming (Michigan) Presbyterian Church asked her to serve as their interim minister for a few months in 1978, and she accepted. "The decision was very, very tough," she says. She served there for one year. Presbyterian rules did not allow an interim pastor to be called to a permanent position. In her resumé Marchiene indicated that what she would most like to do would be to start a new church. Much to her surprise, she received a call to help found Port Sheldon Presbyterian Church in the Port Sheldon area along Lake Michigan near Holland. She was ordained as a pastor/new church developer. There was a positive practical side to this appointment: Port Sheldon was within commuting distance from Jenison, Michigan, where the Rienstras lived, so Marchiene's new position didn't involve moving the family.

For Marchiene, the five good years at Port Sheldon Presbyterian Church confirmed her call. "As I led worship and pastored people, I knew I was doing what God had called me to do. Everything seemed to fit together so well."

For Marchiene, the five good years in Port Sheldon confirmed her call to the ministry. "As I led worship and pastored people, I knew I was doing what God had called me to do," she recalls. "Everything seemed to fit together so well."

On a cold, windy afternoon in October 1983, a phone call marked the beginning of still another stage in Marchiene's ministry. Hope Church, a large RCA (Reformed Church in America) congregation in Holland, Michigan, was looking for a senior pastor. Would Marchiene consider a call? Women had been ordained in the RCA only since 1978, and no woman had yet held the position of senior pastor anywhere. Marchiene agreed to an interview. Port Sheldon was off to a strong start, and she was ready for a new challenge. When Hope Church called her, she accepted.

She brought the resources of many Christian traditions into the worship services. Her ecumenical background had convinced her that the different branches of the Christian church need to enrich each other by sharing their worship styles and spiritual disciplines.

In autumn of 1987, frightening news halted Marchiene's ministry: breast cancer. After undergoing a lumpectomy in October, she took a leave of absence. Chemotherapy weakened her too much to perform her duties, and she needed time to think. For eight months she struggled — with cancer and with her spiritual goals. She realized that the last fifteen years — which had involved breaking ground in the seminary, surviving opposition in the CRC, and coping with the pressures of being in the spotlight and of being "the first" everywhere she went — had taken their toll. After she finished her chemotherapy program and was given a clean bill of health, she returned to Hope Church in August 1988; she left in January 1989. She had been thinking, praying, and reflecting on her life, and she decided to rearrange her priorities. She committed her time to prayer, study, offering spiritual direction, leading retreats, and writing.

Since then, Marchiene has published a Bible study book (in 1990) for the RCA and has been working on several other writing projects. She also helped found the Association for Interfaith Dialogue, a group committed to fostering a better understanding among people of different faiths as part of the effort toward world peace. To date the young group has no headquarters but keeps in touch with its members through newsletters and personal contact.

In June 1990 Marchiene attended the annual meeting of the CRC synod for the first time since that heartbreaking day in 1978. During the twelve years since that day, many women

---

At Synod 1990, Marchiene watched the vote taken on the issue of women holding office in the church. "The most amazing and beautiful part of it all was the spirit in which the vote was taken and announced. There's no doubt the Spirit was moving in the hearts and minds of all the people in that auditorium. I think that moment marked the beginning of a great renewal in the church."

---

had graduated from Calvin Seminary. Seven more study committees had toiled and reported to the synod, and all had concluded that the Bible does not clearly prohibit women from holding church office. At this session, held on June 19, 1990, the synod voted to open all church offices to women (to become effective only when Synod 1992 ratifies the decision).

"I'm grateful I was there to see that moment," says Marchiene. "When I heard the night before that the synod had voted to end the debate and take a vote the next day, I felt that something extraordinary was about to happen. I drove to Grand Rapids the next day. My mother was with me, and many other women were there whose personal heartaches I had shared. For me, it was a very healing experience.

"But the most amazing and beautiful part of it all was the spirit in which the vote was taken and announced," Marchiene continues. "There's no doubt the Spirit was moving in the hearts and minds of all the people in that auditorium. I think that moment marked the beginning of a great renewal in the church."

206

Late in 1990, Marchiene gladly accepted the invitation from Eastern Avenue Christian Reformed Church in Grand Rapids to assist them for a few months while they look for a full-time second pastor. To Marchiene, Eastern Avenue CRC, the church of her parents and grandparents, felt like home. She assisted the congregation with preaching, worship, and pastoral leadership until Easter Sunday of 1991.

During her stint at Eastern Avenue, Marchiene maintained her position as adjunct professor at Western Theological Seminary in Holland, Michigan. Currently her teaching focuses on spiritual formation. "I'm trying to put a circle around myself, though," she says, "to get some writing done."

But circles will never contain Marchiene — and she knows this — because serving God with the many gifts and opportunities she is given will continue to challenge her and bless others.

VIII

Go into all the world
and preach the good news
to all creation.

Mark 16:15

Magdalene Wilson Hollis

Call and Confirmation

*"I was the first black woman to become a missionary in the
Christian Reformed Church without going to Calvin
College. I prayed and praised God. This was not my doing
— it was his!"*

211

She doesn't know where she was born — Tennessee, maybe, but it could have been Arkansas. It was November 18, 1935, when her mother, Melvine Wilson, gave birth to two tiny girls. Magdalene lived, but her tiny sister died. Magdalene had an older sister, and a little brother was born some time later.

"I don't remember much about my father," says Magdalene, better known as Maggie, "and my Mom died when I was seven, so Mrs. Garett became my adopted mother. She was supposed to take care of us. Mrs. Garett, her husband, and their daughter lived on a farm somewhere in Arkansas. Life was happy then."

But Maggie's years of childhood happiness were very few. Her older sister married and moved to St. Louis. Then, when Maggie was ten or eleven, her sister returned to Arkansas and took Maggie and her little brother back with her to St. Louis. During this period Maggie remembers being baptized in a river in the name of the Father, Son, and Holy Ghost. This was a happy event, but life on the whole was hard: Maggie worked, hoeing or picking cotton, from sunup until sundown. She preferred working by herself.

"I never liked being with my sister and her husband," she recalls. "I was supposed to go back to Mrs. Garett in the summer, but before summer came, my sister and brother-in-law left St. Louis and took me and my little brother along. We moved to some place in Arkansas."

Maggie lived under abusive conditions. Her brother-in-law beat her often and confiscated her weekly paycheck. Eventually Maggie rebelled. "I guess I was always rebellious," Maggie says. "One night I asked my sister if I could see my pay. She only showed me the part that had my name on it — it read 'Magdalene McDowell.' I shouted, 'My name is not Magdalene McDowell. It is Magdalene Wilson.'"

Maggie attended church with her sister. "It was a black church, of course," Maggie says, "and people jumped and shouted and danced as they praised the Lord."

Mischief provided some recreation for Maggie — even in church. She remembers one particularly humorous incident.

"All of us twelve-year-olds sat in the back row. One Sunday I went to the outside toilet, and I saw a dog. I let him into the church, and he walked down the aisle. The preacher was shouting, 'And I saw Moses. . . .' He yelled louder with every sentence, and each time he yelled louder the dog barked. 'Get out! Get out!' everyone began shouting at the dog. But the dog didn't leave. When the preacher looked at the dog, the dog just 'woof-woofed' back at him. Everyone was trying to figure out how the dog got in, but of course no one knew. We kids were just rollin'. Finally someone got a little switch, and they switched him out the door!"

But moments of fun were few. Life became unbearable for young Maggie: her brother-in-law abused her frequently. Fed up, Maggie ran away. She soon teamed up with Felipe, a Mexican who spoke very little English and who feared being sent back to Mexico. (Later Maggie learned that Felipe was an illegal alien.) She told him she was eighteen, though she was not yet a teenager. "I was a good actress and liar when I was young," she comments.

Felipe treated her well. One evening she permitted him to kiss her. That was a mistake; not until later did she realize that Felipe then assumed she was his wife. "People didn't get married by law then," Maggie explains. "They got married by just living together." The two found field work together.

One day she decided she didn't want to sit next to Felipe on the truck that carried the workers to the field, so she sat by another worker. Felipe became angry and shouted at the man, and the shouts soon led to blows. The fight continued until Mr. Rogers, the driver and the person at whose home Maggie lived, drew his pistol on Felipe. "Leave her alone," he commanded.

"This is mine!" Felipe shouted. "This is mine! I love her."

"She's not yours," Mr. Rogers said to Felipe; to Maggie he said, "Have you had a relationship with him?" Maggie, a naive twelve, looked at Mr. Rogers questioningly. He persisted. "Have you had intercourse with him?" At that Maggie shouted, "No! No!"

213

"You're sure?"

"Yes, I'm sure."

But Felipe kept shouting, "You mine. You mine." He picked up a hoe and threatened the others. Amid yells, name-calling, and threats, Mr. Rogers took Felipe to the sheriff. Maggie never saw Felipe again.

Some time later at a dance she met Jim Hollis, a truck driver/logger from out of town — Chicago, perhaps. "I loved to dance," Maggie says, "and every Friday night when everybody got done working, we would go to this juke place and dance.

"I met Jim at one of these dances. One night he told me that he'd be coming back only once, and he asked if I would go to Chicago with him. I had liked Jim right away — he was good-looking, clean. He was almost like the father I had always wanted.

"Jim came back as he said he would. I told him I didn't have any folks, which I didn't. And I took off with him to Chicago in the cab of a big truck."

Maggie loved Jim, although they were not married. She soon became pregnant. In Chicago she found work in a small restaurant; Jim was gone on his truck route.

That section of Chicago where blacks lived in the 1940s and 1950s was small — small enough that you could run into someone you knew quite easily. Maggie knew this, and she also knew that by this time her sister had moved to Chicago, so she made an effort to stay out of her sister's way. But one day Maggie's sister, unaware that Maggie was in the city, walked near the restaurant and spotted her. "My sister started following me and calling after me," Maggie remembers. "I didn't look back but I recognized her voice. She followed me to the restaurant and then reported the owner to the authorities for hiring under-aged help — I had lied about my age." The sheriff detained Maggie; she *was* underage, only about fourteen. After she was released, her sister brought Maggie to her home.

Although Maggie and Jim didn't live together and Maggie didn't know where he was at all times, Jim did keep in touch with her. In November 1950, Maggie's first child, John, was born. Little John and Maggie lived with her sister. Both her sister and her brother-in-law loved children, and her brother-in-law especially wanted John. "He didn't have any children of his own," Maggie explains.

Maggie remained stubborn. "My sister tried to make me go

She became disenchanted with her church because it gave her little help yet insisted that she tithe from her monthly Social Security income. "I needed food and clothes and shoes for my family. We could see the pavement below us as we rode down the Dan Ryan Expressway; the bottom was falling out of my car. And I thought, 'How in heck could God give me a raggedy car like this? God don't give people raggedy stuff.'"

---

to church and to school, but I did everything except that. I was still a rebel, I guess. Finally I ran away again, but I left my baby with my sister. I felt completely lost." Lacking money, she hid with different people in the Chicago ghetto and accepted food "from good people all along." One summer she slept in a park every night and was befriended by a man who supplied her with food and clothes. "You want a job?" he asked. He gave her work washing dishes, but soon he said, "You're very good at dishwashing, but you're too good to stay in the kitchen; I need you up front."

"One day I was behind the cash register," recalls Maggie, "and a voice said, 'Can I have a cup of coffee?'" She turned quickly. It was Jim.

"Where's my baby?" he demanded immediately.

She told him her unhappy story. The two went downtown, she lied about her age again, and they married. It was about 1953.

Maggie and Jim wanted their son John, now about three years old. They went to see Maggie's sister and brother-in-law, and after some discussion Jim and Maggie left with their son. Eventually their family grew to include eight children. "I think those were the happiest days of my life," Maggie says. "Sure, we had a lot of problems. He didn't want me to work . . . just kept me pregnant while he was out playing around. That was life, I thought. And he drank. But he always had enough for groceries and clothes for the kids. He taught me how to cook, how to take care of my body as a woman, how to write checks, how to pay bills. . . . He loved me a lot, something like a father loves his daughter."

As a family they began to attend a Baptist church. Jim was an usher and Maggie joined the choir.

In 1964 Jim died. He was only thirty-nine years old.

After that, relentless poverty, loneliness, and single parenting dogged Maggie. She became disenchanted with her church, because it gave her little help yet insisted she tithe from her monthly Social Security income. "I needed food and clothes and shoes for my family. We could see the pavement below us as we rode down the Dan Ryan Expressway; the bottom was falling out of my car. And I thought, 'How in heck could God give me a raggedy car like this? God don't give people raggedy stuff.'" Within a year her pastor told her that she needed a man. After that advice Maggie decided she had to get out of that church.

Nevertheless, within two years of Jim's death, Maggie got married again, to a man named Bill Wrancher. "I was still young then — and stupid," Maggie says frankly. "I thought anyone wanting to marry me with eight kids was great. From the moment I married Bill, I regretted it. But you know, I believe Bill got me into the Christian Reformed Church."

With no job prospects, only a desire to leave Chicago, the family moved to Grand Rapids, Michigan. After several local moves, the family ended up in a house near Madison Square Christian Reformed Church. "I used to sit and watch the people

216

going to Madison Square. People didn't dress up in that church. With ten kids now, and pregnant with my eleventh, I wished I could get into a church like that."

One summer a SWIM (Summer Workshop in Missions) team visited Maggie and "even ate corn bread" with the family. The young girls took the little ones to Vacation Bible School. "They took a deep interest in me and my kids, and sometimes they even took the kids just to give me a break," Maggie says appreciatively.

When the family moved — again — to a different neighborhood, Madison Square church members continued to pick up the children for Sunday school, and they also invited Maggie to attend their church. Maggie decided to go because "I wanted

---

"I thought anyone wanting to marry me with eight kids was great. From the moment I married Bill, I regretted it. But you know, I believe Bill got me into the Christian Reformed Church."

---

to find out what the church was like and what the preachers were preaching about." Rev. Vern Geurkink, the minister then, was "a neat teacher," Maggie recalls. "I started to listen. I learned things about the Bible I had never heard before."

The church gave Maggie a *Reach Out* Bible, and she devoured it. "I could read and understand it," she says. The family started attending Madison Square, even though Maggie wasn't entirely happy there.

That fact came out some time later, when Bill and Maggie met with a committee from the church. "Bill told them at the time that he was ready to go to that church," Maggie remembers. "He said he believed in God. But when they asked me why I wanted to come, I said, 'I don't.'"

If she felt that way, the committee asked, why was she there?

"The Bible says that man is the head of house, and Bill

wanted me here. So here I am. My kids don't want to come —
and besides, you're all prejudiced," Maggie blurted out.

Bill, of course, became very angry with Maggie, and the two
argued heatedly. "You just messed it all up," he accused her.
Maggie just laughed a bit. "Maybe we aren't supposed to belong
to that church, then."

At midnight the telephone rang. It was Rev. Geurkink. "I
could have called tomorrow," he said, "but I couldn't wait to
tell you — you're going to be members of Madison."

"See," Maggie smirked at Bill, "I didn't screw it up."

Soon after this Maggie and Bill discovered that Kathy, their
one-year-old daughter, had leukemia. Maggie learned some
things from the difficult period that followed. "I found out how
important the church was to me," she says. "This was the first
time in my life that people made me see that God loved me no
matter what. So many people helped, with prayer, time, visits,
and meals.

"I never questioned God. Yes, I prayed for Kathy's healing.
But two weeks before she died [on April 7, 1970], I said, 'Lord,
if you're not going to heal her, take her.' In two weeks she was
gone."

But soon Maggie's newfound faith was strangely tested. She
and Bill began to have serious marital problems, and the pressure
of family finances increased. Bill left for a few weeks, and when

---

*Maggie's row in God's vineyard has never been
easy. Having been through times when she had
eleven children to support, little income, and a job
only now and then, always low-paying, she has
found it difficult to always be cheerful.*

---

he returned, he was threatening and abusive. "I'm going to be
a heathen-counselor to you," he said. "I'm going to whip you
morning, noon, and night because you killed my daughter." The

beatings — of both Maggie and her children — were so frequent and so painful, the death threats so ominous, that Maggie moved out. She felt hopeless. Bill, however, did not give up.

"Here the church disappointed me," Maggie says bluntly. "Bill and I finally agreed to get marriage counseling. Bill put up a good front with the counselor. The counselor said things would get better if I wouldn't cater to the kids so much. It made me sick; it was such a big front. The church still had this thing — the male is always right. When it was my turn, I said, 'I'm getting a divorce. If you want to put me out of the church — well, then do it.' I told them all of the things Bill did every day. Before the end of the year, Bill left."

Bill wanted no more of the Christian Reformed Church, but Madison Square never deserted Maggie. "It's funny," she

---

In spite of poverty and discrimination, Maggie never permitted her children to say "I can't."

---

says now. "I still can't figure out why Bill wanted us in Madison Square, but God surely meant it for good. My kids too have been blessed — being brought up in a Christian home and a good church and a Christian school."

Maggie's row in God's vineyard has never been easy. Having been through times when she had eleven children to support, little income, and a job only now and then, always low-paying, she has found it difficult to always be cheerful.

She found herself becoming lonesome in Madison Square, the church that had meant so much to her. She was sick of it. Weary. Discouraged. Lonely. "I saw couples, husbands and wives, and I would think, 'Here sits Maggie and all her kids.' I wanted to be with *my* people. Most people at Madison Square were educated and I wasn't. They were people from Calvin College — even the mothers were Calvin people with kids."

She began attending a church with *her* people, a charismatic group. She intensified her seeking of a Spirit-filled life. Her prayers and those of the group about her housing problems were answered directly by an anonymous gift of a down payment for a house.

Maggie continued to attend both churches, but peace eluded her soul. She struggled. "I thought I was getting too white. I'm black, and I wanted to be black. I was raising my kids to be black, and I was proud of being a black woman. Yes, I have a lot of pride."

This is evident in the way Maggie has raised her children. In spite of poverty and discrimination, Maggie never permitted her children to say "I can't." She wanted them to grow up praising the Lord, so she gave them religious instruction. And she saw to it that all her children got an education. All of her children finished high school; one graduated from college. "They all got much more education than I ever had," she says.

Maggie was proud — but troubled, she remembers. "I stopped going to the charismatic group and to Madison Square. I showed up only once in awhile. Then I got lonely, very lonely again. Depressed. Then better again."

Meanwhile, Rev. David Sieplinga came to Madison Square. "He came looking for me," Maggie recalls. "'You know, Maggie,' he said, 'the Lord has something for you to do. Do come back to church.' So I went back. Dave was always ready to listen. He prayed with me, spent time talking with me, and became really involved with my family.

"Madison Square really became our church again," Maggie continues. "My kids were crazy about Dave — they thought he was the greatest man that ever lived. It was the Lord again, putting someone in my life."

In 1972 Maggie became a bus driver for the Grand Rapids Christian School Association. To her it wasn't simply a job; it was a ministry.

So was her work in the kitchen of Madison Square. "I remember the first meal that Dave and Dante Venegas, co-pastor at Madison Square, cooked at the church," Maggie says.

"Dave made some baked beans and chicken and corn bread, mind you, and I just couldn't deal with it. I said, 'No way! I'll cook next time.' Next thing I knew, everybody wanted my corn bread and whatever I cooked. It made me feel like I could do something in the church that a lot of people couldn't do." She had found a ministry.

Sometimes she dreamed about becoming a missionary. She always remembered Louise, the missionary who had come to hold a revival in the area where she had lived as a child. "When

---

"I was hanging up clothes one day, boys' socks, and they were so nice and white. I stood there admiring how white I had gotten them. Suddenly it seemed like the Lord spoke to me out of a tree in the backyard and said, 'It's time for you to become a missionary.'"

---

preachers came to our house, they ate all the chicken and we got the feet. We had to carry out the slop jars. But Louise took out her own slop jars. You didn't wait on her hand and foot like you did the preachers. She was a powerful speaker, a praying woman." Maggie speaks wistfully of Louise, and the memory of her triggers a related memory.

"I was hanging up clothes one day, boys' socks, and they were so nice and white," Louise recalls. "I stood there admiring how white I had gotten them. Suddenly it seemed like the Lord spoke to me out of a tree in the backyard and said, 'It's time for you to become a missionary.'

"I laughed out loud and said, 'How?' In a black church, becoming a missionary wouldn't be a problem for me. I'd just tell the minister that's what I wanted, and he would put me under the watchful eye of another missionary for a year. Then, if I were qualified (that meant not gossiping or being nosy about other people's business), I could be a missionary. But I was in the Christian Reformed Church, and I knew things didn't go that way.

"Then something happened," Maggie continues. "Several women — and I was one of them — went to a Madison Square council meeting. It was sometime in 1976, I think. It had to do with women's gifts being used in the church. Someone asked me how I felt about women in church office, and I said, 'You

---

"I hit them with a bomb. I told them I wanted to be confirmed as a missionary, even though I knew the CRC didn't confirm women as missionaries. The council appointed a committee to study my request because the elders didn't know what I was talking about. I just went home and prayed more about it. Two months later Pastor Dave told me the church would confirm me as a missionary."

---

lied to me when you said women may take part in all of the church. I wasn't brought up in this church, and when I came you said I could take part, but I can't.'

"And then I hit them with a bomb. I told them I wanted to be confirmed as a missionary, even though I knew they didn't confirm women as missionaries. The council appointed a committee to study my request because the elders didn't know what I was talking about. I just went home and prayed more about it.

"Two months later," Maggie goes on, "Pastor Dave told me the church would confirm me as a missionary in the Christian Reformed Church. For me the title wasn't important, but it is for many black people who don't know the Lord and refuse to be part of any church. So I was the first black woman to become a missionary in the Christian Reformed Church without going to Calvin College. I prayed and praised God. This was not my doing — it was his!"

Maggie joined a small group of Madison Square women — "warriors," she called them — who met to discuss and pray about people's needs and who tried to fill those needs. "We were given a lot of answers," Maggie remembers, "and that made us even more interested in praying."

Maggie kept her job as a bus driver. Sometimes her evangelical enthusiasm startled her passengers. "I get high on Jesus," she told the kids. " 'Don't ask her any questions,' one said. 'She's supposed to keep her hands on the wheel.' I said to them, 'Don't you worry. My angel is driving this bus.' But I do get excited when I'm talking about my Lord."

Sometimes she felt that Madison Square "tightened" her in. "I felt like I was being put in a little box, and I didn't want to be there," she says frankly. "They asked me to be a deacon, but I am not deacon material."

In her mission work Maggie wanted particularly to reach people who did not have television in their homes and who had never heard the Gospel. God's lament, "My people perish for lack of knowledge," kept her going.

"I do get excited when I'm talking about my Lord."

Eventually Maggie with her ministry moved to Kalamazoo, Michigan, where she became an elder in Immanuel Christian Reformed Church. She also became the "missionary staff person" at the House of Hope, a shelter for the homeless, but kept her job as a custodian for Grand Rapids Public Schools. She commuted the 100-mile round trip daily. After three years the heavy commitment and involvement and the constant working with people wore her out. "I couldn't keep it up," she says.

In August 1990, Grand Rapids Public Schools posted a job opening: the position of building manager for custodians of the school system. Maggie applied — with trepidation. She wasn't sure she could handle the responsibility, but she knew the Lord would help her. Maggie got the job, the first woman and the third minority to hold such a position. "I praise the Lord for this accomplishment," she says. This work demanded less of her emotional strength than the House of Hope, and it allowed her to keep her ministry as elder and missionary in Kalamazoo.

"I'm not the little girl who worked in the cotton fields. I can do much more. It took me fifty-four years to get to this point — with God's help and the help of many Christian friends."

Maggie still dreams: she yearns for a high-school diploma. "When I speak, I must first get words into my mind and write them down. Sometimes I get so frustrated," she admits. "But I'm not the little girl who worked in the cotton fields. I can do much more. It took me fifty-four years to get to this point — with God's help and with the help of many Christian friends."

Maggie — the CRC's first black *confirmed* missionary — keeps looking for doors, and God continues to open them. Her journey has taken her from the cotton field to the mission field — and wherever Maggie is, there is her mission field.

Nelle Breen Smith

Majestic Messenger

To Nelle it seemed that she had no other choice. God's word to her was clear: she was to be a missionary. It was a matter of trusting that when the Lord calls, he also provides.

Nelle (pronounced "Nell") Breen, a 28-year-old teacher, had that March day received a contract to teach first grade for another year in the Christian school in Zeeland, Michigan. She loved the children. She loved teaching. The principal and the school board appreciated her. Then why did she hesitate to sign the contract?

She prayed, "Lord, what about this contract? Should I teach another year?" She concluded with the Lord's Prayer.

As she prayed "thy kingdom come," what seemed to her to be the voice of the Lord interrupted her: "Stop!" Nelle stopped. The voice continued. "You can't go on with that prayer. You've been saying this for several months. You ask why? If you really want my kingdom to come, then you must go to Nigeria." It was 1929, and Johanna Veenstra* was a pioneer missionary in Africa under the Sudan United Missions (SUM), a British agency. But at that time the Christian Reformed Church had no mission in Nigeria.

"It was as simple as that," recalled Nelle. "The next morning I said, 'Mom, I'm going to Nigeria.'"

For Nelle all the questions, doubts, and indecision were gone. The Lord wanted her in Nigeria. As she left for school, the unsigned contract tucked into her lesson-plan book, Nelle reviewed her life and the little signals that, she thought now, had pointed to this decision.

Nelle grew up in Holland, Michigan, and attended Hope College there for a year. Subsequently she earned her teaching diploma at Western Normal School in Kalamazoo.

"My decision to go to Nigeria was quite natural, I suppose," she said. "My mother was deeply involved in the Women's Missionary Union. Most of the speakers were missionaries home on furlough, and my mother often invited them to our home."

When Nelle was a young woman, she was struck by the possibility of becoming a missionary herself. With a group of

---

*Stories of Johanna Veenstra, pioneer CRC missionary, are published elsewhere. Her autobiography is entitled *Black Diamonds*.

ten young women, she and her friend, Ann Holkeboer, attended a Bible conference at Winona Lake, Indiana. Two missionaries, Tena Holkeboer from China and Johanna Veenstra from Nigeria, spoke of their work. After the conference, "Jo asked to use our room for prayer and discussion," remembered Nelle. Jo and Tena spoke about the superstitions, the fears, and the pagan worship practices of people in China and Nigeria. "The people are eager to hear, and the need for teachers cannot be measured," Jo said. "I have begged and begged for ordained men." But no ministers had accepted her challenge.

Jo's implication did not escape Nelle — but she did not want to go to Nigeria. She returned to her beloved teaching that fall, but something had changed. Meanwhile, Jo sent her letter after letter. She was certain that Nelle would come to Africa. "We have a whole group of new Christians here who are praying that you will come here to be their teacher," Jo wrote.

Nelle shared her unsettling thoughts with some of her friends, and they began to pray that the Lord would guide her in her decision-making. And he did. To Nelle it seemed that she had no other choice. God's word to her was clear: she was to be a missionary. It was a matter of trusting that when the Lord calls, he also provides.

The first roadblock appeared quickly: a physical examination revealed that Nelle had a heart murmur. Without health clearance, she could not go to Nigeria. "Don't worry," Jo wrote. Nelle didn't. Disappointed but not too discouraged, Nelle continued with her plans.

She wanted a year "away from our people" to broaden her vision and to learn about teaching personal evangelism. Accordingly, she attended the Moody Bible Institute in Chicago. "It's not that I didn't love my church or was disloyal to it," she explained. After that year, she returned to Holland and had another physical examination. The heart murmur was gone. She was thankful but not surprised.

Then a second roadblock appeared: at that time the Christian Reformed denomination was not ready to sponsor Nelle. This did not worry her — and in the end it did not stand in

---

The women were prophets like John the Baptist: they prepared the way for the Lord Jesus Christ. Today thousands of Nigerians worship God in the churches that Jo and Nelle planted.

---

her way. "Friends in my church [Ninth Street CRC in Holland] and others gave generously," she said.

Finally the time came for Nelle to leave. She spent some time at the headquarters of Sudan United Missions in London. Interviews went well; Jo had assured her board that Nelle was "just the right person," and that she especially wanted Nelle as a teacher.

From there Nelle's voyage took her to Lagos, a huge shipping port in western Nigeria. As she disembarked, the equatorial heat beat down on her and ricocheted from the ground beneath her. People, almost all of them black, milled around her, crowding her. Some were dressed in multicolored cloths draped over their bodies. Others wore white, flowing gowns and tightly wound turbans. Hundreds more wore little cloths or rags. "This will be my home," she thought.

The subsequent trip from Lagos to Wukari in an antiquated train tired and tried her. Africans can squeeze more people and possessions into a small space than Americans can squeeze into a spaceship. But when Jo greeted Nelle in Wukari, the strangeness was forgotten. Their celebration soon turned to planning. Jo's next furlough was two years away, and she and Nelle determined to crowd into this time as much as the Lord and daylight would allow.

Nelle tackled the Hausa language. Nigerians use many languages, but Hausa is a bridge language, a "trade language," which many Nigerians know in addition to their tribal language. There was no textbook or trained bilingual teacher to help Nelle; she learned Hausa the way a little child learns to speak a language. Except for the month she spent under the tutelage of a Muslim teacher, Nelle learned Hausa on the job — and she learned to speak the language like a native.

After a couple of months, "Baba" Jo and Nelle went to Lupwe, which would become Nelle's home. Here she too would be a *baba*, a "mama" for the Takum-Lupwe area.

Nelle's stay at "home" was short. She and Jo unpacked all the dirty clothes that had accumulated, washed them, repacked, and went trekking. They wore knee-high leather boots to protect themselves from snakes. They traveled light: they took along tentlike nets to protect them from mosquitos at night, canteens for carrying boiled water, and a few basic foods. These necessities, plus the medical supplies — pills, syrups, salves, bandages, and more — were carried by natives on their heads.

The two women went to village after village. On Sundays they preached, and each morning they held prayer services. Christ was with them. The women drew the villagers, one by one and two by two. Christ the Savior had come, they told the people — and he had come for Nigerians too. He wanted to be their Savior. The women were prophets like John the Baptist: they prepared the way for the Lord Jesus Christ. Today thousands of Nigerians worship God in the churches that Jo and Nelle planted.

Besides declaring the Good News, the women demonstrated its effects. Jo delivered babies and treated tropical diseases. Many were healed, and the people marveled. Through this medical work God also opened the people's hearts. There was so much to do — work was never done. Often seven or eight people came to see Jo and Nelle in the evening. They wanted help with their Bible studies; they had numerous questions; they needed counseling. Jo and Nelle became spiritual mothers to the people.

Although the people in the bush country in which Nelle

and Jo worked had not seen many white people, the women had little fear. But one frightening time stood out in Nelle's memory. She and Jo were spending one night in a small and unfriendly village in the Kuteb, a place where few white people had ever been. Men and women were suspicious; children were curious. Nelle and Jo talked with the people informally. The two women didn't preach but mentioned how God causes crops to grow and how every man, woman, and child is made in God's image.

But the people were not interested, and they said so. When darkness fell — rapidly as it does in Nigeria, with only a moment or two of twilight — the men began to chant. The chanting grew louder and louder. The men danced too, faster and faster. Many became drunk. "They danced around our hut with mad hatred," Nelle recalled. The chants grew still louder, the dancing still faster. "Nelle," said Jo, "it's time to pray." When Nelle opened the Bible, it fell open to God's words to Jonah: "I have many people in this city."

The two fearful missionaries did not sleep much that night. Just as darkness began to disappear, so did the noise. With the quiet came new hope. The women snatched a few moments of

---

"We wanted to give more than just training. We wanted to give ourselves to the Africans so that they in turn would be able, through training, to give themselves to their people."

---

sleep. Shortly after daybreak, they left the village unharmed. Yes, God did have many people here. Today an established church sends its light from the hills of the Kuteb.

Trekking was only part of Nelle's work. For her, daytime soon became a solid schedule of teaching. But there was a problem: Nigerian girls worked mainly in the fields and were not permitted to attend classes. It wasn't that their parents objected so strongly to their being schooled, Nelle pointed out; they just needed to be convinced of education's value. "We finally convinced the tribal chiefs to allow the village girls to attend school. This was several years before Margaret Dykstra [also of Holland, Michigan] greatly advanced the work with women and girls.

"We wanted to give more than just training, however," Nelle continued. "We wanted to give ourselves to the Africans so they in turn would be able, through training, to give themselves to their people." Suspicion of the two white women dwindled as the Nigerians began to understand that the *babas* had no ulterior motives. Gradually the people's confidence in the women grew, and Nelle was able to establish a school in Lupwe. "I used the methods I used in my first-grade at home," Nelle said, "but we wrote our numbers and letters in the sand."

Life settled into a routine of sorts — but an ever-changing routine. One big change involved Nelle's introduction to a young and handsome Englishman, Edgar Smith, a missionary for SUM who had dedicated his life to serving the Lord and the people in Nigeria. After many months, Nelle realized that her affection for Ed had deepened into love. When she shared her realization with Jo, she discovered that Jo had done a lot of thinking about Ed too. "Jo had already analyzed Ed," said Nelle, "and she felt Ed had much to give to the work." Both Nelle and Ed were glad that Jo "approved."

The term of service for missionaries in Nigeria was two-and-a-half years. When Nelle's first term was up, she returned to the United States for her first furlough. Little did she dream that while she was at home, she would lose her mentor, trusted friend, and colleague, Jo. Five days after a successful appendectomy, Jo developed a blockage, and then heart failure caused her death. Nelle wept. Why? Why? She struggled and prayed. Letters from Ed and support from home helped her. She received no answer to her agonized "Why?" But finally she submitted, and she knew in her heart the quiet peace that only God supplies.

On her way back to Lupwe, Nelle stopped in London at

SUM headquarters. "Would your church be willing to take over the work in Nigeria?" officials there asked. "No," Nelle replied, "my church has sent people to China, but it doesn't yet seem interested in Nigeria." In the book he later wrote entitled *Nigerian Harvest,* Ed explained this phenomenon. Synod 1920 had given a number of reasons why Nigeria wasn't being supplied with missionaries, reasons which included the following:

(d) The peoples of the Sudan belong to the types of mankind from which one cannot expect the most in the Kingdom of God. . . .
(f) The close cooperation with churches of less pure confession . . . fills us with fear for the maintenance and propagation of our Reformed principles.

Nelle grieved when she thought of Jo and her close adherence to Reformed principles, to the foundations she had laid so carefully and the vital work she had done in Nigeria.

But some sun shone through these clouds. In October 1934, after Nelle's first furlough, Nelle and Ed were married in Takum, a small town five miles from Lupwe. About a year after their marriage, Alyce Jean was born. With a mother's heart Nelle struggled with her commitment. Could a little white child live in primitive Africa? Bear the heat? Ward off diseases? At that time the nearest doctor was three hundred miles away. After weighing these concerns, Nelle decided to keep Alyce Jean with her and Ed for the time being. Paul, born in 1938, also remained with his parents while he was an infant.

The children had a positive effect on outreach, Nelle recalled. "Nigerians thought that white people came grown up. They were delighted when Alyce Jean was born. One woman just hugged me and said, 'Oh, *baturiya* [white lady], I am so happy that you have this baby. Now I can see that you are the same as we are. Now your God can be our God too.'"

But the questions doubled as Paul and Alyce Jean grew from infants to toddlers. What did the Lord want Nelle and Ed to do? What would be best for them? For their children? The children couldn't remain in Africa. Yet the work must go on; leaving the mission field was not an option for Nelle and Ed. The two talked, prayed, and struggled. On their next furlough, as the time drew near for them to return to Nigeria, Nelle decided she should stay home with the children and Ed should return to the field alone. But Ed did not agree. "We must go and go together," he said. "The work there is for both of us. This is the Lord's work."

Sadly, Nelle consented. Alyce Jean and Paul stayed with their grandparents, John and Jennie Breen. Except for a visit or two to their parents in Lupwe, Alyce Jean and Paul lived with Grandpa and Grandma until they left for college.

When Alyce Jean and Paul were children, living at Grandma's was a part of life that they accepted. "It was all I ever knew as a child," says Alyce Jean. "My parents were called of God; they were very special persons. Grandma and Grandpa did a tremendous job of raising us. At the time I didn't realize what a big task it was for them, but now that I've raised four children of my own, I marvel at them. I asked Mother at one time why she did have children. Mother said she and Dad didn't know how difficult it would be.

What did the Lord want Nelle and Ed to do? What would be best for them? For their children? The children couldn't remain in Africa. Yet the work must go on; leaving the mission field was not an option for Nelle and Ed.

"Later I realized that, yes, this did affect my life. I had to say good-bye so often that I developed a defense system because I didn't want to always hurt when I said good-bye. I just don't allow myself to get too close to people. I love my family dearly, but I do not experience deep grief when I have to say good-bye."

In some ways Paul's experience resembled Alyce Jean's. "As a child, I simply accepted what was. I loved my parents; I loved my grandparents. I accepted the idea that missionary work justified the separations we experienced, but I didn't really understand.

"Numerous people have asked me how my parents could have made the choice they did," Paul continues. "I suspect that they themselves didn't fully understand their reasons, and they acted and chose as they did because their love for God, their concern for the unsaved, and their desire to have a family were all important parts of their being.

"After my father died, Mother continued to handle her own affairs and assert her will until she died. But as she aged, she needed to be ministered to as well as to minister. Yes, there were brief moments when I resented giving her the care she needed, because I remembered that she often wasn't there to give me care when I needed it. But I also remember that in the years between my father's death and my mother's death, my mother did care for and mother her own children in the ways that were familiar to her — through prayer and love and letters and encouragement. She was especially nurturing to me as I went through difficult times of my own."

Months and years raced by. Over time, other missionaries arrived in Nigeria, many of whom brought their children. When the children became old enough, parents sent them to Jos, some three hundred miles away, to attend a school that had been established for missionaries' children. By this time, however, Paul was in junior high and Alyce Jean was in high school; their lives as young adults were well established in the States.

As time went on, God continued to claim hundreds and hundreds of Nigerians as his own. Nelle and Ed saw that the people needed leaders and teachers from among their own tribes, and they began to train individuals accordingly. Fifteen men, fourteen of whom were married, were the first to arrive at Lupwe — with their wives and families — to learn to read, to write, and to become evangelists. Together the missionaries planned the curriculum and trained the men. Nelle taught Bible class for both the men and their wives. She prepared the women for the time when they would be guiding congregations with their husbands.

During the time she spent in Nigeria — nearly four decades — Nelle saw many changes in the mission field. When, in 1940, SUM's Lupwe-Takum field was transferred to the Christian Reformed Church, Nelle and Ed became CRC employees. This

---

"Numerous people have asked me how my parents could have made the choice they did," says Paul. "I suspect that they themselves did not fully understand their reasons, and they acted and chose as they did because their love for God, their concern for the unsaved, and their desire to have a family were all important parts of their being."

---

involved certain policy changes. For one thing, Nelle, as the wife of a missionary, would no longer draw a salary. Yesterday a salaried SUM missionary; today an unsalaried CRC missionary! Same work; different status. "Married women of the CRC mission were no longer considered to be workers but became wives only," Ed later commented. The official rationale went as follows: "It does not mean that wives may not work; many of them do . . . but this is a labor of love and one which is a blessing to the giver." This rationale notwithstanding, Nelle's sponsor, the Ninth Street Christian Reformed Church of Holland, Michigan, petitioned the board to have Nelle's status as *missionary* affirmed. The board granted the request, and Nelle's salary was reinstated.

Nelle and Ed continued to bicycle to areas near and far, but the rigors of trekking and teaching eventually took their toll. Arthritis attacked Nelle's joints, rudely and severely. Particularly affected were her hands and her feet. On one furlough she had several toes amputated.

235

In 1969, Ed and Nelle retired in Holland, Michigan. Both Alyce Jean and Paul had married, and Nelle and Ed became grandparents of seven grandchildren. After Ed died in 1976, Nelle maintained her close interest in missions.

Some time before Nelle and Ed left Nigeria, Nelle's long years of service were recognized. The British government honored her "for distinguished service in Nigeria, administrative, public and social, during his majesty's reign." And in 1989 the Committee for Women in the Christian Reformed Church honored her by establishing a Nelle Breen Smith Scholarship in Missiology at Calvin Theological Seminary in Grand Rapids.

When it became impossible for Nelle to live alone at home, she moved to a residential nursing home in Holland. She suffered increasingly. When she was 85, her right leg was amputated below the knee. Despite such difficult challenges, she never lost sight of her goal: "that Jesus may be my all, in all of my life."

And when she died in April 1990, her goal became heavenly reality.

IX

*Whatever you did
for one of the least
of these [children] of mine,
you did for me.*

Matthew 25:40

Joyce Branderhorst De Haan

Medicine and Mission

Joyce had not made her long journey into darkness for nothing, she knew. She had a new calling now, a new mission field. She would do her best to bring healing and understanding to those who suffered from the disease that had crippled her. She studied everything available on drug and alcohol addiction.

239

"Just a minute. I'll be right back." Dr. Joyce Branderhorst, the 26-year-old medical missionary, was hosting the monthly meeting of a small group of missionaries gathered at her home in Lupwe, Nigeria, in West Africa. The day's heat had lingered on into the evening. Joyce went to her porchlike kitchen to prepare lemonade.

In the kitchen she smelled something strange. Like kerosene. She approached the refrigerator, a small kerosene model designed for areas without electricity. "I wonder if there's some dust or dirt on the burner," she thought. Carefully she stooped, pulled out the reservoir that contained the kerosene, and studied the burner. "Perhaps if I blew gently . . ."

Suddenly flames engulfed her. The kerosene had exploded. She fell to the floor, snatched a small rug, and smothered her face to put out the flames. Rev. Robert Recker and Rev. Ralph Baker, Joyce's colleagues, had heard the explosion and now burst into the kitchen. They tried to grab Joyce, but the fumes and thick smoke choked them. They struggled to help her. When a sudden gust of wind blew through the open door and cleared the air briefly, they grabbed her and carried her to the nearby guest house.

There was no way to stop the fire. It caught hold of the dry grass roof and reduced the house to ashes in a few minutes. Other missionaries gathered and stared, terrified. Second-degree and third-degree burns covered Joyce's face, neck, and arms. What should they do? Joyce was the only doctor within sixty miles.

Still conscious, Joyce began to tell them how to treat her. "Break the window to the dispensary and get some morphine from the drug cabinet," she managed to choke out. Nurses had arrived by then, and Joyce tried to tell them she would probably need a tracheotomy. Then she lost consciousness.

Joyce had come to Lupwe only eighteen months earlier, eager to serve her Lord. The long road to Lupwe had begun in her teen years in Holland, Michigan, where she and her family attended Ninth Street Christian Reformed Church. Nelle and Ed Smith, early missionaries to Nigeria, were also members here.

Joyce listened eagerly to their stories. The more she heard, the more she became convinced: God wanted her to be a missionary.

In 1945, when Joyce was a senior at Holland Christian High School, Dr. John DeKorne, then secretary of Christian Reformed World Missions, spoke at a chapel service. Joyce stayed after chapel and explained to him that she wanted to graduate from Calvin College (in nearby Grand Rapids), become a nurse, and then go to Nigeria. Dr. DeKorne's response took Joyce by surprise: "Well, if education is so important to you, why don't you take it further and become a doctor?"

Joyce had never considered that possibility. She knew no women doctors. But she took Dr. DeKorne's advice. She enrolled in Calvin College, completed its pre-med program, and was subsequently accepted at the University of Michigan medical school. The first two years were tough. In the spring of her second year Joyce asked her parents to prepare her room at home — she didn't think she would pass her exams. But she did. The next year she worked with patients, something she loved.

During her third year at the university, she met her future husband, Ray De Haan, who was studying bacteriology. They walked past each other on campus one day and exchanged a friendly hello. "Who was that handsome man?" thought Joyce. "I've seen him at Calvin. Isn't he a De Haan?" She went straight home to her Calvin yearbook to find out. Somehow the two ran into each other more often after that. Soon they were dating.

As their romance became serious, they began to think about postgraduation plans. Joyce wanted to complete her one-year internship and go to the mission field; Ray was thinking about medical school. Ray's father, Rev. Reuben De Haan, warned his son not to interfere with Joyce's desire to serve in Nigeria. "It's a call from the Lord," he said. It seemed as though the couple's plans were leading them in different directions. They needed time to think over their goals separately, so they agreed not to see each other for a while.

The agreement didn't last very long. By the end of the year, Joyce and Ray were engaged. They would have to wait to marry until Ray finished his medical degree four years later, but they decided they could be patient. Four years would give Joyce time to finish her internship and serve a term in Nigeria — provided, of course, that the mission board accepted her application.

Joyce interned at the Southern Baptist Hospital in New Orleans and studied tropical diseases at Tulane University there.

For Joyce the joy of bringing healing to the people of Nigeria made up for every hardship: the long days, the heat, the bugs, even her loneliness for Ray (well, almost).

Meanwhile, she put in an application with the CRC World Mission Board.

The board welcomed her application. The missionaries in Nigeria desperately needed a doctor. Since Johanna Veenstra's days there in the early thirties, they had been praying for a doctor.

In August 1953, Joyce at last boarded a plane to Nigeria. Traveling to Lupwe, she joined Ed and Nelle Smith there. She soon learned how much the Nigerians needed her. Every morning dozens of patients and their families gathered outside the dispensary. She saw them one by one, all day, communicating with them through an interpreter. She provided whatever medicines she had. About once a month she visited outlying stations, traveling by bicycle with two male Nigerian nurses and packs of medical supplies.

For Joyce the joy of bringing healing to these people made up for every hardship: the long days, the heat, the bugs, even her loneliness for Ray (well, almost). The work went very well. More and more people came to Lupwe and other nearby medical stations to seek medical care. Ed Smith and Joyce began to dream about expanding the medical work in response to the need. Perhaps it could be done. Perhaps they could build for these people a great and lasting gift: a hospital. Joyce and Ed began making preliminary plans.

But then, the accident.

Why? Why did God allow the fire? Wasn't Joyce following his will? Filling a desperate need? Healing people's bodies? Helping to win souls for Christ? The Nigerian Christians' first stunned response: Satan had caused the accident; Satan wanted to take Joyce away. The missionaries wept and prayed with the people. Several months later, their tears turned to laughter and joy. Not only had God allowed their doctor to live, but he had also brought her back to them. Certainly their God was stronger than fire! Word of God's power spread among the people.

Joyce remembers the first few weeks following her accident only dimly, but she knows that God was near her.

God's hand was immediately evident, even on the night of the accident. After Joyce fell unconscious, the other missionaries prayed urgently for guidance. They decided to try transporting Joyce to Dr. Herman Gray, an American doctor sixty miles away in Mkar. To get there, they would have to cross a river. But no barges crossed during the night because darkness made navigation difficult, and there was the danger of alligators on shore. By the time the missionaries arrived at the river, night had fallen. How would they cross? As they neared the river, they received their answer: the headlights of their station wagon beamed on a large boat resting at the river's edge. It was the barge! That night the captain had dreamed that he should return to his post.

It was a miracle.

At Mkar, Dr. Gray administered an intravenous solution and dressed Joyce's burns. She didn't need a tracheotomy; she was breathing fairly well. Dr. Gray sent Joyce by plane to the hospital in Jos for skin graft surgery. In Jos a surgeon performed the grafts, taking skin from Joyce's thighs and replacing the burned skin on her face, neck, and arms.

After the surgery the doctor made a suggestion: "Go back to the States, Joyce." But she chose to stay. The people in Nigeria needed her, she reasoned, and they needed a hospital. Besides, although a network of scars remained, she had healed more quickly than anyone had expected. Just several months after the accident, she returned to Lupwe and began working again. She and Ed chose a site, and their dream for a hospital advanced to the planning stage. The Nigerian government approved the project quickly. A year later, when Joyce's two-and-a-half-year term was completed, hospital construction was underway.

"The Lord was indeed merciful," Joyce reflects now. "He allowed me to finish my work and go home to Ray."

Her struggle, however, was not finished. Although she didn't yet know it, the accident would alter her life.

She arrived home in February 1956; her wedding was

Joyce survived the burns she received when her kerosene-powered refrigerator blew up in her hut in Lupwe. Her struggle, however, was not finished. Although she did not know it, the accident would alter her life. She would become addicted to pills and alcohol.

---

planned for the first of May. She began undergoing the post-accident treatment she still needed. Bumpy scars left from the burns, skin grafts, and infection still covered her face, neck, and arms. To remedy this, she received "planing" surgery, a procedure that literally sands down and smooths the skin. Would the bandages be off in time for her wedding?

For burn patients, the worst part of the recovery process — besides severe psychological trauma — is the relentless, torturous itching. In Nigeria the doctors had given Joyce the drug that seemed to best relieve the itching: alcohol. This remedy doesn't work for everyone, but it seemed to work for Joyce. When the itching became unbearable, the nurses gave Joyce intravenous injections of alcohol or a drink of brandy. Joyce began to experience blackouts and jaw spasms, unfortunate side effects of the medication, she thought. No one then recognized these ominous signs for what they were: typical indicators of alcohol dependence. Without knowing it, Joyce had stepped over the threshold of a nightmare.

After the planing surgery, the horrible itching returned. Sometimes she sought relief in drinking. After weeks of agony and exasperation, Joyce's itching subsided. One week before the wedding, the bandages were removed.

Joyce and Ray married on May 1, 1956. They left immediately for Denver, Colorado, where Ray had arranged to do his medical internship. Over the next few years, Ray completed his internship and residency, and Joyce practiced medicine part-time. Their first two children, Debra and Doug, were born in 1957 and 1958.

Meanwhile, although her alcohol consumption was not as heavy as it had been in the hospital in Nigeria, Joyce did not stop drinking. It didn't seem to be a problem; she drank socially, as others did.

Shortly after Joyce had returned from Nigeria, Dr. John Mulder of Pine Rest Christian Hospital in Grand Rapids, Michigan, had advised her not to go back to Nigeria. The psychological trauma had been too severe, he said. But he hadn't convinced Joyce. Hadn't she returned to her work immediately after the accident? Why would the work and the situation be too difficult for her to handle now? She and Ray would go to the mission field together as soon as Ray finished his residency.

At that juncture, Joyce and Ray applied to the mission board, but there were no openings. Ray subsequently committed himself to two years' government service. Within a year a position opened with the board of missions, but by then Joyce and Ray were not free to accept. Two more children, Dave and Diane, were born. In 1964 Ray accepted a position as a research

245

scientist in the infectious diseases department at the Upjohn Company in Kalamazoo, Michigan. Joyce continued to practice medicine part-time. Their dream of serving on the mission field faded. Maybe when the kids were older . . .

All went well for a time. Joyce continued to drink regularly, but it didn't seem to affect her ability to care for her children or to perform her medical duties. However, in 1969, when she was expecting the couple's fifth child, the first crisis came.

In the sixth month of Joyce's pregnancy, her doctor told her she had an alarmingly rapid heart rate. He sent her to the hospital. For five weeks she received heavy doses of sedatives by injection whenever her heart rate went above the normal level. In addition, she "prescribed" medication for herself: whiskey and sedatives that she had hidden. By the grace of God, Joyce admits, she delivered a healthy baby girl, Darcie, in April 1969.

Behind the joy of Darcie's birth, however, lurked a dark fact: Joyce's experience had plunged her back into deep addiction. She continued to take the drugs at home — a handful of sedatives at night to help her sleep, and a handful of amphetamines in the morning to get her going. The drinking also continued. Debra, her oldest daughter, more or less took over the care of little Darcie. Joyce couldn't manage it.

One evening Ray came home from work and called a greeting to his wife. No answer. She didn't seem to be around. He searched the house and finally found her in bed, half-conscious. "She's really overdone it this time," he muttered. He was furious — he had warned her often about the pills and the liquor. "Write your name," he said, handing her paper and a pen. She couldn't. "You've got to stop. Look what they're doing to you!" he shouted. Joyce promised she would.

The next few days were horrible. One evening, as Joyce and Ray sat quietly reading and talking, Joyce suffered a severe seizure and blacked out. Ray was horrified. This was far more serious than he had imagined; the seizure was certainly a symptom of withdrawal. It meant his wife must be physically addicted to drugs and alcohol. She needed professional help.

Ray got Joyce into bed, where she regained consciousness after a few minutes. He immediately called Pine Rest Christian Hospital for help, and Joyce became a patient there. "But," she recalls, "I had already fallen into the trap of denial. I didn't really admit that I might be addicted. At Pine Rest they counseled me and tried to convince me that my condition was very

---

"Doctors didn't know much about the pathophysiology of drug dependence at that time. I had no idea that certain people are extremely susceptible to drug addiction, and that I was one of those people."

---

serious. Finally I thought, 'Well, yes . . . they're right.' But I never committed myself to quitting entirely.

"Doctors didn't know much about the pathophysiology of drug dependence at that time," she continues. "I had no idea that certain people are extremely susceptible to drug addiction, and that I was one of those people."

Her stay at Pine Rest broke her of her drug habit. But when she got home, she replaced the pills with alcohol. She could drink much more than anyone else and not become drunk. Then came the blackouts. At first they happened occasionally, then more and more frequently. She suspected that her drinking aggravated the problem. "I'll quit for a while," she thought. She did — for five weeks. "See, I can quit any time," she told herself — another of the denials of the drug-dependent person. Meanwhile, she took Valium, not realizing that as far as her body was concerned, either drug would do.

The shakes came next. One morning Joyce woke up feeling weak. "A hypoglycemic reaction," she thought. A glass of milk helped — a little. When the morning shakes continued, she discovered that vodka worked even better. So started her morning drinking.

247

She drank before work. She discovered that cough medicine worked too. A couple of drinks later on warded off the afternoon shakes. Still, she couldn't keep up with her body's demand for alcohol. By the end of the day, the shakes returned. Soon they crippled her. She couldn't use her credit card at the gas station because she couldn't sign her name on the credit-card slips. She needed cash for groceries because she couldn't sign checks.

Finally, finally she began to understand that she had indeed lost control. Waves of guilt washed over her. She was supposed to be a Christian. But only skid-row drunks are really alcoholics, right? She admitted her spiritual life was fading. She became desperate. Driving home from work one evening, she prayed, "Lord, please don't let me drink when I get home." Moments later she walked through the front door straight to the vodka bottle, without even stopping to take off her coat.

God hadn't answered her — at least not just then. "God was really *delaying* his answer at that time," Joyce says now. "I had to sink still further into addiction before I could hear God's answer. When I got into treatment and was able to avoid taking a drink, I realized God was listening to me and helping me."

One evening a bit later, Joyce needed a little help to sleep, so she took a sleeping pill. When she woke later, at two in the morning, she tiptoed to the kitchen. She poured a glass of vodka, added a little orange juice, and drank it down. This time she reached her limit. Struggling toward the stairway, she tried to make her way to bed, but she couldn't manage the stairs. From chair to couch she stumbled, trying to hold herself up. Ray, hearing the racket, ran downstairs. There lay his wife at the foot of the stairs, unconscious.

Joyce came around several minutes later. She opened her eyes and saw Ray staring sadly, intently into her face. The time for denial had passed. "You're an alcoholic," he said.

After twenty-five years, the truth finally sank in. The disease had stalked Joyce slowly, subtly, until finally it possessed her. The only help she and Ray could think of was Alcoholics Anonymous — no other program was available. On New Year's

Day 1980, Ray handed Joyce the phone. The group's next meeting was that evening.

"It was the longest day of my life," Joyce recalls. "I hadn't

---

Joyce came around several minutes later. She opened her eyes and saw Ray staring sadly, intently into her face. The time for denial had passed. "You're an alcoholic," he said.

---

drunk anything all day. I felt awful. I was scared to death. But I went to the meeting. I don't remember much, except their advice: 'Keep the plug in the jug and keep coming back — ninety meetings in ninety days.'"

Joyce attended AA meetings daily for the next three months. It was the therapy, the only therapy, that led to recovery. She learned that the blackouts, the shakes, the denials — all were classic symptoms of alcohol addiction. She also learned that sedatives and alcohol are "cross addictive" — that addiction to one encourages addiction to the other, and that the substances can substitute for each other in meeting the body's addictive cravings.

The first few weeks were rough, but with group support Joyce quit both alcohol and pills. A dense fog seemed to lift from her mind, and she could think again. She began to rediscover long-forgotten pleasures in life — the sun shining in the window when she woke up in the morning, the tangy sweet taste of apples. . . .

One beautiful evening that summer, after an AA meeting, Joyce drove west toward home. The sunset was spectacular. A deep peace embraced her. "I had been so scared to face God again because of my overwhelming guilt for what I had done," she admits. "But that night God told me he had never forsaken me. He wanted me to know that he had been with me all along, and that he still loved me. He created that glorious sunset to celebrate my recovery."

249

Joyce had not made her long journey into darkness for nothing, she knew. She had a new calling now, a new mission field. She would do her best to bring healing and understanding

---

One beautiful evening that summer, after an AA meeting, Joyce drove west toward home. The sunset was spectacular. A deep peace embraced her. "God wanted me to know that he had been with me all along, and that he still loved me. He created that glorious sunset to celebrate my recovery."

---

to those who suffered from the disease that had crippled her. She studied everything available on drug and alcohol addiction.

In recent years a growing awareness of alcoholism and its many unsuspected victims has prompted the health community to begin public education and treatment programs. In Kalamazoo, the Alcohol and Drug Abuse Council, a community group, decided in 1981 to establish Gateway Villa, a 32-bed treatment center. Joyce became the center's medical director, and still serves in that capacity.

In 1984 the Christian Reformed synod addressed the issue of alcoholism and drug abuse. Joyce, three other doctors, and three pastors studied the problem. The 75-page report, issued in 1988, "was our gift to the sons and daughters of our church," Joyce says.

Today Joyce divides her time between Gateway Villa and Kalamazoo College, where she serves as medical director. She has also returned in part to her first love — the mission field. Every February she spends two weeks in Honduras conducting clinics at mission stations there.

In February 1988 Joyce's long journey came full circle. She returned to Lupwe. She toured the now-thriving hospital there. And she thanked God for his faithfulness. "He gave me strength to overcome all the obstacles," she says. "He never let me go."

Debra Dixon Deur

Eyesight and Insight

"Sometimes people are impressed that I left my private practice to work in the clinic. But I don't consider it sacrificial at all. After all, I'm not the typical medical missionary living under mosquito netting in Africa! I'm really very privileged."

When Debra Sue Dixon married Charles Deur during their junior year in medical school, she didn't know that God would eventually use her career to serve him in a volunteer ministry.

Born January 10, 1949, in Indianapolis, Indiana, Debra was the only child of Ralph Emerson Dixon and Margaret (Margo) Benoit. She spent her early years in Munster, Indiana, in the firm and loving care of her parents. Her grandparents lived nearby. Grandpa Joseph Dixon died before Debra was a year old, and his widow, Rose ("Nana") Dixon, enjoyed taking care of Debra each Saturday so her parents could go out.

For many years almost without interruption, Nana, a Baptist Christian, took Debra with her each Sunday morning to Sunday school and church. She lavished time and love on Debra. "Nana always said there were two ways of spoiling little girls — sweet and rotten. She said she was spoiling me sweet," says Debra, "but she got her licks in really early with me." Nana disapproved of the Dixons' "worldly" life-style: they enjoyed smoking and dancing and going out. She used the opportunities she had to influence Debra for the Lord. "From a very early age on, I was learning about the Bible," Debra recalls. "I also learned that I must ask Jesus into my heart." When Debra was about ten, she was baptized by immersion.

Debra's Catholic grandparents, Leo and Marjorie Benoit, got special permission to attend the baptism service. Not wanting to confuse their young granddaughter, the Benoits had deliberately decided not to question Debra's non-Catholic upbringing. Grandma Benoit was — and still is — the epitome of quiet selflessness for Debra. "She loved the Lord and everybody knew it," Debra says of her. "She knew Grandma Dixon was taking me to Sunday school, but she never interfered."

Debra loved school. Grandpa Benoit routinely paid her a quarter for every "A" on her report card. His terms were that he would pay up if Debra could tell him how much he owed her, "but the truth is," admits Debra, "I got the money whether I could figure it out or not." Probably even more important than the quarters was the reward of knowing that Grandpa was pleased. "This may have been the beginning of a primary motivating force in my life — the desire for others' approval," remarks Debra. Paradoxically, although she felt secure as a little girl, her desire to be recognized as outstanding often figured in her efforts. Being an excellent student, being obedient, and doing the right thing reinforced her ego. "I never was competitive with others, though — only with myself," she points out. "Evidently other kids did get jealous sometimes. My best friend later told me she would get angry at her mother for not reading the encyclopedia aloud to her the way she just knew my mother must read it aloud to me!"

Lovetta Dixon, her aunt, introduced Debra to Chicago's Art Institute and several museums, and together they attended the Chicago symphony. Aunt Lovetta helped pay for Debra's piano lessons as well. From her grandmothers, both excellent seamstresses, she learned how to sew.

While in junior high school, Debra was fascinated by things medical. She pored over the transparent anatomical overlays in health textbooks and became a candy striper at the local hospital. All the candy stripers except Debra wanted to become nurses. Debra wanted to become a doctor.

While in high school, she qualified for a language study program for high-school students offered by the University of Indiana, and she spent the summer of 1966 studying German in Krefeld, Germany. For a while her interests turned toward a career in diplomacy. "It was a detour," she says, "but today it looks more like a little bend in the road."

Up to this point, "home" for Debra had meant living with her parents. But her parents, she says, "never had a spiritually secure marriage." Ralph had been raised as a Baptist and Margo as a Catholic; the couple had been married in a Presbyterian church in an attempted compromise. "For a time they attended a Methodist church," Debra recalls, "but the major motivation there was the personality of the pastor and their friendship with him. Eventually, at about the time of Grandpa Benoit's death

253

in 1959, their troubles began. Domestic turmoil followed over the years, and they divorced when I was seventeen."

During this time Debra began to drift away from her grandmother's church. "It was too legalistic," Debra explains. "I wanted to dance, go to movies, and do things Nana disapproved of but which I didn't think were all that bad." When Debra joined a Lutheran church, her parents didn't object. "It was a very good church," Debra says, "and I was much more comfortable with their style."

Debra had always known that she would go to college. Her parents, especially her father, took her around to various Big Ten campuses. In the end, however, Debra chose a school outside the Big Ten circle: Vanderbilt University in Nashville, Tennessee. She liked the school's reputation, its atmosphere, and its strong programs in the liberal arts and foreign languages. Her parents agreed with her choice; they thought Vanderbilt would be a nice, "safe" school.

To Debra, college meant a good time. Although she never stopped believing, her faith in Christ and her religion took a backseat to her other pursuits. She didn't want to concern herself with the daily-life implications of being a Christian. Of course, she studied at college, but she was more interested in the social life there. "I guess I had been the good student for so long that I was just interested in going away and having fun," Debra says now. She had her own agenda; in effect she said, "Thank you very much, God, but I'll handle things myself now."

It was the late sixties then, a time when campuses especially were noisy, turbulent, and filled with activists. Protest against the Vietnam war and the clamor for civil rights and women's liberation were only part of the general unrest that swept across campuses. "Safe" Vanderbilt was no exception.

Campus politics made Debra reconsider her career plans. "I began to think seriously about where I was heading," she recalls. "Somehow, my earlier ideas about a diplomatic career didn't seem too practical or altruistic. I thought I should be concentrating on helping others." She was also being influenced by the fact that helping others would be praiseworthy. "The old need to gain others' approval was reasserting itself!" she says. She realized that she had also sought this approval by spending a great amount of her time and energy becoming someone

---

Debra started out in nursing school but eventually decided to become a doctor. "I began to think that maybe nursing was wrong for me. And I thought, 'I can do what those doctors are doing.'"

---

important on campus, serving in various organizations and offices. As she reflected on it, she began to see that behavior in a new light. "All of a sudden it dawned on me that everything I wanted to do was at heart only an effort to make myself look good," she says. "I detested this in myself." She decided to transfer into Vanderbilt's school of nursing. "I was always interested in medicine, and Vanderbilt had a great school of nursing."

While doing her practical work on the hospital floors, Debra found herself eavesdropping on medical professors and their students. Their doctor talk appealed to her much more than nursing talk. Even at this juncture, becoming a doctor still seemed unattainable — but it was a persistent notion. "I began to think that maybe nursing was wrong for me," she remembers. "And I thought, 'I can do what those doctors are doing.'" She began to see herself as rightfully belonging in the pre-med group.

Eventually that persistent notion won out: Debra decided she would become a doctor.

Not wanting to lose a large number of credit hours, Debra kept her major but added the minimal pre-med science courses required. This meant facing new academic challenges. "The professor that usually taught organic chemistry was tough, a man-eater," Debra says. "The course was kind of a weed-out course for pre-meds. I knew I wouldn't handle organic chemistry well under him, but that summer before my senior year, a kindly visiting professor came to Vanderbilt." He taught "bathtub physics" (a course for non-science majors, not the one expected of pre-meds). Debra passed with an "A."

At this point Debra was still clinging to her own agenda: she didn't attend church, and she didn't want God to interfere with her life. But as she grew more anxious about being accepted into medical school, she began to think differently. "I realized this was going to be rough," she remembers. "I started to bargain with God. I said, 'If you'll just get me into medical school, then I'll let you run the show and I'll turn my life over to you.'" But Debra did more than strike a bargain: she genuinely committed her heart to Jesus Christ. "I realized keenly that I myself should have hung on that cross, and Jesus hung there for me instead," she says. "I could never repay that debt, but I knew certainly that I owed him everything I could be."

In 1971 Debra was accepted at the Indiana University School of Medicine — minorities and women had the advantage then, she explains modestly. "If I had been a male, I might not have gotten in," she says frankly. "Being a woman tipped the scales in my favor a little bit. Of course, my nursing background gave me some credibility too."

"I started to bargain with God. I said, 'If you'll just get me into medical school, then I'll let you run the show and I'll turn my life over to you.'" But Debra did more than strike a bargain: she genuinely committed her heart to Jesus Christ.

It had been months since Debra had attended church. The summer before medical school, she began to attend again, despite the fact that she worked the night shift as a pediatric nurse and was often sleepy on Sunday mornings.

At church she met someone connected with the Christian Medical Society who gave her the names of Christians to contact at I.U. medical school. There she became involved in the "Friday Night Clinic," a fellowship of Bible study, prayer, and praise. "I became a sponge, just soaking up the Bible," she recalls. "Things really took off for me when I began a discipleship course led by Campus Crusade. Looking back, I see God's hand was at work."

She had already met her future husband, Charles Deur, who would also become a doctor. Although they had medicine in common, they were strikingly different in other ways. "Charles was a staid Christian Reformed person, typically reserved," says Debra. "I was pretty high profile as it was, being a female, and my openness about Jesus Christ made me even more so. You know how new Christians are: their convictions and joy just flow out of their mouths — anyplace, anytime. At least I was like that." Charles had to take a lot of heat because of his association with this "religious fanatic."

Debra's attraction to Charles was easily understandable. "The fellows at the anatomy lab table tried their best to embarrass me with crude jokes and rough talk over the naked cadavers we worked on," she remembers. "I stuck with it, and so did Charles. He was interested in me from the first day, and that interest persisted, in spite of everything." Charles and Debra were married on September 1, 1973, by Rev. John Joldersma in the Devington Christian Reformed Church in Indianapolis.

The couple finished medical school and went to Dallas, Texas, to serve their internships and residencies. They became charter members of the Bethel Christian Reformed Church of Dallas.

Debra chose ophthalmology as her specialty, partly because she was intrinsically interested in that field and partly because she thought it would accommodate family life. "It never occurred to me to doubt whether I could do both at the same time," she says now. "It was my old strong ego. It's good that young people are that way, I guess. Otherwise things would never progress." There was precedent for Debra's superwoman approach to life: Debra's mother had worked outside the home in her husband's office when Debra started school, and she had also kept an extremely clean, well-organized home. "I was the original latch-key kid, I guess, and I just accepted that," says Debra. "I took for granted how well my mother managed our home, and not until much later did I realize what a tall order that could be."

In 1980, after finishing their residencies, the couple settled in Arlington, Texas, Charles working in the areas of oncology (the diagnosis and treatment of cancer) and hematology (the study of diseases of the blood), and Debra in general ophthal-

---

As an ophthalmic surgeon, Debra offered to pray aloud for and with her patients before taking them to the operating room. In eleven years of practice she was never refused, although a few patients were surprised.

---

mology. Almost immediately Debra became pregnant, but she worked full-time until her delivery. During that time, God was preparing the way for a Christian Reformed church in the area. Ultimately, Trinity Oaks Church of Arlington grew out of a Sunday-night Bible study in the Deur home.

After baby George arrived in late 1980, Debra reduced her practice to part-time and had domestic help at home. Juliana was born a year and a half later. "With no relatives handy to take care of the babies on short notice, that could have been a big problem," Debra says in retrospect. "You can't put babies on hold. When they need you, they need you. Nor can you put sick patients on hold. When they need you, they need you. It's the first thing I learned in medical school. Personal inconvenience is not an excuse. I did sometimes end up taking the babies with me — infant seats, diaper bags, bottles, and all — to the office after hours to see a patient." On rare occasions

Charles too would take George and Juliana with him after hours to admit a patient. When they were toddlers, he would seat them at the nurses' station with crayons and paper to keep them occupied. Remarkably, despite the times when both Charles and Debra were on call, hardly ever did they both have to leave simultaneously for an emergency. "The Lord handled that for us, I believe," says Debra.

As a surgeon, Debra offered to pray aloud for and with her patients before taking them to the operating room. In eleven years of practice she was never refused, although a few patients were surprised. One Jewish woman agreed to a prayer for her husband, saying, "Sure, go ahead. He needs all the help he can get!" Debra was aware of the delicacy of this situation. "I was careful to close the prayer by saying, 'I ask this in the name of Jesus Christ.'"

Debra's role model is the woman in Proverbs 31:10-31; it is her life's goal to be such a woman. Women sometimes say to her, "It's so great to have a woman for a doctor" or "We need more women in medicine." They assume Debra is a feminist when in fact her outlook is traditional. "My being a physician seems contradictory to that, doesn't it? It's difficult to explain or to generalize from my case," she says. "My heart is in my home. God has given me a special calling *and* provided a sheltered setting in which I can handle these responsibilities and still keep his priorities and commandments."

Relaxing is difficult for Debra, partly because she finds so many activities that beg for her attention. "But I'm learning," she says. "I make plans and do everything I can, and after that I kind of relax in God's sovereignty. After all, he's running the show. Maybe what he wanted me to accomplish in a given situation was just to talk to someone, when my agenda was to complete X,Y, and Z. I used to get frustrated when my plans were derailed, but I'm getting better at remembering that today is always the Lord's day, not mine." Her pastor, Rev. Carl Kromminga, Jr., comments on her spiritual outreach: "She has made evangelism more than a task or a priority; it's a way of life for her. You don't know her for long without realizing her passion to reach others for the Lord."

Her activities include writing feature articles for the Junior League of Arlington, of which she is a member. In addition, she has occasionally contributed guest editorials for the *Citizens Journal,* the local newspaper. But the biggest investment of her time and talent since 1989 has gone to the Lampstand.

The Lampstand is a Christian ministry that provides optical and medical eye care to people who can't afford to pay for it. The name "the Lampstand" is based on Matthew 5:14-16 (NIV): "You are the light of the world. A city on a hill cannot be hidden. Neither do people light a lamp and put it under a bowl. Instead they put it on its stand, and it gives light to everyone in the house. In the same way, let your light shine before men, that they may see your good deeds and praise your Father in heaven."

Started in 1989, the Lampstand, of which Debra is the medical director, serves people from many ethnic backgrounds — but mostly blacks, whites, and Hispanics. If they are employed, they usually receive only minimum wage. Many of the families of those treated have to live each week on an amount equivalent to the cost of an eye examination and a pair of glasses.

The undertaking is sponsored by the Luke Society, a non-profit organization of Christian doctors dedicated to medical ministry to the needy. As a board member, Debra became concerned about the problems of people who couldn't afford eye care. "I realized that we had this problem right here in Arlington, a city of 250,000 people," she comments.

The Lampstand is a project oriented toward providing a specialty service in that it provides ophthalmological care, Debra explains. It dovetails nicely with the new community clinic nearby that provides primary ambulatory care.

In the field of ophthalmology, doctors often choose surgery as their specialty — and that means that certain basic eye-care needs can be slighted. "There's a cataract surgeon on almost every corner," Debra observes. "In my profession we're good at doing the flashy things, but we're not very good at doing the most needed work for a vulnerable population — such as detecting glaucoma or preventing vision suppression, which hap-

---

"In my profession we're good at doing the flashy things, but we're not good at doing the most needed work for a vulnerable population — such as detecting glaucoma or preventing vision suppression in children. . . . I think the Lord has put me in this special spot because my skills fit both the need and the opportunity for ministry."

---

pens when a child ignores one eye that for some reason isn't functioning well. If that defect isn't treated before the child turns ten, that eye may be permanently impaired. I think the Lord has put me in this special spot because my skills fit both the need and the opportunity for ministry."

Despite being unable to gather good statistics to document the need for a place like the Lampstand, Debra went ahead and set up the clinic with the help and cooperation of many. The response quickly confirmed the need for the services provided. So great was the need, in fact, that it later became clear that Debra would have to give up either her practice or the clinic. "I just wasn't able to give this ministry the time I needed to really do it right," she says.

Faced with this choice, she gave up her practice to devote herself to her vision. "Charles and I are comfortable financially. God put me here in Arlington for some reason. Sometimes people are impressed that I left my private practice to do this. But I don't consider it sacrificial at all. After all, I'm not the typical medical missionary living under mosquito netting in Africa! I'm really very privileged," she points out.

Housed in rent-free space provided by the predominantly black Mt. Olive Baptist Church, the Lampstand is staffed by volunteer receptionists and assistants from other churches, including Debra's own. A pastor from another Baptist church regularly contributes his expertise, developed during his days in the Air Force when he was an optician and ophthalmic scrub nurse. He and others perform vision checks, put in eyedrops, and help the process move faster so more patients can be examined.

The clinic offers basic eye care, but it is more than a clinic: it's a Christian environment in which patients are shown concern and love in the name of Jesus. Opportunities for witness arise frequently, although Debra's time to chat is very limited because she treats so many people. However, because the clinic is so small (654 square feet), she can often hear what is being discussed. When a volunteer has an opportunity to talk about spiritual matters with a waiting patient, Debra starts praying silently.

Debra hopes and plans one day to expand the Lampstand ministry to include literacy tutoring for adults and Bible study for novice readers, in addition to a well-stocked Christian reading room. "It seems to me that eye care, literacy, Bible study, and Christian reading material would all make sense as a package," Debra says. Before this vision can become a reality, however, the Lampstand needs more space.

Sometimes Debra is a bit frightened, feeling as if she's out on a limb. Her future is uncharted, her vision still unfolding. But she is not without guidance, as she herself points out: "Today is the Lord's day. The clinic is a faith venture, and God seems to be confirming it."

With God's blessing and Dr. Debra Dixon Deur as the lamplighter, the Lampstand will grow in its ministry and glow ever brighter.

X

"Master," [s]he said,
"you entrusted me
with five talents.
See,
I have gained five more."

Matthew 25:20

Doris Tuinstra

Chrysanthemums and Currency

"Talk about materialism! When you're in business, you do think about the bottom line — frequently. . . . There were times when I'd watch the cash register — so vital to our business — tally up the sales. Sometimes I wondered about it all. A Christian businesswoman has to keep her perspective."

She was born with a green thumb and a penchant for work. Doris Tuinstra is retired today, but her thumb is still green and her industry has not slackened. Doris never felt that the Lord had specifically "called" her to business, but as she looks back on her life, she sees that by both incident and indication the Lord led her into the world of business.

As a teenager she helped her father sell produce, getting up at four in the morning to go to the wholesale market with him. From this insignificant beginning she worked her way through six decades in the nursery business. Recently, upon retiring, she sold her stock in a business that had grown to three major stores in Grand Rapids, Michigan.

Born on August 31, 1917, Doris was the oldest of the five children of Jacob and Jennie Tuinstra. Her father, faced with the choice of entering the army during World War I or growing vegetables, chose gardening rather than fighting. Besides selling his produce at the farmers' market, he soon expanded his market business to include supplying vegetables to Grand Rapids restaurants and hotels. Never did he dream, as he directed his vegetable-filled wagon to market, that his oldest daughter would become his "right-hand man" and eventually a successful businesswoman in her own right.

Doris's mother taught school — all eight grades — for seven years before she married Jacob. As a Christian teacher in the public school of that era, she freely integrated her Christian beliefs and principles into her teaching. She told Bible stories, led the children in prayer, and imbued her teaching with her Christian philosophy. "She was an excellent teacher," Doris recalls. "My mother was capable and wise. She knew her Bible and she knew her Lord. She was a good homemaker too. She liked people as much as she liked her students. Sunday dinners were special. Extra plates were always on hand. Dad always read the meditation from *The Banner*."

Just when Doris was old enough to enter kindergarten, she contracted scarlet fever, which at that time was a very scary illness. While she recuperated, the family visited California.

266

They stayed for three months, during which time her father's business was nearly ruined.

"The effect that my illness and the Depression had on my father have influenced my life greatly," says Doris now. "I some-

---

"I identified with my father more than with my mother during my growing-up years. I loved getting up at four in the morning and going to market with him. I helped him load the truck. I liked physical work."

---

how felt partly responsible for my father's financial problems because of my illness. So from the time I was about ten or eleven years old, I either helped Dad or cared for my brothers and sisters while Mom went with him to market."

The Depression was hard on all businesses, and as restaurants and hotels closed, Jacob's wholesale produce business died. Discouraged but not daunted, he decided to retail fresh fruits and vegetables.

"I identified with my father more than with my mother during my growing-up years," Doris recalls. "I loved getting up at four in the morning and going to market with him. I helped him load the truck. I liked physical work."

Eventually Doris graduated from Grand Rapids Christian High School and began attending Calvin College, all the while continuing to work with her father. She helped him trim the produce before morning market time, assisted him at the market, and worked evenings in the store her father ran. While attending Calvin she continued to work a full forty-hour week; she read and studied even while traveling to and from school on the bus. Dr. Henry Schultze, president of the college at that time, understood the difficulties of working full-time and attending college. "He let me take my exams early or late, whatever worked out for me," Doris remembers.

Then her father's assistant became ill and couldn't work, so Doris left school for a while in order to help out. "My father needed me," says Doris. "He was an excellent buyer, but he wasn't very good at merchandising. So I ran the store."

Later Doris returned to Calvin and considered going into education, but eventually she nixed that idea. "I would have had to take several education courses to get an education degree, and somehow I couldn't see that," she says. "Looking back now, I know I am not and never was a teacher." She chose not to graduate.

Besides, it was wartime. The Pearl Harbor debacle had catapulted the United States into World War II. Two of Doris's brothers and her brother-in-law were serving in the armed forces. Doris also enlisted — in the WAVES, the women's branch of the Navy. After basic training and three months in Boston, she and two of her friends, who graduated at the top of their class, were given their choice of assignments. Doris remembers how they chose their location. "One of my friends looked at a huge wall map. 'California is so far away,' she said. So we chose Philadelphia. Maybe if the map had been smaller, we would have landed in California."

Philadelphia was a good choice. Doris's mother "knew of" Professor R. B. Kuyper and encouraged Doris to call him for directions to the Orthodox Presbyterian church there. Doris did so, and after attending Sunday services she enjoyed dinner with the Kuypers. The friendship grew. "Sunday was a change of pace for me, and it removed me from the mentality of the service," Doris recalls appreciatively. "You would think that people participating in war would be very serious-minded, but that simply wasn't true. On weekends they tried to put the war behind them with drinking and carousing. I was fortunate, though. My two roommates, a Catholic and an Episcopalian, were faithful in their Christian life.

"I had planned to finish college after the war," she continues, "but I didn't. I decided to wait to go back to college until the spring term because one of the women with whom I lived during the war was to be married in October in Worcester, Massachusetts. It sounds funny now, but I didn't want to miss that! I guess that's how the Lord opens and closes doors."

In 1946, when Doris returned from serving in the WAVES, she talked about renting an apartment or buying a house. Her parents wouldn't listen. Unheard of! Nice, respectable young women didn't do that; Doris should live at home. Although Doris was at first disappointed, "I soon realized how convenient it was to live at home," she says. "Mother always had meals ready. *Everything* was ready for me. This allowed me to work twelve- and fourteen-hour days."

Not surprisingly, Doris returned to work with her father. The wholesale market had lost its appeal, but business, specifically horticultural business, was in Doris's blood. Eventually she and her brother teamed up and went into business together. "Besides being brother and sister, my brother Bob and I were always good friends," Doris explains. "Dad had told him to look for investment property. One day Bob and I had lunch together; he told me he had found a good location. We said to each other, 'What if we would buy it instead of Dad?' We looked into it, liked the location, and eventually bought the property. The owner agreed to build us a store on the land. Although he was a good builder, he kept moving the promised completion date — from April to May and then to June. Meanwhile, nursery stock and bedding plants that we had ordered arrived. The store didn't open until July, and we ran out of money. But Dad bailed us out and became our silent partner.

"Eventually Dad became the buyer for the business," Doris continues. "He was an excellent buyer and innovator, and I was good at marketing."

Marketing, Doris explains, is "the movement of goods from their source through to their replacement. It consists of several challenging steps: choosing, purchasing, processing, displaying, and then replacing the merchandise when it is sold. Purchasing good products, choosing the right sizes and colors, displaying them, and seeing items drop into the customers' shopping carts — that's exciting," she says. This was her area of expertise in the store she and her brother opened. "I enjoyed taking customers through the store. I enjoyed making the store the place where customers *wanted* to make purchases."

Business, particularly horticultural business, was in Doris's blood. So eventually she and her brother Bob teamed up and went into business together.

Now retired, Doris lives in a warm and spacious home in Grand Rapids, but she doesn't live alone. One section of her house is always open to missionaries on furlough and to people who have some reason for living in Grand Rapids temporarily. Some have remained as long as three months.

Her friend and house companion is Mag (Magdalene) Van Tol, a Reformed Bible College (formerly Reformed Bible Institute) graduate, evangelist, and retired nurse. In 1948 she became a missionary-evangelist at the Griggs Street Chapel in Grand Rapids, where Doris was then serving on the board. Mag worked long hours — "day and night," Doris says — and her health broke down. The president of the board called Doris. "You're the only one who can take time off from work. Can you take a trip with Mag and get her away from here for a while?" Yes, Doris could — and thus began a friendship that continued throughout their careers. They talked about sharing an apartment or home together if the Lord spared them for retirement.

Yes, the Lord has opened and closed many doors for Doris. Her childhood illness, the Depression, the war, the illness of her father's assistant, her postponement of college for a wedding, her business partnership with her brother, her friendship with Mag. "Even the fact that I've never liked doing things inside the house has had a bearing on my life," Doris says. This may well have contributed to her zeal for business.

Doris's zeal was rewarded — but success came gradually.

"Sometimes I thought it would be nice to have some extra money to use in the business, but that didn't happen very quickly, so we had to work very hard," Doris recalls. "Fortunately, I was given boundless energy and very good health."

The business grew slowly but steadily. Doris, Bob, and their father kept setting new goals and objectives. Their business expanded, gradually embracing multiple functions: from selling fruits and vegetables, to offering bedding plants and nursery stock, to offering all the equipment needed to grow plants and flowers, to stocking products that would sell year-round to compensate for the slow winter season.

Doris recalls an exciting challenge that involved a particularly difficult decision. "We had to decide whether we wanted to start offering toys or go into Christmas decorations for the off-seasons," she explains. "I spent two or three months using every means possible to decide which was better — toys or decorations. I prayed about it. So often in our decision-making we found that the Lord made the answer clear. We decided to go into decorations, finally, and we felt good about our decision.

"However," she adds, "talk about materialism! When you're in business, you do think about the bottom line — frequently. We concentrated on Christmas decorations, and the products sold well. There were times when I'd watch the cash register — so vital to our business — tally up the sales. Sometimes I wondered about it all." She sits quietly for a few minutes. "A Christian businesswoman has to keep her perspective."

She recalls opening the second store in 1973. "It was a deep and moving experience," she says. "I felt as though the struggles of many years were now behind us. We invited many friends to share our thanksgiving to God. We wanted to acknowledge publicly, 'We have come this far, and hereto the Lord has helped us.' We wanted to dedicate our store to him. Marie [the poet Marie Post, Doris's sister, who died in 1990] wrote a special litany for the service."

Keeping a Christian perspective is never easy, Doris points

out. Personally, she tried to counteract the materialistic effects of profiting from Christianity's special days by taking time to read devotional books geared to the season, listening thoughtfully to a recording of *The Messiah,* and attending a performance

---

"Most nursery stock increases in beauty and in value over the years. It's an exciting business to be in. Of course, you can make some awfully big and expensive mistakes — and I did. In those situations I had to admit I'd made a big boner and get out from under it as fast and as well as I could."

---

of the oratorio. But these efforts were secondary to Doris's principal way of keeping her equilibrium. The foundation for maintaining her spiritual balance had been laid in her early childhood and had supported her since then. "Dad and Mother often had supper separately," Doris recalls, "but we always had devotions together when I got home. As long as I can remember, we children would all be home on Saturday nights by ten o'clock. At eleven, we had devotions. Dates were invited and were always welcome. Not that my parents ever said, 'You have to be home' — it was more that we *wanted* to be home."

Doris's balanced perspective was evident in her attitude toward work and toward her employees. "Work isn't drudgery for me," she explains. "Each new day is a gift. Quite often I went into work looking for opportunities. Business is an exciting challenge for Christians — it's multifaceted. Through it God provides many blessings. It's a resource for those who are in it. It gives one a deep sense of accomplishment, it provides employment, it furnishes goods and services to many, and it provides opportunity for outlet and growth.

"Every day I looked forward to the next," Doris continues. "We maintained an open-door policy for our employees, and we were always willing to listen. It was surprising how often they would openly tell us something about their family or their church or whatever."

Horticulture particularly thrilled Doris — and still does. "It's alive; it concerns living things. It isn't something that's consumed. Most nursery stock increases in beauty and in value over the years. It's an exciting business to be in. Of course, you can make some awfully big and expensive mistakes, and I did," she recalls. "When that happened, I had to admit that I had made a big boner and get out from under it as fast and as well as I could."

Doris never married and doesn't regret that. "It's a blessing to be single," she says frankly. "I couldn't have accomplished what I have if I had a family. I would have had to share my time and energy. My parents never seemed to think everyone had to marry, and they never particularly encouraged me to marry. Besides, I was always able to enjoy my nieces and nephews, since two of my sisters lived nearby. On days off I usually worked in my garden, and I always kept two sets of tools. One was for me, and one was for whichever child wanted to work with me — and usually I had a niece or nephew working with me."

"It's a blessing to be single. I couldn't have accomplished what I have if I had a family."

According to her sister Marie Post (who died recently), Doris has always been deeply interested in the children's education. She has set up scholarships for her nieces and nephews, and for their children: now, whenever a grandniece or grandnephew earns a B-plus or better semester average, she provides him or her with a "unit" of education (a monetary unit in Calvin's scholarship plan). In addition, in honor of her parents, Doris has established a scholarship fund at Calvin College for women in business.

Her interest in education is only one of the ways in which

Doris reaches out. She believes in practicing the commandment to "love thy neighbor." David Crenshaw, a young black man, attests to that. "She's my friend — a real friend. Sometimes we have breakfast together. She helps me with my problems, and she teaches me about using money [of which David has very little]." In addition, Doris has been a member of the Urban League for nearly twenty years and has served as a board member for more than ten years. "I've always been concerned about racial problems," she says, "but when Martin Luther King was murdered, it really hit me. Although I had never said anything against blacks, I had never done anything overt to help them either. I suggested to my minister that we all go downtown and support our black neighbors in a march. Well, he didn't want to go quite that far, so I marched with my niece."

A two-term member of the Christian Reformed Synodical Committee on Race Relations (SCORR), Doris has served on the education and the scholarship committees. "It has made me realize deeply not only the need minorities have for education but also their need to be assimilated into society," comments Doris. "If you put minority students in any CRC college, they feel isolated. I know how I feel when I attend a meeting at which I'm the only woman. Calvin College is now working on the problem."

Besides helping at Dégagé, a downtown Grand Rapids ministry for the homeless, Doris has served on the Christian Reformed World Relief Committee (CRWRC). Through that association she became and still is deeply involved in the Cottage Industries program. This arm of the CRWRC strives to teach people how to start and maintain small businesses that enable them to become self-supporting. In 1983 Doris took time off from business to travel to Sri Lanka and Indonesia as a representative of this program. As a board member, she accompanied the CRWRC planning director and the CRWRC area director. Together the three of them surveyed potential areas for CRWRC service. Doris also spent several days in the Philippine Islands looking at the CRWRC's self-support programs there.

"You either feed the poor and keep them dependent, or you help them become self-sufficient," Doris comments. "The CRWRC establishes such programs in the name of Christ."

Doris visited several homes in Negros where women made saleable craft and clothing items. Here a "house" — home for six to eight people — is an 8 × 10 foot room made of any kind of scrap found on the edge of the dump. The woman of the house cooks on an outdoor grate. If she finds she has enough money for soap, she can buy a handful of soap bits from the storekeeper. She keeps her poor family clean and neat.

In Barcolod Doris visited a church where women were weaving baskets. She climbed to the second-story workshop and was greeted by a large sign that said "WELCOME." Forty-four women asked her to pick the prettiest basket from among the ones they were making. "I couldn't do that, of course," she says. "That day we purchased forty-four baskets."

As Doris returned to the home of the CRWRC worker who was her host, she winced at what she saw: naked or scantily dressed little children with protruding stomachs and scrawny legs; skinny dogs; shelters balancing on stilts. Her emotions were in turmoil. Amid the squalor and poverty, her horticultural eye caught sight of a gorgeous native orchid plunked into a discarded and battered gallon can. "We surround ourselves with beauty so lavishly and easily," she says sadly, "and we forget that these people love beauty too. They try so hard with so little."

As she walked along, a few women approached her. An older woman said, "Mum, we need education. We need teachers. We need to learn." The woman's eyes filled with tears, as did Doris's. "That woman understood part of the deep roots of entrenched poverty," Doris says. This experience confirmed her determination to spend her retirement serving the poor, the hurting, and the uneducated.

Doris retired on January 1, 1984 — but her service to many continues. Her work for the CRWRC has included offering help after catastrophes in Mississippi, Missouri, West Virginia, and California. "My work was mainly advocacy or needs assessments. The areas were being restored, but sometimes people were wound up and bewildered; they didn't know how to go on or where to turn. So we called on people to see how they were progressing and to see what remained to be done. Usually there were ways and resources available to them, but the people just needed to be energized and encouraged to seek help.

"I'll soon be leaving on assignment again," Doris says, "and I'm looking forward to that." Assignments are what retirement is about. For this retired businesswoman, retirement spells strength and experience to be used and God-given time in which to use them — for the Lord.

[Their] master replied,
"Well done,
good and faithful servant[s]!
You have been faithful
with a few things;
I will put you in charge
of many things.
Come
and share
your master's happiness!"

Matthew 25:21